Especially for

KJ

From

Grandpa & Grandma

Date

April 2023

Daily Encouragement
FOR KIDS

• • • • • • • • • • • • • • • •

3-Minute Devotions and Prayers
for Morning & Evening

BARBOUR **kidz**
A Division of Barbour Publishing

Text compiled from and inspired by *Daily Wisdom for Boys* and *Daily Wisdom for Girls*, © 2018 by Barbour Publishing, Inc. All rights reserved.

Scripture quotations marked NIV are taken from the HOLY BIBLE, NEW INTERNATIONAL VERSION®. NIV®. Copyright © 1973, 1978, 1984, 2011 by Biblica, Inc.™ Used by permission. All rights reserved worldwide.

Scripture quotations marked KJV are taken from the King James Version of the Bible.

Scripture quotations marked NKJV are taken from the New King James Version®. Copyright © 1982 by Thomas Nelson, Inc. Used by permission. All rights reserved.

Scripture quotations marked NLT are taken from the *Holy Bible*. New Living Translation copyright© 1996, 2004, 2015 by Tyndale House Foundation. Used by permission of Tyndale House Publishers, Inc. Carol Stream, Illinois 60188. All rights reserved.

Scripture quotations marked MSG are taken from THE MESSAGE, copyright © 1993, 2002, 2018 by Eugene H. Peterson. Used by permission of NavPress. All rights reserved. Represented by Tyndale House Publishers, Inc.

Scripture quotations marked ESV are from The Holy Bible, English Standard Version®. Text Edition: 2016. Copyright © 2001 by Crossway, a publishing ministry of Good News Publishers. The ESV® text has been reproduced in cooperation with and by permission of Good News Publishers. Unauthorized reproduction of this publication is prohibited. All rights reserved.

Scripture quotations marked NLV are taken from the New Life Version copyright © 1969 and 2003. Used by permission of Barbour Publishing, Inc., Uhrichsville, Ohio 44683. All rights reserved.

Scripture quotations marked CEV are from the Contemporary English Version, Copyright © 1995 by American Bible Society. All rights reserved.

Scripture quotations marked NCV are taken from the New Century Version of the Bible, copyright © 1987, 1988, 1991, Word Publishing. Used by permission.

Scripture quotations marked AMP are taken from the Amplified® Bible, Copyright © 2015 by The Lockman Foundation. Used by permission.

Scripture marked GNT taken from the Good News Translation® (Today's English Standard Version, Second Edition), copyright © 1992 American Bible Society. All rights reserved.

Scripture quotations marked NASB are taken from the New American Standard Bible ®, Copyright © 1960, 1971, 1977, 1995, 2020 by The Lockman Foundation. All rights reserved.

Scripture quotations marked NRSV are taken from the New Revised Standard Version Bible, copyright 1989, Division of Christian Education of the National Council of the Churches of Christ in the United States of America. Used by permission. All rights reserved.

Published by Barbour Publishing, Inc., 1810 Barbour Drive, Uhrichsville, Ohio 44683, www.barbourbooks.com

Our mission is to inspire the world with the life-changing message of the Bible.

Printed in China.

001230   0622   HA

Daily Encouragement for Your Heart Begins Right Here.

• •

My theme song is God's love.
PSALM 101:1 MSG

• •

This encouraging morning and evening devotional will inspire and comfort your heart with regular reminders of God's love. Each day's reading touches on a life topic that is important to you—like faith, forgiveness, friendship, and more. Inspiring prayers and easy-to-understand scripture selections will motivate you to grow up the very best way—God's way!

Read on. . .and experience God's amazing, unending love for you all 365 days of the year!

DAY 1
Catch Some ZZZZZZs

Do you ever have trouble sleeping? You toss, you turn. You roll around and get tangled up in the covers. You stare at the clock. You stare at the ceiling. You need to sleep, but you just can't. The truth is, you're worried about *so much stuff*. And your mind won't shut off. You worry that you won't pass your math test. You worry that your friend is still mad at you because of the disagreement you had yesterday. Worry, worry, worry!

Well, guess what? You don't have to worry anymore. You have a promise from the Bible that guarantees restful sleep. Proverbs 3:24 says that you will not be afraid and that your sleep will be sweet. Isn't that good news? No more sleepless nights for you!

> *When you lie down, you will not be afraid;*
> *when you lie down, your sleep will be sweet.*
> **PROVERBS 3:24 NIV**

God, sometimes my thoughts and worries keep me up at night. Then I struggle the next day, feeling grumpy and tired. The next time I start the whole tossing-and-turning-and-can't-sleep routine, remind me to say out loud, "I will not be afraid, and my sleep will be sweet." I can trust this, because it's in Your Word. And Your Word is truth! I will quit worrying and start dreaming! Right now, I give all of my worries to You. Thanks for a good night's sleep, God. Amen.

DAY 2
Ready to Catch You

Sometimes life feels mean, like when the kid on the bus teases and pesters you until you feel like you're going to burst. Or the teacher accuses you of cheating on a test when you really didn't. Or your parents have a heated argument, and it leaves you feeling sick all over.

Life can be unfair and painful and scary. Life can feel lonely too, as if you've fallen into a deep black hole. When you worry that your tomorrows will feel the same as today and nothing will *ever* change, what can you do?

Think of God. Reach out to Him. Run to Him like a child who runs to his or her daddy. God's shoulders are big enough to carry you!

> *God is our refuge and strength,*
> *an ever-present help in trouble.*
> **PSALM 46:1 NIV**

Father, life just isn't fair sometimes. There are days when I feel worried or afraid or unsure—and sometimes I feel all these emotions at one time! When the day is dark, I am so thankful I have You. Your never-ending love is bright enough to fill all the dark places with a light that is warm and safe and just right. Please be near me in my scary times and lonely times. Let me feel Your presence, know Your love, and feel Your arms around me like a warm and cozy blanket. Amen.

DAY 3
Follow Your Creator

MORNING •

Did you know that a baby zebra knows its mother by her stripes? When the baby is born, the mother makes sure the baby sees only her stripes first so that the little one will know how to find her if they get separated.

We have a Creator that we can identify with too. God made each of us unique, but we have the ability to know who He is and to recognize Him if we get lost. We have a special relationship with Him because He made us in His image.

Our friends and family know our habits, our likes, and our dislikes. But they can't possibly know the deepest parts of us. Only God knows those things. That's why we can trust Him with everything that concerns us.

> *You created every part of me; you put*
> *me together in my mother's womb.*
> **PSALM 139:13 GNT**

EVENING •

Dear Father, help me to not be distracted by the world. I want to follow only You. I know You created me and have given me signs that point to You. And I will stick close to You, because You know exactly what I need. Don't let me ever get too far away from You, God. If I ever do get separated from You by my bad choices, all I need to do is look for Your stripes! I know You will be watching out for me! Amen.

DAY 4
It's Not about STUFF

When you first read Matthew 7:7–8, it kind of sounds like everything you want is just a prayer away, doesn't it? But here's the deal: this verse isn't talking about "stuff"—material things that everyone else is getting. Nope. It's definitely not about that. God *does* promise to take care of *all* our needs, but this verse is about seeking after God and wanting what He wants for you.

It's not wrong to wish for a new bike or a new phone. It becomes wrong when you let your desires consume you so much that you become discontent with all the other blessings in your life. God gives you everything you need to live a great life. So count everything you have as a blessing, and keep seeking after Him.

"Ask, and it will be given to you; seek, and you will find; knock, and it will be opened to you. For everyone who asks receives, and the one who seeks finds, and to the one who knocks it will be opened."

MATTHEW 7:7–8 ESV

Dear God, I'm sorry for all the times I've had an ungrateful heart because I've wanted more than I have. I am truly thankful for all the blessings in my life. Even though it's not wrong to want new things, please help me not to be consumed with "stuff." Remind me that with You in my life, I'll always have everything I'll ever need! I want to seek after You, and I trust You to take care of me today, tomorrow, and in the future. Amen.

DAY 5
God's Word Is Light

Have you ever tried to walk through your house when it's dark? You bump into furniture and stumble over toys or shoes, don't you? It's even more difficult to walk through someone else's house in the dark. You haven't had time to memorize where things are before you find yourself stumbling through the darkness!

Just like trying to walk through a dark house, many people are stumbling through life. They have not discovered the truths of God's Word. In the Psalms, we read that the Bible is a lamp to light the way for us. Wherever we go and whatever we do, we can rely on God's Word to guide us. Even in unfamiliar places or at difficult crossroads, you don't have to be afraid or confused.

Your word is a lamp that gives light wherever I walk.
PSALM 119:105 CEV

God, when I'm in the dark, I can't see clearly. And I can't take the right path for my life. Thank You for the light You have provided through Your holy Word. Teach me as I read my Bible. Wherever I am, whenever I find myself needing Your light, help me to look to the Bible and allow it to shine on the paths I travel. I trust that Your Word will provide light for all the days of my life. Amen.

DAY 6
Clueless

Everywhere you go, people are encouraging and instructing you to read the Bible. What's the big deal?

When God inspired the authors of the Bible to write, He knew there were three things every person should understand. First, as our Creator, He wanted us to realize how we were created from His love. Second, He wanted us to have something to turn to when we weren't sure what to do about certain situations in our lives: *How are we supposed to treat others? What is the true meaning of love? How do we know right from wrong?* Finally, He needed to show us Jesus came, died on the cross, rose again, and will come back for us someday.

Without the Bible, we would be clueless. God's Word gives us the answers we need.

> **"The grass withers, the flower fades,
> but the word of our God stands forever."**
> ISAIAH 40:8 NKJV

God, the Bible is a very big deal! It's a big deal because it's from You! Without Your Word, I wouldn't have the confidence to make good decisions. I wouldn't feel Your love and blessings because I wouldn't be able to recognize what they are. I wouldn't pray for help if I couldn't read about the amazing ways You have helped people. God, I promise to read Your book as often as I can! Amen.

DAY 7
What God Wants

Even though some of the details may not be clear yet, we already know what God wants us to do every day for the rest of our lives: He wants us to do the right thing.

We may not know what career path to take, but we know God wants us to be kind to others—even when they're not kind to us. We may not know if we'll get married—but we know God wants us to be honest, no matter what. Starting at this very moment, and every moment for the rest of our lives, God wants us to show compassion and mercy. He wants us to stand up for what is right and good. And He wants us to love Him with all our hearts.

He has shown you, O man, what is good; and what does the Lord require of you but to do justly, to love mercy, and to walk humbly with your God?
MICAH 6:8 NKJV

Dear Father, although I can't see into the future—and there's no way for me to know what will happen tomorrow or next month or next year. . .I can know HOW You want me to live—Your best way! Thank You for showing me the very best way to live. . .with You by my side with every step I take. I am so thankful that You show me what You want me to do—the right thing! Help me to always follow Your lead. I want to please You, Lord. Amen.

DAY 8
Jehovah Jireh—Your Provider

The Bible is full of promises. One of them is that if you remain in Him and His words remain in you, you can ask whatever you wish, and it will be given to you (John 15:7). You don't have to worry about what you're going to eat or wear because God knows you need these things, and He will provide them (Matthew 6:31–32).

But His promise to meet your needs and give you the things you want comes with a condition. The condition is that you seek after God and His righteousness first, and then all these other things will be given to you (Matthew 6:33).

Putting God first will satisfy you in every way. And that's a promise the world can't make or keep.

I was young and now I am old, yet I have never seen the righteous forsaken or their children begging bread.
PSALM 37:25 NIV

Dear God, the promises of Your Word are so wonderful. The Bible is full of them! One of my favorite Bible promises is that You will provide for Your kids. So thank You for being my provider, Lord. Give me a heart that follows after You so I won't become focused on the things of this world. Instead, I want to be focused on You. I trust You to provide the things I need. Please let the things I want be the things You want for me too. Amen.

DAY 9
Quiet Time with God

When you go to God in prayer, do you ever wonder if He hears? Do you wonder exactly what it is He wants *you* to hear from *Him*? Do you sometimes rush through your prayers so you can focus your attention on something else? Try sitting quietly in your room while you pray. Don't answer your cell phone, don't turn on the TV, and stay off the computer. Just concentrate on you and God. Pray; pour your heart out to Him. And when you say "amen," don't rush away. Be still and listen. You just might be surprised at how God makes His presence known to you. The Creator wants you to be still and fully know that He is God, and He will guide you through every step of every day.

> *Be still, and know that I am God; I will be exalted among the nations, I will be exalted in the earth!*
> **PSALM 46:10 NKJV**

Dear God, I admit that sometimes I wonder if You really hear every word of my prayers. I know what Your Word says—that You do listen to every word—but it seems almost too wonderful to believe! Please help me know that You are always with me, that You have answers for me if I will only listen for them. Please help me to be patient and listen for Your guidance instead of rushing off to do what I want to do. You are so good, and I am so thankful! Amen.

DAY 10
I've Got the Joy!

Some days are hard. But our God is so amazing—He's given us His never-ending fountain of joy. It's there, every day, ready for us to dip into. Just like He is always there, ready for us to cast our burdens on Him.

Isn't it awesome to think that the God of the universe loves you? That He knows everything about you? He knows that life here on earth isn't easy. He understands the trials and hardships you go through—even homework! And He's longing for you to reach out and grab onto His joy, which cannot be taken away. *No matter what.*

So next time you find unhappiness knocking at your door and the blues threatening to overtake you, remind yourself that you have access to the heavenly Father's joy, anytime, anywhere.

> ***When anxiety was great within me,***
> ***your consolation brought me joy.***
>
> **PSALM 94:19 NIV**

God, I know I will have good days and bad days. There's no way to avoid hard times in this life. But even on the hardest days, I can be thankful. So thank You, Lord, for being with me each and every day. Thank You for Your joy. Help me to grab onto joy every day and sing praise to You, because Your joy is overflowing in my life. And as it overflows out of me, help me to be Your light to those around me. Amen.

DAY 11
Just Wait!

The Bible tells us that if we seek good and not evil, the Lord God Himself will be with us! Don't you want to live each day knowing that God loves you and He is watching over you? Then think twice before you try to bend the rules even just a little.

There will be a lot of temptations around each corner as you get older. Just remember to seek good, not evil, and seek the Lord with all your heart! God promises to always be with you (Hebrews 13:5), He promises to provide a way of escape from temptation (1 Corinthians 10:13), and He promises to protect you from the evil one (2 Thessalonians 3:3). With the promises of God in your heart, He makes it a whole lot easier to "be good."

> **Seek good, not evil, that you may live. Then the LORD God Almighty will be with you, just as you say he is.**
> **AMOS 5:14 NIV**

God, sometimes I get so tired of listening to everyone tell me to behave...to be good. Some days I don't want to follow one more rule—even when I know the rules are put in place to make my life better. When I run into temptation, please remind me of the importance to stop and think before I do something I'll regret. Thank You for Your love and guidance. I really do want to be good—for You, Lord! Amen.

DAY 12
What Prayer Should Sound Like

Does the screeching sound of fingernails on a chalkboard send shivers up your spine? Oddly enough, God is set on edge by something way more serious—a prayer that tells God how much you don't need Him. Then what should a kid's prayer sound like?

One day at the temple, Jesus told the story about the man who tried to impress God with his own good deeds. Jesus explained to the crowd that such a prayer does not make a hit with God. Another man, Jesus said, simply begged God to show kindness to him, a sinner. God gladly listens to that prayer.

As God's child, ask Him to step in and give you His goodness. Now that's a prayer that'll sound much better than fingernails on the chalkboard.

"But the tax collector stood at a distance. He would not even look up to heaven, but beat his breast and said, 'God, have mercy on me, a sinner.'"
LUKE 18:13 NIV

Lord, talking to You every day is so important! I am so thankful for Your Word that gives reminders of how to pray. Help me to spend daily time in meaningful conversation with You. It's so wonderful to know that I can talk to You like my very best Friend—because that's what You are! You love me, and You can be trusted with all my worries, cares, and fears. Help me speak to You. . .and to listen as well. I need You in my life, Lord. Amen.

DAY 13
Just Do It!

The old Nike commercial slogan "Just Do It" is a great reminder for Christians. We read God's Word. . .we hear it at church. . .we sing about the scriptures in songs—but none of it means a thing if we don't do what it says!

"Actions speak louder than words" is a true and common phrase used to help people understand the idea of letting your beliefs or words show through your actions. Founding Father and inventor Benjamin Franklin is credited with the phrase, "Well done is better than well said." It's wonderful to hide God's Word in your heart, but if it isn't changing you. . .if you aren't actively doing something about it. . .your faith won't seem very important.

But don't just listen to God's word. You must do what it says. Otherwise, you are only fooling yourselves.
JAMES 1:22 NLT

God, please help me to talk less and do more. My words only mean so much if I don't take action to obey Your Word. I want to hide Your Word in my heart, but I also want to go into the world and use that to make a dif-ference in other people's lives. If I truly believe Your Word, then it will change me from the inside out! Father, use Your Word to help me grow and change and take action. Help me to "Just do it!" Amen.

DAY 14
Waiting with Hope

Have you ever had to wait for something that you really wanted? Waiting for God to give you what you want can be really hard. But if you have hope, waiting can feel exciting because you know something great is coming.

If God has promised you something and you believe that He keeps His promises, you will have hope. You will have hope because you know that something good is going to happen—in God's time, in God's way. When you trust Him, the tough part of waiting can be easier. Because when you wait with hope, it means you believe that God is working in ways you can't see. And you dream about the great things that will happen when your wait is over.

Blessed are all who wait for him!
ISAIAH 30:18 NIV

Lord Jesus, sometimes it's really hard to wait for what I want. I'm not a very patient kid. I want everything...RIGHT NOW! I do know that there are times I can't avoid the wait. So please help me to trust You and wait for Your plans for my life with hope. Help me to believe that You are working in ways that I can't see and this is why I can be hopeful. I trust You. I know You have only good things in store for me. Amen.

DAY 15
Bless the Lord!

If you're breathing, you should be praising! Sure, there are problems, sorrows, and big disappointments in life, but everything doesn't have to be perfect for you to praise God. Think of your blessings. When the God of the universe is supplying your needs, it's hard to keep track of them all!

Take a deep breath. Then throw your head back and sing to the Lord. Praise Him for life and strength, food and shelter. Praise Him for liberty. For friends and family. Thank God for the birds, trees, sunshine, and clouds. Thank Him for blessing you with talents and for giving you a bright, healthy mind. Thank Him for keeping His promise of providing everything you need. And most of all, thank Him for sending a Savior to die for your sins so that you can have eternal life.

Let every thing that hath breath praise the Lord.
PSALM 150:6 KJV

Lord, thank You for giving me another day. Each day is a day to experience the exciting things—and all the blessings—You have planned for me. Thank You for loving me and supplying all my needs. Thank You for showering me with more blessings than I could ever count. I am amazed by Your love and care every single day. You are worthy of all my praise. With everything I have, I praise You, Lord. Amen.

DAY 16
Every Day's a Holiday

MORNING •

Did you ever tear open a big Christmas present and then groan inside? Maybe you got a sinking feeling when you saw the gift because it wasn't what you wanted or it was the wrong brand. You had high hopes, but then you had to make do with what you received—which is a not-so-wonderful gift.

The good news is that you're receiving wonderful gifts and blessings from your Father in heaven all the time. Prayers are being answered and mercies given every day. And God knows exactly what to give you because He knows what you need better than anyone else. You won't be forced to just "make do" with an off-brand gift. What God has to give is the best quality, and it won't ever break or go out of style.

"But seek first the kingdom of God and his righteousness, and all these things will be added to you."
MATTHEW 6:33 ESV

EVENING •

God, thank You for showering me with gifts, even when I don't deserve them. On days when I feel like nothing is going my way, help me to remember all the things You've given me and all the ways You take care of me. Because You know me better than anyone else, You always know exactly what I need. Your gifts are the very best! I will celebrate Your good gifts today and all year round! Amen.

DAY 17
God Knows My Thoughts

MORNING •

God knows everything. He sees everything. He even knows your thoughts. God is there when you're playing in the neighborhood or enjoying His creation at the park or lake. If you travel across the world to a foreign land where a different language is spoken, God is right there with you as well!

You have a heavenly Father who knows your name. The Bible says that before you were born, He saw you in your mother's womb. He created you and watched as you developed. He is watching still.

Nothing brings God greater joy than when one of His children chooses to spend time with Him. Talk to God throughout your day today. Understand that He is constantly with you. You can whisper a prayer to Him at any time!

***You know when I am resting or when I am working,
and from heaven you discover my thoughts.***
PSALM 139:2 CEV

EVENING •

Thank You, Lord, for knowing me. . .for knowing my name! It's a comfort to know You are always with me. You know me and You love me no matter where I am or what I am doing. I am so thankful that You know my thoughts and concerns—even if I don't speak them out loud. Thank You that I can talk to You any time of the day or night. . .and You hear me! Amen.

DAY 18
Plant Seeds of Joy

MORNING •

Joy is contagious. It's hard to stay in a bad mood when everyone else is happy.

Praising God is a good way to capture joy in your heart. His Word tells us to clap our hands and sing songs. It's a solid plan to get you going on the path to joy.

The Bible also tells us that joy is a fruit of the Spirit. To get fruit, you must first plant a seed. And God wants to give you all the joy you can handle.

God loves to hear our praises, and He sends us joy when we show Him our love and gratitude. When you are filled with this fruit, others will see and want what you have. Think of what a better world it would be if we all shared this kind of joy.

Clap your hands for joy, all peoples!
Praise God with loud songs!
PSALM 47:1 GNT

EVENING •

Heavenly Father, I want to have more joy in my life, and I want to share it with others. I want to have so much joy in my life that others take notice—and they become joyful too! Thank You for giving me the fruit of joy. I will praise You in the good times and even when things aren't quite going my way. I want to have a thankful heart every day of the year. Amen.

DAY 19
Living in Christ

Living in Christ isn't as hard as you might think. All you have to do is believe in Jesus, love others, and obey His commands. When you do that, you will feel Him living inside of you. Wow! What a great feeling!

Some days you may end up doing things *your* way instead of *Jesus'* way, and He knows that. What Christ wants is for you to try every day to do the things He wants you to do. And He will help you. Just ask Him. Before you know it, you'll be growing in Him and finding it easier to do things His way.

You'll know it's working when you feel His Spirit deep inside of you and when you become more like Jesus, your King, each day.

The one who keeps God's commands lives in him, and he in them. And this is how we know that he lives in us: We know it by the Spirit he gave us.
1 JOHN 3:24 NIV

God, I am so sorry for being demanding. . .for always wanting my way. Remind me that Your way is always better because You know what's best for me. Your way will always bring blessings and joy to my life. I believe You, Lord. I love others. And I will obey Your commands. I want to do all the things Your Word asks me to do. Thank You for showing me Your very best plans, Father. . .to live in YOU! Amen.

DAY 20
My Treasured Delight, Part One

Psalm 119:9 says, "How can a young man keep his way pure? By keeping it according to Your word" (NASB).

Everything you need—guidance, comfort, character-trait examples, good stories, and more—are in God's Word, the Holy Bible. By "keeping" your way according to it, you're able to keep your way pure!

"All Scripture is inspired by God and beneficial for teaching, for rebuke, for correction, for training in righteousness; so that the man or woman of God may be fully capable, equipped for every good work" (2 Timothy 3:16–17 NASB). The Bible isn't just a collection of stories, letters, and prophesies. It's God-breathed— God-inspired. It is your guidebook for. . .*everything*!

God has given you His Word to study, delight in, treasure, and apply. His grace is overflowing and abounding. . . . Thank Him today.

I have treasured Your word in my heart,
so that I may not sin against You.
PSALM 119:11 NASB

Father, thank You for Your Word. Thank You that everything I ever need is right there. I know the truth. I know that You love me, died for me, and are preparing a place for me up in heaven. You've poured out Your life, Your love, and Your Word for ME! Thank You for Your grace. I love You, Lord. In Jesus' name I pray. Amen.

DAY 21
My Treasured Delight, Part Two

God's Word shouldn't be taken for granted. There are many people in restrictive countries who don't have the privilege of sitting down and reading the holy Word of the Most High God.

In our souls, there's a thirst for His Word, and we should cherish every tidbit we can get. Why? Because God's Word is everlasting; it will never pass away (Matthew 24:35). It's our guideline, our comfort, the weapon of the armor of God (Ephesians 6:17).

Therefore, memorizing God's Word is one of the best things you can do. Do you think God meant for His Word to be read then forgotten? Use the magnificent weapon He's supplied by dwelling on it!

"On the glorious splendor of Your majesty and on Your wonderful works, I will meditate" (Psalm 145:5 NASB).

> **But his delight is in the Law of the LORD,**
> **and on His Law he meditates day and night.**
> **PSALM 1:2 NASB**

Lord, it makes me sad to know that people in some countries aren't free to read and study Your Word. Please help them come to know You and gain access to scripture. I am thankful to live in a country where I can praise You and read the Bible whenever I choose. Thank You for the ability to memorize scripture. I will take up the "sword of the Spirit" and use it, Lord. Please help me to study and remember Your Word continually, faithfully, diligently. I love You, Father. In Jesus' name I pray. Amen.

DAY 22
Do You Know His Voice?

MORNING •

When you're at school and your best friend yells your name from down the hall, don't you immediately hear it? It's because you've spent so many hours with your best friend; you know that voice.

It should be the same way with God. But you won't be able to know God's voice if you don't spend time with Him. And if you don't know what He says in His Word, then you won't know if it's actually Him speaking to you.

No, He won't talk to you in that big, booming "Darth Vader" kind of way. Instead, you'll have a thought and you'll wonder, *Was that me, or was that God?* If your thought is in line with the Bible, it's probably God. If it doesn't line up with God's Word, then it couldn't have been His voice.

> *"My sheep listen to my voice;*
> *I know them, and they follow me."*
> JOHN 10:27 NIV

EVENING •

God, it's hard to imagine that You love me so much that You'd take the time to speak to me. But I know You will—and You do! Lord, I'm listening! Please help me to know and recognize Your voice. The more I spend time with You and in Your Word, the stronger Your voice will be. Help me to always follow You. Today and for the rest of my days, I will be listening. Every Word You have for me is worth hearing. Amen.

DAY 23
Road Map

God's Word helps us know the right things! When we're not sure which way to go or how to handle a certain situation, the Bible serves as a road map to guide us.

If you're having a disagreement with a friend, the book of Proverbs is filled with wisdom for relationships. If you're mad at your parents, Ephesians says to honor them and treat them with respect anyway. If you're tempted to make fun of someone, or lie, or cheat on a test, God's Word teaches that we should avoid those behaviors.

Reading the Bible helps us to see more clearly so we don't mess up. And when we do make mistakes, God's Word helps us pick ourselves up and get back on the right track—every time.

Your word is a lamp for my feet, a light on my path.
PSALM 119:105 NIV

Dear Father, thank You for Your Word. I am grateful that when I have questions about life...or I have a big decision to make...or I just need hope and encouragement, I can read the Bible and get exactly what I need. Your Word helps me see life more clearly. Help me to read it and understand it, and then put Your commands into action. I want to obey You. Amen.

DAY 24
An Answer That Is Always "Yes!"

MORNING •

A lot of times it's easier to think about the wrong things other people do to us rather than the sins we commit. But *everyone* misses God's mark of perfection. No one can live their life without sinning.

God made a way to fix the broken relationship with Him that sin causes. He sent His Son, Jesus, to take the punishment we deserve.

But the forgiveness isn't automatic. We need to remember to confess our wrongs to God—and the sooner the better! With as busy as life can get, it's easy to forget to ask for His forgiveness.

Because Jesus died for all of us, His answer to our request is always *yes*! He is faithful to forgive our sins.

If we [freely] admit that we have sinned and confess our sins, He is faithful and just [true to His own nature and promises], and will forgive our sins and cleanse us continually from all unrighteousness [our wrongdoing, everything not in conformity with His will and purpose].
1 JOHN 1:9 AMP

EVENING •

Dear Father, I'm sorry for the sins I've committed today. Thank You for forgiving me and for not having a limit on how many times You'll do that. Please help me to remember to say I'm sorry each time I sin. I am so thankful that You love me—and that Your love never changes. I'm far from perfect, and yet You love me the same yesterday, today, and forever! Amen.

DAY 25
Seek, and You Will Find

MORNING •

God loves you. He truly wants a special relationship with you, but He will never force Himself upon you. He wants you to desire His presence in your life too. He has promised that if you seek Him with your whole heart, you will find Him. He won't hide in hard places; you just need to go to the right place to discover Him.

Spend some time with God today. Talk to Him in prayer. Talk to Him just like you would your best friend—that *is* what He wants to be after all. Share your joys with Him. Share your troubles. Let Him experience everything with you. Then choose a passage from the Bible to read, and let God speak to your heart.

Seek Him—you *will* find Him!

> *But if from thence thou shalt seek the Lord thy God, thou shalt find him, if thou seek him with all thy heart and with all thy soul.*
> **DEUTERONOMY 4:29 KJV**

EVENING •

God, I want to spend time with You. Remind me that You're my very best friend in the whole world. Thank You for always being there just when I need You. I know You'll never hide from me and that You truly want to be with me...always. Whenever I seek You, God, I will find You. Thank You for loving me so perfectly! Amen.

DAY 26
Freedom

Christ set you free so that you would live in *His everlasting freedom*.

What *is* freedom? Freedom is:

Being released from the "certificate of debt consisting of decrees against us" which Jesus has nailed to the cross (Colossians 2:14 NASB).

Being freed from the sins that so easily and strongly hold you down (see John 1:29; Romans 6:6–7, 11, 14; 1 John 1:7).

Walking away forever from the worldly life and living the never-ending, pure life Jesus has given (see John 3:16; Titus 2:11–14; 1 John 2:15–17).

God is so good! As David put it, "He restores my soul. . . . And my dwelling will be in the house of the LORD forever" (Psalm 23:3, 6 NASB).

> *It was for freedom that Christ set us free;*
> *therefore keep standing firm and do not*
> *be subject again to a yoke of slavery.*
> **GALATIANS 5:1 NASB**

Lord, thank You for freedom. Because I am free, I can enjoy Your peace, love, and joy every day of my life. Thank You for saving me so I can spend eternity (FOREVER!) with You. I love You, Lord. Please help me to live freely and not under "a yoke of slavery." I am thankful for each promise in Your Word. When You say something is true, I can believe it 100 percent! I love You, Lord. In Jesus' name I pray. Amen.

DAY 27
The Bible Will Guide Me

MORNING •

When you feel confused and aren't sure what to do. . .when you feel pressured to do things you just don't feel quite right about. . . remember that you have a fantastic guide to help you with any decisions you must make in this life. You have the Bible, God's Word! There is no other book that can help you live the life God has called you to live. Its pages hold everything you will ever need to know in this life. God has a plan for us, and if we stay in His Word and read it often, He will speak to us through it and show us the way to go. Guard it. Appreciate it. Love it.

> *Jesus commented, "Even more blessed are those who hear God's Word and guard it with their lives!"*
> **LUKE 11:28 MSG**

EVENING •

Dear God, when I'm confused, I'm thankful for the guidance of Your Word. Thank You for showing me what to do through Your scriptures. Please help me to read the Bible and understand what it is You would have me to do. Please help me to keep reading so that I may always be able to know Your will and be open to receive Your guidance. If Your Word says it, I'll do it! Amen.

DAY 28
You Are God's Best Work

Of all God's creation, man is the only one created in God's image for the purpose of being His friend. Man was God's final creation, a combination of His best designs. . .His masterpiece.

And before Adam ever took his first breath, God had already planned *YOU* too. Your days were already written in His book before you were born (Psalm 139:16). God planned you before the world began and then waited with eager anticipation for the day when you made your grand entrance.

You are exactly the person God planned you to be. You are His workmanship. On the day you chose Him as your Lord, you melted His heart. There is nothing He wouldn't do for you, because He's crazy about you!

> *For you created my inmost being; you knit me together in my mother's womb. I praise you because I am fearfully and wonderfully made; your works are wonderful, I know that full well.*
>
> **PSALM 139:13–14 NIV**

Dear God, it's amazing to me to think that I'm Your masterpiece. You knew me before the world even began. I am just the person You had in mind. . .perfectly created by You. Even though there are times when I feel like I've messed things up, help me remember I am exactly who You planned for me to be. I'm Your child. Thank You for making me who I am and loving me no matter what. Amen.

DAY 29
Your Best

MORNING •

Slackers. You know who they are. . . . Whether it's phys ed class, home economics, art, or math, slackers do the bare minimum— they scrape by just enough to get a passing grade. But any extra effort on their part, *no way*!

While God has given each of us special gifts and talents, that doesn't mean we should ditch everything else, not bothering to try those things outside our comfort zones and interests. Just because science isn't your thing doesn't mean you shouldn't put energy into learning it. And just because you're not into running doesn't mean you should walk the entire mile in gym class.

Every opportunity we have is from God. And He expects us to give our all in everything we do!

> **Don't you realize that in a race everyone runs,
> but only one person gets the prize? So run to win!**
> **1 CORINTHIANS 9:24 NLT**

EVENING •

God, I'm sorry for all the times I've been lazy instead of doing my very best for You. Show me all the areas in which I'm tempted to slack off and take shortcuts. I need Your help to stay motivated. With You by my side, cheering me on, I know I can give 100 percent in all I do. I know You won't let me down. Please help me run the race to win. I want to run the race of life like I'm running it only for You, Lord. Amen.

DAY 30
The Master of You-ology

MORNING •

Think you're an expert when it comes to Y-O-U? There's One who knows better—God!

He knows whether you prefer plain vanilla or triple chocolate with sprinkles, and whether your brain is geared more for reading or math. He also sees the part that no one else does—the inside.

Why do you react to certain things the way you do? What is it about that particular person that gets on your nerves? The answer is clear to God. Best of all, He knows how to change you. God has all the right tools for tweaking.

The next time you're troubled over a personality quirk, talk to your Maker. Ask Him to perfect your flaws. You'll never go wrong by putting yourself into the hands of the One who knows—and loves—you best.

> **But the very hairs of your head are all numbered.**
> **MATTHEW 10:30 KJV**

EVENING •

Lord, I am a work in progress. You understand everything about me, including the things that still need improving. Show me what I need to change today. I know I have attitudes and habits that don't always honor You, Father. And I need Your help in those areas. Give me the desire to change when I need to so that I become more and more like You. I want my life to always bring glory to You. Amen.

DAY 31
Do You Know God's Will?

MORNING •

Do you ever hear this statement and feel a bit overwhelmed?

"God has a plan for your life."

Do you ever fear you just might miss it?

Consider this: God has given *everyone* unique strengths. Are you organized or mathematically gifted? Do you have an outgoing personality? Do you work well with your hands? Maybe it is none of these things. There are thousands of possibilities.

As a Christian, in addition to talents, you also have spiritual gifts. God wants you to use your gifts and abilities for His glory. When you do, you are fulfilling His will for your life.

> *Each of you should use whatever gift you have received to serve others, as faithful stewards of God's grace in its various forms.*
>
> **1 PETER 4:10 NIV**

EVENING •

God, thank You for my talents! If there's something I've missed, please show me those unique gifts and abilities. I know You've gifted me in areas that are a true match for my personality—they're all things that I love to do too! It amazes me that You had my purpose in mind before I was even born. May I always use everything You've given me for Your glory. Amen.

DAY 32
Need Wisdom?

MORNING •

The Bible says that wisdom is worth more than jewels, and nothing else you desire can compare with it (Proverbs 8:11)! Having wisdom means that you know right from wrong, and then you choose to do the right thing. The book of Proverbs talks a lot about the importance of finding wisdom and understanding. Many people seek wisdom, but few find it. Why? Because they are looking in all the wrong places!

James 1:5 tells us that if we want wisdom, we have to look to God and ask Him to give it to us. And when you do ask God for wisdom, never doubt that He will grant it. Trust that He will give you all the wisdom you need to accomplish the plans that He has for you—at just the right time.

> *If you need wisdom, ask our generous*
> *God, and he will give it to you.*
> **JAMES 1:5 NLT**

EVENING •

Dear God, I definitely need a lot of wisdom. I'm growing up, and I want to know how to follow You better. I want to serve You and do the right thing. I have a lot of choices to make every day, and sometimes I'm confused about what to do. Please give me the wisdom to make the right ones. Help me to trust You more. Show me all the truths of Your Word. Amen.

DAY 33
God's Love Is My Support

MORNING •

Friends may come and go, schools may come and go. . .sports teams, churches, even family members come and go. But as a child of God, you can rest assured that He will always be your constant. It doesn't matter where you are—He's there and He loves you.

His love is greater than anything you or I could ever dream of—it's deeper than the deepest ocean, wider than the span of the earth, and bigger than the universe itself. And on days when you feel alone, His love will support you. Even if the earth crumbled around you, His love would still be there!

> *When I said, "My foot is slipping," your*
> *unfailing love, LORD, supported me.*
> **PSALM 94:18 NIV**

EVENING •

Jesus, thank You for never leaving me. Thank You for dying for me so that I might live. Today as I'm walking to school, or eating my lunch. . .or whatever I'm doing, remind me that I've got all the support I'll ever need in the best friend I'll ever have—You! Help me to lean on You, and help me to be a friend and support to someone else today so I can share all You've done for me. Amen.

DAY 34
Chase Comfort

Have you ever lost a loved one or had a falling out with a friend?
If you have a troubled heart or a burdened spirit, God wants
to heal you.

Peace is the gift of God that comforts our hurting souls.
Peace is easy to receive when things are going well in life and
the future looks bright. But when life presses in and hard times
come, peace can seem so far away.

As Christians, we need to be still and let the truth of God
wash over our hurts. Even though stillness is quiet and physically
inactive, it is an intentional action that pursues God's peace.
Today, quiet your busy mind, and let the peace of God soothe
all your hurts.

> **The Lord is close to the brokenhearted;**
> **he rescues those whose spirits are crushed.**
> **PSALM 34:18 NLT**

Father, my heart is hurting, and I need Your peace today.
I cry out to You and trust that Your perfect peace will
soothe my pain and heal my heart. You are so, so good.
And I am so thankful for that! I know You alone can
provide all the peace I need today. Please comfort me
in my sorrow. I trust You for all my needs, Lord. Amen.

DAY 35
The Dream Giver

God has big plans for His message to be shared, and it takes all kinds of dreamers to get the job done. If you don't know what your dream is, ask yourself what you are good at and what you love to do. It may not be obvious at first, so ask God to show you the best dream He has for you.

Our dreams are part of who we are, but sometimes we're afraid to think we could do something big. Our confidence needs to grow to catch up with our God-sized dreams. It may take awhile, but if we believe God wants our dreams to come true, we just need to wait for Him to open the doors to make them happen. . .because He will!

> *For we are God's masterpiece. He has created us anew in Christ Jesus, so we can do the good things he planned for us long ago.*
> **EPHESIANS 2:10 NLT**

Dear God, I want to explore the dreams You have put in my heart and see where they—and You!—might take me. With Your help, I can fulfill my purpose. Show me the way I should go. I can trust You to lead me to all the great big wonderful things You have in store for me. If it's in Your plans, I can do it! Thank You for making all my dreams come true. Amen.

DAY 36
Only a Phone Call Away

Have you ever thought about the purpose of prayer? Do you ever feel like you're praying to the wall instead of to God? Sometimes you may wonder where your prayers even go—if they float away, like cartoon thought bubbles into oblivion, or if your heavenly Father really is listening to your whispered words.

It might help to imagine that you're talking on the phone when you're praying. God has His ear pressed to the phone on the other end of the line, wanting to listen. . .desiring a connection with you. You can talk to God like He's your best friend. And even if your mind wanders or you're half asleep, God will still be on the other end of the line, listening to your prayer.

Pray without ceasing.
1 THESSALONIANS 5:17 ESV

Father, thank You for the gift of prayer. I invite You to be a part of my life as my constant friend and companion. It brings me so much joy to know that You want to know me. . .that You want to be close to me. Today, and every day, I want to spend time in conversation with You. Thank You for always listening. . .for always caring for me. Amen.

DAY 37
I Don't Want To!

Mom thinks your room should be cleaned at the worst possible times. And so you put her off. Maybe you choose to ignore her all three times she asks. And if that doesn't work, you head to your room like you intend to follow through, but then you start playing a game on your phone. The next thing you know, Mom is majorly upset and you're grounded. Now what?

God created parents to protect us and teach us to obey. He expects us to learn how to hear and take action, no matter how we feel. It's the only way He can help us fulfill the plan He has for our lives. There will always be days when our feelings will pull us one way, while in our heart and spirit we know we shouldn't be listening to those feelings. By practicing with small things, like cleaning your room, you will have the ability to make better choices when bigger, more life-altering decisions come along.

> **"And this shall come to pass if you diligently obey the voice of the LORD your God."**
> **ZECHARIAH 6:15 NKJV**

God, I know there are things I should do. . .but sometimes I just don't want to! I'm sorry for dragging my feet and for being difficult. Help me to make better choices about being responsible. Remind me that it's important to obey even when I don't feel like it. I know that learning to obey is a part of growing up into the person You created me to be. Amen.

DAY 38
God Knows

Sometimes it feels like nobody in the world understands us. That's a pretty lonely feeling. But even when our parents or our friends misunderstand us, we can always talk to God. We never have to worry that He will misinterpret our thoughts or our words. He knows us! He knew us before we were born, and He's been with us every moment of our lives. He knows our thoughts even before we have them.

It's comforting to know God understands us. Sometimes our attitudes are right, but others misunderstand our intentions. If we ask God, He will help us communicate our true feelings to others in a way that they'll understand us better.

Other times, our attitudes may be wrong. We may be angry or hurt or annoyed about something. When we talk to God, He understands, and He helps us get our attitudes right.

You have searched me, LORD, and you know me.
PSALM 139:1 NIV

Dear Father, when it seems like no one on earth understands, I'm so glad You get me. Help me to think like You think. I know that as long as I come to You and ask for help, You'll never judge me or make me feel bad about talking to You. You understand me completely, and You want to help me live the best life I can live. Thank You for being such an awesome God! Amen.

DAY 39
The Greatest Love

MORNING •

There are so many ways and opportunities to express your love to others. You might exchange cards with your friends on a special holiday. You might give your mom a stack of homemade coupons for household chores or hugs and kisses. Maybe you'll make a great big batch of chocolate chip cookies for your dad. These are all beautiful expressions of love, but as heartfelt as they are, they cannot come close to the perfect love God has for you.

Did you know that even when your heart was black with sin—when you were hard to love—God gave the greatest possible gift of love? He gave His perfect, holy Son, Jesus, to pay a sin debt that you wouldn't want to pay. What an amazing love that is! Have you accepted it?

Herein is love, not that we loved God, but that he loved us, and sent his Son to be the propitiation for our sins.
1 JOHN 4:10 KJV

EVENING •

Dear heavenly Father, thank You for always loving me...especially on those days when I am hard to love. And thank You for the greatest gift ever—Your Son, Jesus! Every single day of my life, I can count on You. You never let me down, and I am forever grateful. Help me to love others with that same kind of love. You're the perfect example to follow! Amen.

DAY 40
A Giant Eraser

Have you ever messed up so badly that you felt like the Lord couldn't forgive you? Here's the good news: God has a giant eraser. When you mess up (like all people do), you can ask for His forgiveness. Once you ask, He grabs that giant eraser of His and gets to work, wiping away all of that icky stuff. Ah! Doesn't it feel good to have a clean slate, a fresh start?

Don't beat yourself up when you mess up. Just ask for forgiveness and then imagine God wiping away that bad stuff and giving you a chance to replace it with good. He will, you know!

Let all that I am praise the LORD; may I never forget the good things he does for me. He forgives all my sins and heals all my diseases.
PSALM 103:2–3 NLT

Lord, You do so many wonderful things for me. One of the very best things is that You forgive me when I do something I shouldn't. I'm so glad You have a giant eraser to wipe away all my mistakes! Whew! What a relief to know that my mess-ups won't mess up my relationship with You. It feels so good to know that when I ask, You'll always give me a fresh start. Thank You for that. Amen.

DAY 41
Courage to Face the Hard Times

MORNING •

What happens when you face a hard time? It won't disappear on its own, so the only option is whether to run from it or face it head-on.

The easiest choice is to run from a difficult situation. Jonah did that when God told him to go to Nineveh. But even during the storm at sea, throughout his time in the fish's stomach, and when he eventually traveled to Nineveh, the Lord went with Jonah.

God doesn't want you to run from challenges; rather, He wants to face them with you. He inspires you to be strong because He will confront the hard time with you. No matter how rough it gets, there's nothing that can make Him leave you. He is with you through it all.

> *"Be strong and courageous. . . . For it is the Lord your God who goes with you. He will not leave you or forsake you."*
> **DEUTERONOMY 31:6 ESV**

EVENING •

Dear Jesus, I want to be strong and courageous. Help me to face the hard times with determination because I know that You will stay by my side through it all. Because You are always with me, I will never run away from my problems. Instead, I'll stand strong. Thank You for being such a faithful friend and encourager. You're the best Friend a girl could have! Amen.

DAY 42
The Lord, Your Hero

MORNING •

Sometimes the world is a scary place. . .and it seems to get scarier every day. There are so many things you have to watch out for, not only at school but on the internet, in your neighborhood . . .maybe even in your own home.

No matter where life takes you, you can be sure that God goes with you. He is the ultimate dad. He loves you and watches over you every moment of every day. His ears are always open to your prayers (1 Peter 3:12). Because of your relationship with Him, you can be confident that He will keep you safe. When you go to sleep at night you can sleep peacefully. You don't have to be afraid because the Lord, your protector, is on the job (Proverbs 3:24).

Though I walk in the midst of trouble, you preserve my life. You stretch out your hand against the anger of my foes; with your right hand you save me.

PSALM 138:7 NIV

EVENING •

Dear God, thank You that You are my protector. Thank You for loving me and going with me everywhere I go. Thank You for keeping me safe. Even though the world is a scary place, I know I can count on You. And every night I can go to bed and sleep peacefully. When You're there watching over me, I don't ever have to worry. You're like a great dad—the very, very best a girl could ask for! Amen.

DAY 43
Sometimes Love Means Stop

MORNING •

There was once a middle-school boy who drew a bright red STOP sign with the word *compassion* scrawled above it in bold, black letters. Compassion means that you feel kindness and concern for someone's trouble. Sometimes it's compassionate—it shows kindness—to tell someone to stop.

If you see someone running out in the street and a bus is coming, you don't just sit there; you yell for them to stop.

It's the same way with God. Because He loves you, there are times when He will tell you to stop. And sometimes the way He will get you—and me—to stop doing something that is hurtful for us is to discipline us. His discipline is always done in love because He cares for us and He doesn't want us to get hurt.

Sometimes love means stop.

The Lord disciplines the one he loves.
HEBREWS 12:6 NIV

EVENING •

Lord, thank You that You discipline me. You know what's best for me, so I can trust when You discipline me, it's because of Your love for me. I am so very grateful that You don't allow me to do everything I want, especially when You know something is bad for me. I'm glad that You're a good daddy who cares for me. Thank You for telling me to stop when it's the best thing for me. Amen.

DAY 44
Words of Comfort

When your friends hurt your feelings. . .when you feel left out. . . when you're sick or feeling bad. . .remember the One who will never leave you, the One who knows you better than anyone else. Remember that our God wants only what is best for you, and then turn to Him. He is the Great Comforter. Reread today's verse from Psalm 119 and familiarize yourself with other scriptures about God's comfort. Be assured that He is *always* ready and willing to comfort you.

> *This is my comfort in my affliction,*
> *for Your word has given me life.*
> **PSALM 119:50 NKJV**

Dear heavenly Father, my day had a less-than-stellar start—I haven't been feeling well and I didn't feel like going to school today, but I couldn't afford to miss any more days. So I went. Then I found out my friends are having a party and didn't invite me. Oh, they said they thought I was still sick and meant to call me to see if I could come, but now I'm not sure they really want me to. But I want to go, Father. Please give me comfort so that I can quit crying and get past my hurt. And please help me to comfort others when they feel like I do right now. Amen.

DAY 45
If His Eye Is on the Sparrow...

MORNING •

God sees the birds as they soar and as they pluck little worms out of the fertile soil, when they make nests for their little ones. . . If God sees and feeds the birds of the air, you can be sure that He sees and takes care of you!

God understands whenever you're going through a hard time. After all, Jesus came as a human. He suffered every temptation we do (see Mark 1:12–13 and Matthew 4:1–11). He understands. He sees what you're going through, and He's there to help you, strengthen you, and carry you through (see Matthew 6:30; 1 Corinthians 10:13; Philippians 4:13; 2 Corinthians 12:9). He wants you to trust Him and know that He has everything under control. God will never abandon you—no matter what!

> *"Look at the birds of the sky, that they do not sow, nor reap, nor gather crops into barns, and yet your heavenly Father feeds them. Are you not much more important than they?"*
> **MATTHEW 6:26 NASB**

EVENING •

God, I know You care about the birds. And I know You care for me even more! Thank You for loving me so perfectly. Thank You for seeing me. Thanks for Your understanding, protection, and help. You are always there when I need You—even when I don't realize it myself! I trust You, Lord. And I will keep trusting You for the rest of my life. In Jesus' name I pray. Amen.

DAY 46
Reading and Growing

The Bible may have been written centuries ago, but its principles apply to your life today. No matter what situation you find yourself in, God's Word has the answer for how to handle it. Having trouble with a bully? Check out Romans 12:19–20. Struggling with temptation? Read 1 Corinthians 10:13. Whatever you need, the Bible has a verse for you.

The Bible is a big book with a lot to say. If you're not in the habit of reading it, you can get a little overwhelmed. Start with something familiar, like the creation account in Genesis or the birth of Christ in Luke. Use a highlighter to mark the verses that stand out to you. Write notes in the margins. Most importantly, make a daily effort to read God's Word.

Search the scriptures.
JOHN 5:39 KJV

Dear God, put a love for the Bible in my heart. Remind me to set aside some time each day to read the scriptures, and most of all, help me to obey what I read. It's true that when I read Your Word and spend time talking to You, my faith grows, and grows, and grows some more. Your Word always speaks directly to my heart. Amen.

DAY 47
Joy in Troubles

MORNING •

Consider it *joy* when problems come into your life? That's what God's Word says. This doesn't mean you have to act happy and be fake when problems happen. It just means that you "get" that this world isn't perfect and problems will come—and that you trust in God to give you joy in spite of the bad stuff!

Consider this. . . . Let's say you move to a new school and you don't know a single person. You have a not-so-good first day, and you are treated badly by some mean kids. You don't have to be happy about it; but God does want you to remember that He is always with you, and He has you at the new school for a reason. He wants you to be a shining light for Him wherever He allows you to go. Ask Him to give you His joy to make it through, and He will!

Consider it pure joy, my brothers and sisters, whenever you face trials of many kinds, because you know that the testing of your faith produces perseverance.
JAMES 1:2–3 NIV

EVENING •

Dear Jesus, I know that the world isn't perfect. And some-times I'll have to go through difficult times. Help me to grow up knowing, loving, and trusting You—even when life is hard. With You by my side, I can always have joy in my heart. . .even on my worst days. Thank You, Father. Amen.

DAY 48
Always, Always

Have you ever been in a situation where you felt lost or alone? A time when you got a panicky feeling in your stomach and you felt vulnerable, like something bad was about to happen? In times like these, it's easy to forget that there is Someone who loves and protects you, who will never forget you or abandon you. But your Father in heaven is *always* watching over you, even when it feels like no one is there.

God knows when you are scared or lonely. He knows you better than anyone else on earth ever could, and His love and protection are constant reminders of that. He never tires of hearing from you, and He desperately wants to give you comfort when you need it.

> ***It is God who arms me with strength
> and keeps my way secure.***
> **PSALM 18:32 NIV**

Heavenly Father, thank You for always watching over me and giving me strength when I feel weak. Help me remember to talk to You when I'm feeling lost or scared. I can always tell You exactly how I feel, and You will understand. You're always ready to take my worries away, and You can comfort my heart like no one else can. You provide courage and strength—and whatever else I might need—to deal with any situation. Amen.

DAY 49
Do Not Be Afraid

MORNING •

Everyone feels afraid sometimes. But the Bible tells us that God has not given us a spirit of fear. He wants us to be courageous. There will be times in life when you have to face things that make you nervous or even scared. And in each one of those experiences, God will be with you.

God assures us in His Word that He knows the plans He has for us, and those plans are to bring us hope and a future. . .never to harm us (Jeremiah 29:11). Nothing can touch your life without first being filtered through the fingers of your heavenly Father.

Be strong in Jesus, and when you are afraid, tell Him about it. He will help you face your fears.

For God has not given us a spirit of fear,
but of power and of love and of a sound mind.
2 TIMOTHY 1:7 NKJV

EVENING •

God, sometimes I feel so afraid. Help me to remember that You have put a spirit of courage within me. It's comforting to know that nothing gets to me without going through You first. I couldn't ask for a better protector. Today I will be strong. . .I will face my fears with boldness. . .because of You. Thank You, Father! Amen.

DAY 50
The God Hug

Some days it seems like everyone is against us, doesn't it? Friends are mean. Mom gets onto us for leaving our towel on the bathroom floor. Even the dog won't sit in our lap when we call him. On days like that, we feel like there's no hope, no comfort anywhere.

But God, who loves us more than anything, wants to be our comforter. No matter what's going on around us, we can always find that still, small voice in our spirit that says, *"I love you. I'll never leave you. I think you're special, and I want you to trust in Me and have peace."*

Just as God comforts us, He wants us to comfort others. Today, look for someone who might need comforting, and offer your friendship. It just might make both of you feel better.

> *Praise be to the God and Father of our Lord Jesus Christ, the Father of compassion and the God of all comfort, who comforts us in all our troubles, so that we can comfort those in any trouble.*
> **2 CORINTHIANS 1:3–4 NIV**

Dear Father, when life is hard, sometimes I feel like I'm all alone. Like no one cares about me or what I'm going through. When negative thoughts enter my mind, please nudge me. . .remind me that my thoughts and feelings are sometimes unreliable. Remind me that I am never alone because I have You! Thank You for being my comforter. Help me comfort others as You comfort me. Amen.

DAY 51
Me, Strong?

You may be just a kid, and you might think you are small and weak. But did you know you are also a soldier for the Lord? And that He gives you all the strength you need to face each battle that comes your way? It's true!

When you keep your attention on God and on what *He* has for your life, the bumps, hurdles, roadblocks, and even wars that come your way will be easier to tackle. He's given you a very special set of armor to wear, and He has unlimited strength to help you through even the most difficult of days.

So when you feel weak, don't allow feelings of insignificance to overwhelm you. God has given you *His* strength for each day. And His strength is perfect.

> *It is God who arms me with strength*
> *and keeps my way secure.*
> **PSALM 18:32 NIV**

God, thank You for today and even for all the chal-
lenges that come my way. When I begin to feel over-
whelmed by life, thank You for giving me Your strength.
Remind me in the hard times that Your strength is all
I need—and Your strength isn't limited. For that, I am
so very thankful! Help me to keep my focus on You
today, tomorrow, and all my days to come. Amen.

DAY 52
How Much Is Too Much?

Did you ever sin so much that you thought God could never forgive you? That God would abandon you because you'd gone too far? What if you lost your best friend and it was all your fault? What if you told a lie that hurt your brother or sister? What if you stole something or even hated someone in your heart? Would God give up on you? Would He be unwilling to forgive you?

The answer is no! When you say you're sorry to God, He forgives you for all the bad stuff. All those hurtful things are wiped away. Your past becomes like a pile of dirty laundry that gets thrown into the wash. Those clothes come out clean, ready to be worn again.

For I am convinced that neither death nor life, neither angels nor demons, neither the present nor the future, nor any powers, neither height nor depth, nor anything else in all creation, will be able to separate us from the love of God that is in Christ Jesus our Lord.

ROMANS 8:38–39 NIV

Lord, sometimes it feels like my sins are too big. Like maybe—just maybe—You won't be able to forgive me for things I've done. But Your Word gives me hope by reminding me that nothing can keep me from You. Nothing is so big that You won't forgive it. So please forgive me today, Father, for all the things I've done that make You sad. Help me to live closer to You each day so I can know Your peace and joy! Amen.

DAY 53
My Eternal Home

Do you think a lot about your home? It's probably your favorite place to be. . .your room is exactly the way you like it. . .all of your favorite things are exactly where you like them to be, right? Well, do you ever think about your ETERNAL home? If we have accepted Jesus as our Savior, we get to live in heaven with Him forever after our life on this earth is over.

Jesus tells us in John 14:2 that He has gone to heaven to prepare a place for us! He is getting our room ready in heaven. Heaven is a perfect place, and it will be filled with all your favorite things. So whenever you are having a rough day or feeling down about this life, imagine what life will be like in heaven!

One thing I ask from the Lord, this only do I seek: that I may dwell in the house of the Lord all the days of my life.
PSALM 27:4 NIV

God, thank You for thinking of me. . .for creating a home in heaven for me. . .for loving me so very much. I can only imagine what heaven will be like. And while I don't know exactly what my forever home will be like, it's sure fun to think about. No matter what, it will be perfect because You are there. And I will be able to worship You for eternity. I am so thankful to be Your child! Amen.

DAY 54
In His Care

These days, many families are struggling financially. Maybe yours is one of those families. When you see all of that and can do nothing about it, it can lead to a lot of fear.

It's true you can't do much to change the financial situation of your family right now, but there are things you can do to help.

First, work on having a great attitude. Let your parents know that you're content with what you have. Next, be creative about ways to stretch what you have, yet still make it interesting. Why not trade outfits with a friend or have a movie night at home instead of going to the theater?

Finally, pray. Pray for the financial situation of your family, and pray for the security your parents feel in God. Be sure to thank God for all your blessings. When you have a thankful heart, the emptiness fades away.

"That is why I tell you not to worry about everyday life—whether you have enough food and drink, or enough clothes to wear. Isn't life more than food, and your body more than clothing?"
MATTHEW 6:25 NLT

Lord, forgive me for being jealous when other kids have things I want. Remind me that things will never bring me joy because things are temporary. What really matters in life can't be bought. Help me to remember—and be grateful for—all of the wonderful blessings You've given me. I want to focus on the important things in life, not the "stuff." Amen.

DAY 55
Needs and Wants

MORNING •

It's quite easy to confuse wants with needs. Sometimes the line between the two can get a little blurry. But even when there's confusion on our part, God knows what His children need and has promised to provide it.

We should not grudgingly trudge through life, sulking because we don't have the "certain thing" we feel we *need* to have. If there's something that God chooses to equip us with so that we can better serve Him, then He will bring it to us.

Because God is our God of unconditional love, He will give us some "wants" too. He is a loving Father who joys in showering blessings on His children.

> ***And my God will supply all your needs according to His riches in glory in Christ Jesus.***
> **PHILIPPIANS 4:19 NASB**

EVENING •

Dear heavenly Father, I admit sometimes I act more like my wants are actually needs. Help me to know and recognize the difference. Thank You for giving me all that I need. Thank You too for many of the "wants" You have provided. Help me to trust that You will take care of me. . .and help me to know and understand that You have perfectly good reasons for not giving me everything I want. You are so good to me! Amen.

DAY 56
The Cowardly Lion

MORNING •

If you've seen *The Wizard of Oz*, you know that Dorothy met several people on her journey down the yellow brick road. One of those people was the Cowardly Lion. He sure seemed like a scaredy-cat, didn't he? Talk about being afraid!

Maybe you've felt like a scaredy-cat at times too. You wanted to run and hide from your troubles instead of facing them. Here's the good news: God will give you the courage to face the things you're scared of. It's true! You can get back on the yellow brick road and walk with courage and confidence, knowing the Lord is walking with you.

"Be strong and of good courage, do not fear nor be afraid of them; for the LORD your God, He is the One who goes with you. He will not leave you nor forsake you."
DEUTERONOMY 31:6 NKJV

EVENING •

God, sometimes I feel so afraid. I try not to, but I just want to crawl under the covers and hide. I don't want to be like the Cowardly Lion, Lord. So on days when I struggle, please give me Your courage. Thank You for encouraging me and giving me strength to face the hard things! How wonderful to be able to look fear in the eye and say, "You don't scare me anymore!"...and to really mean it! Amen.

DAY 57
When You Lose a Friend

Have you ever lost someone that was really special to you? It can be especially hard to lose close friends because we don't think we are supposed to lose them. We expect them to always stay with us. We have to remember that when God brings people into our lives, sometimes it's for a long time and sometimes only a short time.

When they leave, it hurts because you may feel alone or like no one is going to love you again. Maybe you feel angry. Maybe you blame yourself or you blame them for what happened.

No matter how you feel—if you are mad, sad, or frustrated—God cares. When you lose someone special to you, God wants to comfort you. He is always there. He wants to heal your broken heart.

The Lord is close to the brokenhearted
and saves those who are crushed in spirit.
PSALM 34:18 NIV

Lord Jesus, I am so thankful that I can always tell You exactly how I feel—the good, the bad, and the ugly. It is so hard to lose a good friend. But I do know that sometimes friends come and go in our lives. And that's okay. But when my heart is broken, help me to trust that You will heal me and help me to keep my heart open so that I can keep loving others. I know You will bring new friends into my life. Thank You for loving me so very much! Amen.

DAY 58
A Special Kind of Hope

MORNING •

There is a recipe for success in Romans 12:10–13—a recipe for success in the Christian life.

One ingredient mentioned in these verses is hope. Not just any hope, but *confident* hope. There is a difference between plain hope and *confident* hope. You can hope the wind doesn't blow today, but you don't know for sure that it won't. You can hope those shoes you've been wanting will go on sale, but there is no guarantee they will. *Confident* hope is a sure thing. . .like the hope of God's love and a future home in heaven. These things are guaranteed if we have chosen to follow Jesus. We can have this kind of hope all the time. It's a special gift—a gift that God gives to us as a promise.

Aren't you happy to have God's special kind of hope?

Love each other with genuine affection, and take delight in honoring each other. Never be lazy, but work hard and serve the Lord enthusiastically. Rejoice in our confident hope. Be patient in trouble, and keep on praying. When God's people are in need, be ready to help them. Always be eager to practice hospitality.

ROMANS 12:10–13 NLT

EVENING •

Dear Lord, thank You for showing me how to live a good life—the kind of life You mean for Christians to live. Thank You for the gift of hope. Help me to share it with others and give them hope through the way I live my life. I want others to see You reflected in all I say and do. I will always rejoice in the hope You have given me. Amen.

DAY 59
Watch Your Words

Sometimes words can hurt much, *much* more than sticks and stones. A scrape on the knee will heal pretty quickly, but wounds that come from hurtful words will stay inside your heart for a lifetime if you let them.

God wants us to be an encouragement to the people in our lives. He wants us to be helpful and to say things that make Him smile. He doesn't want us to use bad words or gossip about others either.

If you've had unkind things said about you, forgive the person who said them and then ask God to heal your heart. If you're the one speaking unkind words, ask God to forgive you, and use your words to lift people up instead.

> ***Don't use foul or abusive language. Let everything you say be good and helpful, so that your words will be an encouragement to those who hear them.***
> **EPHESIANS 4:29 NLT**

Dear God, it's true that words can hurt. . .but words can also heal and bring hope. I want to be an encourager—both in my actions and my words. Please help me to be wise in the way I talk to and about others. Forgive me for unkind things I've said in the past. And please help me to be forgiving of others who have said mean things about me too. Help me to always honor You—and others—with my words. Amen.

DAY 60
How Hungry Are You?

When you get home from school, are you totally starving? Have you ever been that hungry spiritually? Have you ever longed for God so much that you really hungered for Him?

Some people think if they read the Bible once a week, they're good to go. But if the Bible is our spiritual food, we're going to be pretty skinny spiritually speaking if we only feast on the Bible once a week. We need to "eat" of it daily! As Christians, we should literally crave God and His Word.

If you're less than hungry for more of God, ask Him to increase your spiritual hunger. Once you begin "snacking" on the scriptures, you'll find it's a lot like potato chips—completely addictive! So go ahead—dig into God's Word today. It's full of good stuff!

> **For he satisfies the thirsty and**
> **fills the hungry with good things.**
> **PSALM 107:9 NIV**

Thank You, God, for giving me physical food to feed my body. I am also thankful for the spiritual "food" I can find in Your Word. Please increase my spiritual hunger so that I may grow closer to You. When I feast on Your Word every day, I will grow wiser and stronger in my faith. I want more of You every day, Lord! Amen.

DAY 61
Please Forgive Me

MORNING •

When you know you've done wrong—kept the truth from your parents, lied to your friends, cheated on a test, or anything else you know you weren't supposed to do (even in secret)—remember that God knows *all* you do and *nothing* is hidden from Him. But He is a God of mercy and forgiveness. All you have to do is ask!

I acknowledged my sin to You, and my iniquity I have not hidden. I said, "I will confess my transgressions to the Lord," and You forgave the iniquity of my sin.
PSALM 32:5 NKJV

EVENING •

Dear God, please forgive me for my sin. I thank You for being a forgiving God. I know I was wrong. I know You and my parents love me and will forgive me. I don't know what came over me! And now I can't get it off my mind, and I feel so guilty. You know everything I do, Father—I know I can't hide anything from You. I am so very sorry. Please give me strength and wisdom so I won't disappoint You or my parents again. Amen.

DAY 62
I Think I Can; I Think I Can!

Do you ever feel like you just "can't"? Maybe you're struggling in school or you're crumbling under heavy responsibilities. Or maybe the Christian walk is a burden on your heart right now: "Don't give in to temptation." "Stay pure." "Be an example."

You may want to say *NO* when the Holy Spirit is prompting you to invite a friend to church or to tell someone about Jesus. Maybe you want to run away when a friend comes to you for help with a struggle you don't feel equipped to face.

But God promises to be there with you through all of those hard times and to carry your fears. He will give you the strength you need to live out His call in your life, and He'll never ask you to do anything that He won't equip you to do.

> *"Fear not, for I am with you; be not dismayed, for I am your God. I will strengthen you, yes, I will help you, I will uphold you with My righteous right hand."*
>
> **ISAIAH 41:10 NKJV**

Dear God, I want to follow You, but sometimes it's hard. Sometimes I want to say no. Other times, I feel like running away...even when I know it's not the right thing to do. When I'm struggling, thank You for being here. I know You won't leave my side. Please give me the strength today to do the things You ask me to do. Amen.

DAY 63
The Real Hope

There doesn't seem to be much hope in the world today. The news is full of depressing stories. The friends we once thought would be there through anything turn away. The game that was a sure win turns out to be a loss. *Where is the hope?*

Hope is heard in a lot in conversations. "I *hope* I can go this weekend." Or, "I *hope* it doesn't rain today." Or, "I *hope* my mom/dad will let me [fill in the blank]."

But the only real hope comes from Jesus Christ. He is always right there—He doesn't move away or leave us on our own. That's hope we can count on!

He will *be* our true hope and will *give* us true hope—especially in those times that seem to be hopeless.

> *For God alone my soul waits in silence and quietly submits to Him, for my hope is from Him.*
> **PSALM 62:5 AMP**

Dear Lord Jesus, I need Your hope. The world needs Your hope too! Sometimes things are so bad that I wonder if they will ever get better. But then I remember I have You, Lord. And You are all I'll ever need. You are exactly what the world needs! So I ask You today to be in control of my life. Thank You for being my true hope and for giving me true hope. In Jesus' name, amen.

DAY 64
The Right Thing–Every Time

MORNING •

Ever had one of those days? You didn't study for a test right after school. Then you had practice. After practice, you went home, ate dinner, helped with the dishes, and then went to your room. Exhausted from a long day, you fell asleep in your school clothes.

Several hours later you wake up and think, *I'll study tomorrow, during recess or in study hall.* Defeated, you put on pajamas and crawl into bed for the night.

The following day, things don't go quite as planned. And when test time arrives, you are scrambling to think of a way to save yourself from the impending F. *Susan always gets As*, you think. *I could probably cheat off her, and no one would know the difference. . . . But I would know, and my heavenly Father would know. And He wants me to do the right thing—every time.* So with a shrug and a quick prayer—*Thank You, Jesus, for giving me the strength to do the right thing!*—you begin.

> ***. . .because you obey the Lord your God by keeping all his commands that I am giving you today and doing what is right in his eyes.***
> **DEUTERONOMY 13:18 NIV**

EVENING •

God, thank You for giving me the courage and strength to do the right thing. Help me to always do my best to be prepared—and to choose the right thing, even when I'm tempted to do what's wrong. Forgive me, Lord, for all the times I've failed to listen to Your voice. You will never lead me in the wrong direction. Thank You! Amen.

DAY 65
Give Him Your Dreams

I once watched a movie in which a tiny girl held a handful of shiny pennies. An adult held out a five-dollar bill, inviting her to trade. Convinced she had what was best because it looked like the most, she told him no and hugged her pennies close.

This reminds me of how we can sometimes be when Jesus wants to trade what we want for what He wants. Maybe He asks us to move to a new school or to join a new club. But we want to hold on to our old thing, like our old school or our old club. We hold on and won't let go because we think that what we have is more.

Remember that God always knows best. Also remember that He will never ask you to give up something without giving you something in return that is His best plan.

Humble yourselves before the Lord, and he will lift you up.
JAMES 4:10 NIV

Lord, sometimes it's hard for me to give up what I want for what You want. And I have a tight grip on the "old" thing. Help me to loosen my grip. . .to trust You and not demand my own way. Your plan may not be easy—but I know it will be right. I know I will have joy in my heart if I follow You. I trust Your plan, Father. And I love You. Amen.

DAY 66
You're Gonna Live Forever!

Someone once said there are only two things you can be sure about: death and taxes. Everybody pays taxes. . .and everybody dies. Or do they?

God never intended for you to die. God created you to be His friend and live with Him forever. But when Adam sinned in the Garden of Eden, death came into the world for the first time. For a long time after that, death had authority over every living thing on the earth. It didn't matter if they were good or bad or worshipped the one true God or not.

When God sent Jesus to die on the cross, Jesus paid the price for Adam's sins and everyone who came after him—including you. Adam may have allowed death into the world. . .but Jesus kicked it out (1 Corinthians 15:21–22). Through Jesus Christ you can have a relationship with the Creator of the universe and cheat death at the same time!

> **And this is the testimony: God has given us eternal life, and this life is in his Son.**
> **1 JOHN 5:11 NIV**

Dear God, thank You for the promise of eternal life I have through Your Son, Jesus. Thank You for making a way for me to escape death and live a life of joy and peace with You. I can't wait to see what heaven will be like. I just know it will be wonderful! And I can't wait to spend forever worshipping You! Amen.

DAY 67
God's Workmanship

MORNING •

You're God's workmanship—His *masterpiece*! God doesn't make mistakes (Genesis 1:31). He made you and didn't mess up in the process. He didn't have a blooper moment.

He knows exactly who you were, are, and will be. He knows why He made you the way you are. And He made you that way for a *reason*!

Everyone is unique and special in their own way. God wants it that way! How boring would it be if everyone looked exactly the same?

God sees you as His workmanship and craftsmanship. He loves you beyond measure, precious one. Trust Him. He knows what He's doing. (See Proverbs 3:5; Ephesians 4:20–24; Colossians 2:13–14; Proverbs 31:20; 1 Peter 3:3–4.)

> *For we are His workmanship, created in Christ*
> *Jesus for good works, which God prepared*
> *beforehand so that we would walk in them.*
> **EPHESIANS 2:10 NASB**

EVENING •

God, I am special. I am unique. I am Your creation. And I know that I'm "just right" in Your eyes. Thank You for loving me, covering me with Your fingerprints, and having a perfect plan for me. I love You. Thank You so much for loving me enough to make me, me! You love me—in fact, because You created me, You love everything about me. And I am so thankful for that! In Jesus' name I pray. Amen.

DAY 68
The Great Comforter

Who do you talk to when you're hurt? Sad? Lonely? Afraid? You might talk to your parents, your brother or sister, or friends. God has put these people in your life to help comfort you in times of trouble. God Himself can comfort you too. When you open your heart and pray to Him, don't be afraid to tell Him exactly how you feel.

The Bible teaches us that God is full of mercy. This means that He is compassionate. He wants to comfort His children.

The more you turn to God and feel His comfort, the better you will be able to comfort those around you. When you see someone hurting, you can reach out in love.

All praise to God, the Father of our Lord Jesus Christ. God is our merciful Father and the source of all comfort. He comforts us in all our troubles so that we can comfort others. When they are troubled, we will be able to give them the same comfort God has given us.

2 CORINTHIANS 1:3–4 NLT

God, sometimes life is hard. When it is, I am so thankful You have placed good people in my life to help me. My friends, my family, my teachers. . .I have so many people I can count on when I need them. And best of all, I have You! When I am hurting, Lord, be my comforter. I know You will always make me feel better. You love me with an everlasting love. Amen.

DAY 69
What Do I Have to Look Forward To?

Some days, you wonder if there's anything good at all coming in your future. Is there any point?

There is! And it's so much brighter than the most incredible future you could dream up for yourself. It's eternal life. And God offers it freely to you. Don't you love that? That He sent His Son to die for you and me so that we could live with Him forever. That's love. That's sacrifice.

So no matter where you are today—excited about the future or not—remember that the very best is yet to come. An eternity without pain or sorrow or sadness.

Now that's something to look forward to.

> *"For my Father's will is that everyone who looks to the Son and believes in him shall have eternal life, and I will raise them up at the last day."*
> JOHN 6:40 NIV

EVENING •

God, sometimes I don't feel I have much to look forward to, but that's just not true. Not when I have You in my heart. When I have hopeless, hard days, please help me remember that the best in life is yet to come. My future will be wonderful because You are my Savior. Thank You for offering me eternal life. Please help me to share Your gift with someone else today. I look forward to forever life in heaven with You, Father. Amen.

DAY 70
All Prayed Out

MORNING •

Do you ever feel like you're all out of prayers? Like you don't have enough energy to speak one more word to anyone, let alone share your feelings with God? Or maybe you're all prayed out because you've been asking God for the same thing over and over again, and you feel like He's either not listening or has decided not to answer.

In Luke 18, Jesus gives us a picture of how He wants us to pray. The widow wears down the judge with her persistent request until one day, he finally gives in. No matter what you are praying about, don't give up! Keep talking to the heavenly Father. The process of persistent prayer will change your heart to be more like His. And at times when you feel all prayed out, remember that God is *always* listening and working in your life.

Then Jesus told his disciples a parable to show them that they should always pray and not give up.
LUKE 18:1 NIV

EVENING •

God, sometimes I feel like this widow lady in the Bible when I come to You over and over again about the same thing. And I wonder if You're tired of hearing from me. I worry that You're not listening. Help me to get rid of those untrue thoughts. I know You hear my prayers, Father, and I trust that You will always do what is best for me. Help me not to lose heart but to remember Your love and faithfulness. Amen.

DAY 71
A Giant Treasure Box

Have you ever waited for Christmas morning, hoping you would get a certain gift? Maybe you asked your parents or grandparents for a new video game or bike. Maybe you secretly hoped for a new gaming system or computer. You planted lots of hints, convinced they would get you what you wanted. Then Christmas morning arrived. . .and no video game! No bike! No games or computer!

When you don't get the things you want, why not take your requests to God? The Bible says that He owns everything in the world. He's got a huge treasure box filled with all sorts of unimaginable things!

The cool thing about God is that He doesn't give us what we *want*—He gives us what we *need*. Sure, it won't always be some cool gadget or gaming system, but it will always be His very best for you.

> *My God will use his wonderful riches in Christ Jesus to give you everything you need.*
> **PHILIPPIANS 4:19 NCV**

EVENING •

God, I know that I don't always get what I want. Sometimes I ask my parents for things and don't get them. But You know what I really need. Today—and every day—I will share my wants with You. Then I will wait with a patient heart, and know that whatever You provide, it's the perfect thing for me. Thank You being my great Provider! I trust You fully for everything. Amen.

DAY 72
Lesson from the Sea

MORNING •

God sees the bright promise of your future. He also knows that poor choices could spoil it. That's why He gave you parents, spiritual leaders, and a conscience. It's why your internet use may be limited and you're not allowed to hang out with certain people.

Staying within your boundaries might mean missing out on some fun. It could even make you unpopular with some of your peers. But when you're tempted to sneak over the line of protection that has been drawn for you, remember that God placed it there for your good. Remember too that when the sea oversteps its bounds, it takes a lot of effort and expense to repair the damage.

> *He gave the sea its boundary so the waters*
> *would not overstep his command.*
> **PROVERBS 8:29 NIV**

EVENING •

Lord, sometimes I have a really bad attitude about rules. Sometimes I don't understand why we need them; other times, I just don't want to follow them. I certainly don't always like—or agree with—the restrictions that my parents and others place on me. When my attitude needs an adjustment, Lord, please remind me that the rules are for my good—to keep me safe from the dangers of the world. Amen.

DAY 73
Who Could Know You Better?

MORNING •

We hear the word *know* all the time. We can say we "know" about many things or know certain people. And it's true. But there is a different kind of knowing that only God has.

Because He is the one who created you, He knows *everything* about you. He knows you in a way that no one else can. Like the artist who creates a beautiful painting and knows each stroke of the brush and the tiny specks that make it special, God knows each part of you. He is proud of His special creation—the perfect picture of you. He also knows your thoughts and dreams. . . the desires of your heart. God's knowing goes far deeper than we can even understand. And because His knowing is so deep, His love is deep too. And that's the best blessing of all!

> *"And the very hairs on your head are all numbered.*
> *So don't be afraid; you are more valuable to*
> *God than a whole flock of sparrows."*
> **LUKE 12:7 NLT**

EVENING •

Heavenly Father, a lot of people know me. My parents know nearly everything about me. I even have some friends who know me almost as well. And I sometimes forget that You know me better than anyone ever will. You alone know me best of all. Please help me to be the special person You created me to be. Thank You for knowing me and loving me—no matter what. Amen.

DAY 74
Invite God

You probably know people who are always ready for a party. They're the ones who make their way to every gathering and are always ready to hang out with anyone and everyone. Social by nature, they enjoy spending time with people and cannot wait for an invitation so they can mingle with others.

God's the same way. He yearns for the time when two or three people gather together to pray, study His word, offer help to others, or simply spend time together in Christian friendship; and then the Holy Spirit shows up, just like that. He arrives for the smallest of meetings and the biggest of corporate worship services—they're all important to Him.

> *"Where two or three gather in my name, there am I with them."*
> **MATTHEW 18:20 NIV**

God, thank You for showing up whenever I ask. . .before I even ask. I can always trust that when I look for You, I will find You. I am so thankful that what matters to me also matters very much to You. While I will always talk to You—just You and me, Lord—I'd like to invite others to pray with me too. Help me to have the courage to invite friends and family members into my prayer time. It's not always easy, but I know it's important. Amen.

DAY 75
More than Cherubs

What comes to mind when you think of heaven? Are there any chubby cherubs reclining on clouds and stroking golden harps in your vision? If so, the idea of angelic beings lounging around for all eternity might strike you as, well. . .boring.

But if the God who created rainbows and mountains and music and color also created the heavens, then how much more breathtaking and exciting will your eternal home be than earth? As a Christian, you have so much to look forward to. No one really knows for sure what heaven will hold, but you can rest assured that it will be beyond your wildest dreams. There will be infinite joy, overwhelming beauty, and—best of all—you will get to see Jesus face-to-face.

> *"I give them eternal life, and they will never perish,*
> *and no one will snatch them out of my hand."*
> **JOHN 10:28 ESV**

God, thank You for reserving a spot for me in heaven. When I get discouraged or anxious, help me to remember that this isn't my true home. Spark my imagination when I think of heaven, Lord. Lead me to the portions of Your Word that give vivid descriptions of my forever home. I'm looking forward to eternity with You! It's going to be amazing! Amen.

DAY 76
Don't Give Up!

MORNING •

Have you ever started something that you didn't finish? We're not very good at following things through to completion sometimes, are we? But aren't you glad that God is? He doesn't start something and not finish it. That should give you hope!

God began a good work in you, and He's going to complete it! He's no quitter! So don't give up, even when you feel hopeless about things. Keep going. God hasn't given up on you, and you shouldn't give up on yourself either. Keep on hoping! Keep on believing! Keep on trying. The Lord is working inside of you right now, at this very moment, and He won't stop—no matter what!

> *God began doing a good work in you, and I am sure he will continue it until it is finished when Jesus Christ comes again.*
> **PHILIPPIANS 1:6 NCV**

EVENING •

Lord, I admit I'm a quitter. Sometimes I start things but then don't finish them. They seem too hard! And then I give up hope. But that's not like You at all, Father. You never quit. You never give up on me. You have a plan for my life, and You won't stop until You see it through. Thank You, God, for never giving up on me! I want to learn from Your perfect example! Amen.

DAY 77
A Fresh Start

MORNING •

Mess-ups are a part of life. Everybody messes up. *Every single one of us.*

Sometimes we mess up on accident, like when we drop our lunch box and the contents spill everywhere, and we lose our temper about the whole thing. Other times we mess up on purpose. We decide in our heart that we don't want to clean our room, even though Mom has asked us four times already, and so we shut our door and read a book instead. Whether it's an accident or on purpose, God calls those kinds of mess-ups "sin."

But when we realize we've messed up, tell God we're sorry, and sincerely promise to try not to mess up like that again, God wipes the record clean. He forgives us. The verse below says He removes our sins as far as the east is from the west. And since the east and west never meet each other, that's a pretty long way.

> ***He has removed our sins as far from
> us as the east is from the west.***
> **PSALM 103:12 NLT**

EVENING •

Dear Father, sometimes I worry that I went too far. That my sin is too big—even for You. I know You can handle a lot, but can You handle super-duper big mistakes? Thank You for Your Word that lets me know, without a doubt, that You are the very best forgiver. If I tell You I'm sorry for my mistakes, You'll always give me a fresh start. Thank You, Jesus! Amen.

DAY 78
A Joyful Heart

What does it mean to be joyful?

Being joyful is the ability to rest in God's goodness, no matter what's going on in life. Not everything that happens will be good, but He will let us rest in Him while we get through it. And that's something to smile about!

Those with illnesses take medicine to feel better, but the Bible says that a joyful heart will have the same results on the body as a good medicine. It can keep a person from having a "broken spirit," which "saps a person's strength." Joy sounds like a much better option!

Whatever today brings, try to keep an attitude of joy. It may change the results of your situation, or it may not. But either way, resting in God and trusting that He will work everything out for His good is always the best way.

> *A cheerful heart is good medicine, but a*
> *broken spirit saps a person's strength.*
> **PROVERBS 17:22 NLT**

Dear Jesus, I admit that sometimes I just don't feel joyful. When I don't get what I want. . .when I have a bad day. . .when I just don't feel well. . .I allow those things to get in the way of my joy. Please help me to trust that You are working good in my life, whether I can see the results right now or not. I want to be known as a person who always has a joyful heart. Amen.

DAY 79
Band-Aid Moments

Imagine this: You're zooming down the street on your skateboard. You've done it a hundred times, at least. So often, in fact, you're not really paying attention. So instead of watching where you're going, you check out the neighbor's new puppy. Then, *BAM!* You collide with a mailbox. Head trauma plus scraped elbows and knees don't bother you as much as the embarrassment of lying on the curb, crying in front of the entire neighborhood. It's a Band-Aid moment in more ways than one. You could limp back home, whining about how life isn't fair. But *you* were distracted by the pup, weren't you? When things go wrong, God often prevents situations from being far worse. What would have happened if that mailbox had been a car?

The next time you encounter a bad situation, try to view it from God's perspective. Your attitude might change from "Life isn't fair!" to "Thank You, God! That was a close one!"

I will speak with the voice of thanks,
and tell of all Your great works.
PSALM 26:7 NLV

God, when things go wrong, I often feel like You're far away or not even there at all! Please change my view on things. Help me to see the big picture in my "Band-Aid" moments, so I recognize Your presence, even when life isn't perfect. I'm glad You're always here, loving and protecting me. You are the best! Amen.

DAY 80
He Hears Me

Do you ever wonder if God hears your prayers for help when everything seems to be going wrong? When you feel sick or sad? Or when you don't get everything you ask for? Sometimes we forget all that God has done for us or how many prayers He's answered. Remember when you thought you wouldn't be able to play in the soccer tournament? You'd been sick all week and prayed, but you thought God didn't hear. And yet by the time the game rolled around, you were just fine and played one of your best games ever. Or the time when you were scared you'd fail the test and you prayed. . .and you somehow remembered all the right answers and made an A on the test? Thank God for answered prayers!

When the righteous cry for help, the Lord hears and delivers them out of all their troubles.

PSALM 34:17 ESV

Dear God, thank You for all the prayers You've listened to. Thank You for all the prayers You've answered. Please help me to always remember how You've worked in my life—including Your many blessings and all the times You've listened to my whining and complaining—and know that You do answer my prayers (even if You might not answer the way I'd expect You to). Please help me to trust You all my days. Amen.

DAY 81
Join the Clutter-Free Club

MORNING •

Is your life cluttered? Do you leave the house early in the morning and arrive back home just in time to go to bed? If so, you are probably a member of The Clutter Club. With lots of extracurricular activities, homework, school, and church—there's not much time for anything else.

You know what happens when you have too much clutter in your life? You get stressed out, and then you freak out!

But there's good news! God is the best organizer, the best planner, and the best at time management. (He did create the whole world in less than a week!) The Bible says to seek Him first. When you do, all of the clutter just seems to fall away, and God supernaturally organizes your day.

> *The wicked are too proud to seek God.*
> *They seem to think that God is dead.*
> **PSALM 10:4 NLT**

EVENING •

God, I feel like I have no time for anything, and I am s-t-r-e-s-s-e-d out! I am having to take shortcuts to get everything done—and I feel like I'm doing nothing well. Life is just one exhausting day after another, with no end in sight. I need Your help! Please help me declutter my life. Where there are things I need to let go, please show me. Thank You! Amen.

DAY 82
The Lord Is Faithful

MORNING •

No matter what, God promises that He will be faithful. He'll strengthen you, protect you, and perfect the good work that He began in you (see 2 Thessalonians 2:16–17; 1 Timothy 1:12; Philippians 1:6, 4:13; Ephesians 2:10).

God has given you His armor to boldly wear. Paul says, "Stand firm then, with the belt of truth buckled around your waist, with the breastplate of righteousness in place, and with your feet fitted with the readiness that comes from the gospel of peace. In addition to all this, take up the shield of faith, with which you can extinguish all the flaming arrows of the evil one. Take the helmet of salvation and the sword of the Spirit, which is the word of God" (Ephesians 6:14–17 NIV).

You're given truth, righteousness, the Gospel of peace, faith, salvation, and the magnificent Word of God—all of these to put to good use, in faith that God has provided and will protect you.

> **But the Lord is faithful, and He will strengthen**
> **and protect you from the evil one.**
> **2 THESSALONIANS 3:3 NASB**

EVENING •

Father, thank You for keeping me safe, no matter what's going on in my life or in the world. You promise to keep me from harm. Thank You for protection and peace. Thank You for Your Word, salvation, truth, and righteousness. I trust You, Lord, with all my heart. You are always faithful to me. In Jesus' name I pray. Amen.

DAY 83
Text from God

Is your main means of communication verbal, email, or text message? The majority of us have most of our conversations via text today. It's fun; it's easy; it's fast.

What if God texted you? How would you feel about that? Would you feel like He took a shortcut if you wrote to Him with a deep need and He wrote back, *IDK*?

Did you know God hears every word you speak and every need on your heart? And what's better is that He replies with an active response. *Every single time.*

He either meets that need by giving you exactly what you asked for, or He meets it with *no* or sometimes a *maybe*. But even in the *no* and the *maybe* there is still action. He decides what's the very best for us, and He is going to provide that even if it means saying *no*.

Now this is the confidence that we have in Him, that if we ask anything according to His will, He hears us.
1 JOHN 5:14 NKJV

Dear God, thank You for always having an answer to my prayers. Your answers may not be quite what I expect, but I do trust You to always do what's best for me. Please help me to accept Your no's and the not-yets with grace. Thank You for always hearing me and always responding to me. I love You, Lord. Amen.

DAY 84
God Provides

The Bible promises that God takes care of His children. He cares for the birds, providing food for them in nature. Will He forget about His children? No way!

You may not always have everything you *want*, but consider all your *needs* that God meets every day. Ask Him to help you be content. It's a dangerous thing to always want more. Some children grow into adults who are never satisfied. They are constantly on the lookout for the next thing that might bring them happiness.

True happiness doesn't come from our belongings but from a genuine relationship with God. Start today by thanking Him for the way He provides all that you need. Then challenge yourself to say a prayer of thanksgiving whenever you begin to feel even the slightest tinge of jealousy.

"Look at the birds of the air; they do not sow or reap or store away in barns, and yet your heavenly Father feeds them. Are you not much more valuable than they?"

MATTHEW 6:26 NIV

Heavenly Father, I want to experience true happiness . . .true joy. Remind me that I can have joy even when I don't have all the things I want, because You truly care for me. And help me to have a grateful heart for everything You've given me, Lord. I have experienced so many blessings in life. For each one, I am so thankful. Amen.

DAY 85
A Special Message

Are you happy, sad, excited, or disappointed? Celebrating or feeling depressed? Lonely, loved, worried, nervous? No matter what you're feeling, God's Word *always* has a message for you— a message that will help you with anything and everything you care about, whatever's on your mind. Your life is important to the One who created you!

So pick up your Bible, and get reading! Set aside a special time of day to spend with the One who loves you more than anyone or anything. Highlight, underline, or circle the passages that speak to your heart.

When you're through spending time in God's Word, you'll have time to reflect and write in a journal. And the best part? . . . You'll find yourself growing closer to the heavenly Father *every day*!

> **The people read it and were glad
> for its encouraging message.**
> **ACTS 15:31 NIV**

EVENING •

*God, being busy is no excuse for not spending time
with You. There is so much for me to learn by spending time in Your Word. Please help me to stay faithful.
Help me to set aside time each day to read my Bible
and have conversations with You. Lead me to scriptures that will speak directly to my heart. I need more
of Your Word in my life. Thank You, Father! Amen.*

DAY 86
In the Garden

Do you like growing things? In school you probably learned about planting seeds and watching them grow. Jesus liked to use gardening illustrations in the Bible to help people understand what He was teaching too! John 15 is a good example of one of these illustrations. Jesus says, "Yes, I am the vine; you are the branches. Those who remain in me, and I in them, will produce much fruit" (verse 5 NLT).

You can learn a lot by hanging out in a garden. But if you're not a big fan of digging in the dirt, just soak in all the beautiful flowers and plants that God created. View them as reminders that God wants you to do the right thing and grow into a young person who harvests "love, joy, peace, patience, kindness, goodness, faithfulness, gentleness, and self-control" (Galatians 5:22–23 NLT).

> *You will always harvest what you plant. Those who live only to satisfy their own sinful nature will harvest decay and death from that sinful nature. But those who live to please the Spirit will harvest everlasting life from the Spirit.*
> **GALATIANS 6:7–8 NLT**

God, thank You for creating so many beautiful things for me to enjoy. . .for the different kinds of plants and flowers. Each leaf, every bud and bloom. . .Your creativity is awesome! Use nature to remind me of Your teachings to do the right thing and grow into the kind of person You created me to be. I want to be all You created me to be, Lord. Amen.

DAY 87
A Man of His Word

Believe it or not, there are some things God *CAN'T* do. God can't lie. He can't sin. He can't break a promise. God is perfect in every way. He is always with you, always hears you, always knows what you are going through, and always has the answer. God would never do anything to violate His perfect nature. He is good, all the time, in every situation. If He were to do or be anything else, He would not be God.

That's good news for believers. If God says He will always be with you. . .He will. If He says He will protect you from your enemies. . .He will. If He says He will provide for your needs. . .He will. God keeps His word. What He says He will do. . .He does!

> *If we are faithless, he remains faithful,*
> *for he cannot disown himself.*
> **2 TIMOTHY 2:13 NIV**

Dear God, none of the people in my life are perfect—not one. Sometimes even the people I love the most let me down. And while that's a bummer, there is some great news! And it's this: there is someone I can always count on. . .it's You! Thank You, Father, for NEVER letting me down. You are 100 percent perfect in every way. Thank You for keeping all Your promises. Amen.

DAY 88
God Won't Break His Promises

Do you ever wonder if God really saved you? If He's really there? If He really has a plan for you?

It's easy to doubt God in our humanness. We are imperfect, so it's hard to understand how He can be perfect and all-knowing, all-powerful, all-present, and love us so much that He sacrificed His own Son to die for us.

But in Titus 1:2, we get a huge affirmation—God doesn't lie!

When you learn how to study the Bible, you learn that scripture doesn't contradict itself, and scripture always backs up scripture. So when God says He will never leave you nor forsake you—it's true. When it says that you are fearfully and wonderfully made—it's true.

Other people may break their promises, but God won't. He doesn't lie.

> *Let us hold unswervingly to the hope we profess, for he who promised is faithful.*
> **HEBREWS 10:23 NIV**

God, I sometimes find myself doubting the truth of Your Word. Please forgive me and help me to remember Your promises. When I asked You into my heart, You saved me! You're always there for me. . .in every situation. And You have a wonderful plan for me! You never lie. You're not capable of telling lies. So every single word of Yours is true. What a comfort to my heart. I love You, Lord. Amen.

DAY 89
Forgiven: No More Bad Labels

Have you ever done something wrong and felt like you have been labeled "bad," "not worth keeping," or "not worth loving"?

Sometimes when we sin, people will stick a label on us. They will say we are bad, but God always forgives, and He always gives us second chances.

In Exodus 2:14, after Moses killed a man, a Hebrew made fun of him and said, "Who made you ruler and judge?" (NIV).

More than forty years later, God did send Moses to rule and deliver His people. Acts 7:35 says, "He [Moses] was sent to be their ruler and deliverer by God himself" (NIV).

What is wonderful is that even though Moses had done something bad, God still used him. God didn't let a bad label stick to Moses. He forgave him. Then God sent him to be a ruler and deliverer over the Israelites.

If we confess our sins, he is faithful and just and will forgive us our sins and purify us from all unrighteousness.

1 JOHN 1:9 NIV

Lord, how wonderful to know that You will always forgive me when I ask. No matter what I say. No matter what I do. Nothing is beyond Your forgiveness. And I am so grateful! If I do something wrong today, You don't permanently stick a label on me that marks me as not good enough. I am so thankful You're a God of second chances. I know You'll continue working in my life every day, according to Your perfect plan. Amen.

DAY 90
Where Is God?

There are lots of things that we know exist, even though we can't see them. Things like the air, our beating heart, love, and even the sun on a cloudy day. . . We often take these things for granted but still trust they are there.

How do we know that God is always around? The Bible tells us He is with us all the time, but how can we be sure? Is believing what the Bible says enough? Sometimes. When we have some sort of evidence, we are satisfied. God provides evidence in many ways, but the most precious proof is when He speaks the truth to us personally. When we know God in a personal way, He will speak softly to our hearts, telling us He is there. He will always be there to answer questions and hear our cries twenty-four hours a day.

He will *never* leave you. Learn to listen for His voice.

"I will never fail you. I will never abandon you."
HEBREWS 13:5 NLT

Dear Father, I know You are with me, and I want to hear You speak to me. Help me turn to You when I am in trouble. Whenever my heart feels like You're very far away, remind me of Your nearness. Thank You for being by my side every minute of every day. I will listen for Your voice today and every day. I want to hear Your message for me. Amen.

DAY 91
Just Trust!

Have you ever lost hope, been so disappointed and discouraged that you just didn't think it was possible for things to get better? Everyone has moments like this at some point in their lives, and it's at those low points that God wants to reach out and give you hope. Having hope means that even if your situation doesn't get better immediately, you have complete faith and trust that God is still in control and will work things out. Holding on to hope and trusting that God will take care of you isn't easy; it takes patience and time. But if you do put your hope in the Lord, He will give you a peace that passes all understanding and joy in any situation.

God, treat us kindly. You're our only hope. First thing in the morning, be there for us! When things go bad, help us out!
ISAIAH 33:2 MSG

Dear God, I don't know why I'm going through something hard, but You do. Please help me get through this and to put all my hope in You. I trust that You are in control and will give me peace and joy in any situation. When I am feeling discouraged, I will rely on You to bring me hope. I know You love me and want the very best for me. Thank You. Amen.

DAY 92
Got the Giggles?

Have you ever had this happen? You're with your friends and you get the giggles. One person starts laughing. . .and then another. . . and then another. Before long, everyone is cracking up! That's kind of how it is when you let the joy of the Lord take over your life. Even when you're going through a tough time, God's joy can bring a smile to your face. It's true! And your smile can be contagious! Others see it and start smiling too. Before long, the joy that's inside of you has spread to the people around you! Everyone is soon feeling better.

So don't worry about the tough stuff you're going through. Just ask God to give you His joy so that you can laugh your way through the tough times.

May the God of hope fill you with all joy and peace
as you trust in him, so that you may overflow
with hope by the power of the Holy Spirit.
ROMANS 15:13 NIV

Lord, I don't always feel joyful. Sometimes I get sad.
But now I know that I can ask for Your joy and You will
put a smile on my face! If I ask, You'll do it. And I'm so
glad! Your joy can bubble out from my heart and spread
to others who also need to feel Your joy in their lives.
Help me to laugh my way to pure, lasting joy. Amen.

DAY 93
God Is Always with Me

Are there days when you are afraid of just about everything? Afraid of going to class on your first day at a new school? Feeling tongue-tied when the teacher asks you to tell the class a little about yourself? Or what about the time you were late for class and got sent to the principal's office? What about the day you embarrassed yourself by giving the wrong answer to a question the teacher asked you? When any of these things happen, remember that God loves you and He will *always* be with you. He doesn't want you to fear a thing!

> *"And the Lord, He is the One who goes before you. He will be with you, He will not leave you nor forsake you; do not fear nor be dismayed."*
>
> **DEUTERONOMY 31:8 NKJV**

Dear God, I never have to be afraid—of anything! Please help me never to forget that You go before me—You know all that I am doing and all that will happen to me. Please help me to remember that I don't need to be afraid or worried about what will happen because You are always here with me and will never leave me. Amen.

DAY 94
Head Scratchers

Have you ever tried to understand—really, truly understand—God? Little kids ask their parents, "Who is God's mommy?" and "Could there ever be a rock so big that even God couldn't lift it?" The answers to these questions go against everything we know as humans: God doesn't have a mommy; He has always been there. God can lift the biggest rock that there ever could be.

God's love for us sinful humans is just as confusing. How can the Master Creator love His creation so much?

Someday in heaven the fog of confusion will lift. We'll understand God's will and His plan for all of creation. We'll know why He answered our prayers the way He did. And we'll fully understand how big His love is for us.

We don't yet see things clearly. We're squinting in a fog, peering through a mist. But it won't be long before the weather clears and the sun shines bright! We'll see it all then, see it all as clearly as God sees us, knowing him directly just as he knows us!
1 CORINTHIANS 13:12 MSG

God, there are so many things I just don't understand about You—even though I pray and read my Bible. Yet while it's impossible to understand everything about You. . .for now I will just trust You with all my heart. I'll have all the answers I'll need when I get to heaven. Until then, I'll keep talking to You and spending time in Your Word. Amen.

DAY 95
Hello? Are You There?

At the end of a hard day, after dealing with bullies, temptations, and stresses of life, it's comforting to walk in the front door of your own home, isn't it? The soothing smells of comfort food. The familiar sounds of Mom tinkering in the kitchen. It's comfortable. It's always there, and you trust it will always be the same.

That's how it is with God. He promises that He is always there with us and that He will never change. Sometimes it's hard to believe that because we can't see Him. But we do hear His voice in our hearts when we pray, we feel His presence when someone offers comfort in His name, and we feel Him surrounding us when we praise Him.

Today, let God reveal His presence to you. Be aware of what He's doing in your life right now.

He has never let you down, never looked the
other way when you were being kicked around.
He has never wandered off to do his own
thing; he has been right there, listening.
PSALM 22:24 MSG

Father, I need Your comfort today. The world is a hard
place to be sometimes. It doesn't feel friendly or safe.
Spending time with You feels like home to me. It's com-
forting—a place where I can just be myself. Please
show Yourself to me today. Help me see You clearly.
Thank You for never leaving me alone. Amen.

DAY 96
Do-Over

MORNING •

Video games are addictive. From old-school PAC-MAN to the very latest in gaming technology—there's nothing quite like getting the highest score or advancing to the next level. But when you get blown up or eaten in the very first minute or two, it can make you so mad, right? If you're not too far into the game and nobody is watching, do you ever just restart the game?

In real life, we don't get many do-overs. When you say something hurtful to your best friend, you can't rewind and start again. So isn't it nice that with God we always get to start over? All we have to do is tell God we're sorry, and then we get to start over and move forward with our heavenly Father. With God, we always win!

> *Count yourself lucky, how happy you must be—*
> *you get a fresh start, your slate's wiped clean.*
> **PSALM 32:1 MSG**

EVENING •

Lord, thank You for forgiving my sins and giving me a new beginning. No matter what I've done, You still love me and forgive me. Psalm 103 tells me that You have removed my sins as far as the east is from the west. That's a very l-o-n-g way, Lord! I am thankful that with You, my slate can be wiped clean! Amen.

DAY 97
Father Knows Best

"But I prayed about it! Why didn't it work out?"

Rest assured that God hears His children each and every time they call. But like all good parents, your heavenly Father decides whether or not your petition is a good one. Some answers to prayer are delayed until the timing is right. Other prayers are denied because they don't fit into God's plan for your life. And sometimes God thrills your heart by opening the windows of heaven and pouring out blessings.

Before you pray for something, ask yourself if your desire is a godly one. If it is, then pray and wait patiently to see what God will do. Remember that when you trust Him with your life, everything will work out for the best.

Your Father knoweth what things ye have need of.
MATTHEW 6:8 KJV

Dear God, I admit that I'm disappointed when You don't answer my prayers the way I want You to. The things I ask for are really important to me. . .and I know that You understand me, Lord. You know how I feel. Help me not to question Your motives when You don't give the answers I seek. You are a good and loving Father. Thank You for loving me enough to choose what's best for my life instead of spoiling me with what I want. Amen.

DAY 98
Escaping Temptation

There are many different temptations. Some are really big ones. Others are quite small. Some are easy to avoid. Then others trap you. . .and sometimes they trap you over and over again.

Jesus was tempted by Satan while He was on earth. So He knows what it's like to be faced with a really difficult choice. But unlike His creation, He didn't give in to temptation.

The Bible says that you will be tempted. You'll be stuck in that moment when you know what you should do but pause to decide what you will actually do. It's in that split second that God wants you to know there is an escape—a right choice to make. He will be faithful in helping you to overcome it. Just look to Him!

No temptation has overtaken you that is not common to man. God is faithful, and he will not let you be tempted beyond your ability, but with the temptation he will also provide the way of escape, that you may be able to endure it.

1 CORINTHIANS 10:13 ESV

Dear Jesus, You understand what it's like to be tempted, so I know it's not unfamiliar to You. You know and understand what it's like to be me. When temptation is really strong, You will always provide a way out for me—even though it might not be easy. Please give me the strength to overcome temptation. Thank You that You will always make a way for me to get through it. In Your name, amen.

DAY 99
Just Be You!

Dr. Seuss wrote, "Today you are You, that is truer than true. There is no one alive who is Youer than You." And that's a fantastic thing! God created each of us to be unique on purpose! Not even identical twins are exactly alike. God made us all just the way He wanted us to be.

Take a few minutes and open your Bible. Read Psalm 139. Ask God to help you understand these verses and believe them. Print out the words and hang them on your wall or on your bathroom mirror as a special reminder that God made you to be YOU! He doesn't want you to change to be more like one of your friends. He gave you special gifts and talents and ideas that nobody else has! Be thankful and use them to honor Jesus!

> *I praise you, for I am fearfully and wonderfully made. Wonderful are your works; my soul knows it very well.*
> **PSALM 139:14 ESV**

Dear God, it's so wonderful to know that every single person on earth is unique because You created us all so differently. Our differences make the world a more beautiful place. Thank You for the one-of-a-kind gifts and ideas that You have given me. Remind me when I try to be like someone else that You created me to be me—nothing more, nothing less. Help me have the courage to be myself. Show me how to use my personality to bring You joy! Amen.

DAY 100
Dangerous!

Have you noticed that being alive is dangerous? You get sick. Your friends have accidents. Your grandparents grow old. But God cares about each of us. He knows everything there is to know about you, and He watches over all your comings and goings.

The Bible doesn't guarantee us a perfect life here on earth. In fact, Jesus said we will have many troubles, but the Lord is right here with us. He may not sweep away every misery or heal every wound, but He has promised to give you strength to handle whatever life throws at you.

God can take something that was meant for evil and turn it into something good. He is the master at turning shadows into a sunrise. We can rest in that promise until He takes us home to be with Him for eternity.

> *The Lord will watch over your coming and going both now and forevermore.*
>
> **PSALM 121:8 NIV**

Jesus, I know that every day I spend on earth won't be easy. You never promised a perfect life—even with You in it. But You did promise to be there for me and to help me have joy even in the hard stuff. So help me to trust in You—that no matter what happens each day, I know You'll stay beside me, helping me with every choice I make and every step I take. Amen.

DAY 101
God's Masterpiece

MORNING •

Artists paint. Sculptors sculpt. Musicians compose. Many of them dedicate their entire lives to creating a *masterpiece*, the work of art for which they will be remembered.

Now think about everything that God created—He created the entire world! Imagine that. Every flowering tree, each unique animal, the brilliant stars, and the clear blue water were designed by your heavenly Father.

But none of that brought Him complete satisfaction. It was not until He created humankind that God had crafted His greatest work, His *masterpiece*. We were created in order to bring glory to our Creator. When you begin to worry about your appearance or wonder if you have enough talent, remember. . .God made you to be just as you are. And you are His masterpiece!

> *For we are God's masterpiece. He has created us anew in Christ Jesus, so we can do the good things he planned for us long ago.*
> **EPHESIANS 2:10 NLT**

EVENING •

Heavenly Father, when I look at Your creation, I am amazed. What a wonderful artist You are, Lord! But I admit that sometimes, I don't feel so special. Sometimes I feel quite ordinary. Help me to remember that there is nothing ordinary about me—because I was created by You! I'm Your daughter. . .and I am perfect in Your sight. I am Your masterpiece. Amen.

DAY 102
You Can Do It!

Ever have one of those weeks when you feel like everything has come crashing down on you at once? It makes you want to pull your hair out and scream, "I CAN'T DO THIS!"

The truth is. . .you probably can't. Not by yourself, that is. The great thing is you don't have to because you are never alone. You've got God on your side. The Bible says you can do all things through Christ who strengthens you (Philippians 4:13).

Take a few minutes every day to spend time with God in prayer and worship. When you do, you'll find you really *CAN* do everything you need to do because God will give you the strength you need right when you need it (Isaiah 40:31).

> *"The Lord is my strength and my defense; he has become my salvation. He is my God, and I will praise him, my father's God, and I will exalt him."*
> **EXODUS 15:2 NIV**

Dear God, sometimes I get overwhelmed with all the stuff I'm supposed to do. I REALLY can't handle everything all on my own. Sometimes I need more strength, more courage, more of YOU! Help me to remember that everything I need comes from spending time with You, Father. I can give all my cares to You—and You'll take them and handle them for me. Thank You for being a loving God who gives me strength. Amen.

DAY 103
The Wages of Sin

God has given us a gift—a marvelous and undeserved gift. He sent His one and only Son to earth so that we could be saved from eternal suffering.

Jesus was born in a stable, despised and rejected by His own people, flogged in a synagogue, and died on a rugged, splintery cross—even though He was sinless.

His sacrifice was no small undertaking. The devil didn't want Jesus to go through with His purpose. We can safely assume that he made it as hard as possible. But Jesus persevered through everything—because He loves the world and everyone in it (John 3:16). He extended His grace to *everyone* so we can have hope for a future of *everlasting* bliss where we can worship Him and live to the *absolute* fullest.

> **For the wages of sin is death, but the gracious gift of God is eternal life in Christ Jesus our Lord.**
> **ROMANS 6:23 NASB**

Father, I can't comprehend why You sent Jesus to die for me. I can't even begin to imagine what it was like. Your love is bigger than anything I can fathom. You really do love every person in the entire world. Please help those who don't know You yet find their way to You, Lord. Show me how I can help make that happen! I thank You with everything in me. In Jesus' name I pray. Amen.

DAY 104
Eat Your Spinach!

There are some days when we just don't feel very strong. We're spiritual wimps! But we don't have to stay that way. We can get strong in a hurry, and it doesn't even require eating healthy foods or working out at the gym! All we have to do is pray and read our Bibles and as a result, God builds our spiritual muscles! In other words, we get strong from the inside out.

Do you need to be strengthened today? Reach for your Bible and swallow down as much as you can! Write down your favorite verses on pieces of paper and put them on your bathroom mirror. Memorize them and say them out loud. Before long, you'll be the strongest kid in town!

He gives strength to the weary and
increases the power of the weak.
ISAIAH 40:29 NIV

God, sometimes I get so tired! I don't even want to get
out of bed in the morning. I need Your strength on all the
days I feel weak, Lord. Lead me to Your Word and pull
me closer to You every day. I know that I will grow stron-
ger in my faith by spending more time with You. Thank
You for giving me the strength to keep going, even when
I really want to pull the covers over my head! Amen.

DAY 105
Learn to Use Your Sword

MORNING •

In Ephesians 6, we're given the rundown of the amazing armor of God that is available to each and every believer. Isn't it cool to know that He's provided that for us? We have a way to stand firm, every moment of every day.

But all too often, we hide behind our shield of faith because we're doing good just to survive the attack of the enemy, right? Guess what? God's given us a sword as well. And one we're supposed to be using.

The sword is the sword of the Spirit, which is the Word of God. We need to be studying the Word, hiding it in our hearts, so that we are ready to use it when God calls us to.

> *Study to shew thyself approved unto God, a*
> *workman that needeth not to be ashamed,*
> *rightly dividing the word of truth.*
> **2 TIMOTHY 2:15 KJV**

EVENING •

Lord, I want to know You better, and I want to study
Your Word so that I can be prepared to serve You better
each day. Help me to memorize a verse from Your Word
each week. Show me where I can set aside time each
day to read my Bible. There are probably things I should
give up so I have more time to spend with You, God.
You're worth it! I want to be a kingdom worker. Amen.

DAY 106
A Hopeful Tomorrow

MORNING •

On those days when you think there is nothing left to hope for, or when you feel down and out of sorts—maybe the day didn't turn out quite like you had hoped, or something you'd been wishing for fell through—remember to look to the one true Hope. God will always give you new hope for a new day. After all, He gave each one of us the hope of eternal life in heaven with Him through His precious Son, our Savior. How can we have a down day when we think of that?

"Why are you cast down, O my soul? And why are you disquieted within me?" (Psalm 42:5 NKJV).

> *Hope in God, for I shall yet praise Him*
> *for the help of His countenance.*
> **PSALM 42:5 NKJV**

EVENING •

Dear God, I didn't make that A like I thought I would. And I was late for one of my classes. Now I have to do extra work, which means I won't get to spend time with my friends this afternoon. And tomorrow isn't looking good either—I feel so frustrated inside, mostly at myself. Please help me to get past this down feeling and be able to hope again like I did this morning. Amen.

DAY 107
Does God Like Me?

You have probably heard a lot about how much God loves you in your lifetime. But *love* and *like* are a little different, right? Do you think God likes you?

When you come to know Jesus as your Savior, God washes all your sins away and He sees you as the perfect kid you are. And you can say with confidence: "God likes me!" He rejoices over you, and the Bible says He even sings about you! You are liked. You are loved. You are His!

"The Lord your God is with you, the Mighty Warrior who saves. He will take great delight in you; in his love he will no longer rebuke you, but will rejoice over you with singing."
ZEPHANIAH 3:17 NIV

Dear God, wow! Knowing how You feel about me makes my heart smile. Thank You for loving me. . . and for liking me just the way I am. I am so thankful You like hearing me pray. . .and that You like me spending time in Your Word. Thank You for loving me enough to send Jesus. Thank You for seeing me as perfect. I love You. I like You a whole lot too. Amen.

DAY 108
God's Yearbook

MORNING •

Did you know God has His own yearbook? If you turn to the year you were born, your face would be there. He picked that specific moment in time for your birth. He wanted to create you exactly at that moment so you could be right where you are today. He continually looks through His book and says to the angels, *"Isn't My child wonderful? Look how smart and kind! This is My child, whom I love so much!"*

God enjoys celebrating your life as much as you do. He takes pride in all you do and say. . .in your adventures and how you handle your challenges. He doesn't even care if you're the one in the school yearbook with bed head. You are His treasure!

See what great love the Father has lavished on
us, that we should be called children of God!
1 JOHN 3:1 NIV

EVENING •

God, thank You for adding me to Your yearbook. When I
feel like I don't belong, remind me that You created me
for this specific time and place. I celebrate life with You
and plan to make the best of today—and the rest of my
life. Walk beside me every moment, Father. I want to feel
Your presence with me. I will do my best to obey You,
Lord. May all I do and say be pleasing to You. Amen.

DAY 109
Changed Plans

MORNING •

You're getting ready to leave for vacation. You've packed, fed your fish, and went to bed early so you could be up at the crack of dawn. You can't wait!

When you come downstairs the next morning, your parents tell you that something has come up—and now you can't go on your camping trip. Your grandmother has fallen and will need help getting around for the next few weeks.

Instead of telling Mom and Dad that you understand, you stomp upstairs and throw your suitcase. Its contents spill out all over the floor. After putting all your stuff back in order, you realize how horribly you've behaved. You ask your parents to take you to see your grandma—and after seeing her, you realize how much worse her fall could have been. And you give thanks to God for your family. . .and for plans that can change when others are in need.

> **"For I know the plans I have for you," declares the Lord, "plans to prosper you and not to harm you, plans to give you hope and a future."**
> **JEREMIAH 29:11 NIV**

EVENING •

God, I know You have plans for me—and Your plans aren't always my plans. Remind me of this when things don't go my way. Help me to keep my cool when I don't get exactly what I want. This doesn't mean I won't be disappointed for a time, but with Your help, I will see that everything will be okay. Thanks for always understanding how I feel and for wanting the best for me. Amen.

DAY 110
Here's How God Sees You

VeggieTales creator Phil Vischer wrote a rhyming script called *A Snoodle's Tale* about a small, unique creature struggling with self-image. The snoodle feels unloved, unwanted, and unimportant because of his differences and because of the way others are treating him. Eventually, the snoodle's creator shows him a picture of what he really looks like and says, "Here's what you look like. Here's how I see you. Keep this in your pack, and you'll find it will free you from all the pictures and all the lies that others make up just to cut down your size."

When you take your eyes off Jesus—just like Peter did—your self-image will begin to sink. You'll feel "less than." You'll feel unloved. Your differences will stick out. Your faith will grow weak. But when you keep your eyes on Christ, you'll begin to see yourself as He sees you! Perfect. Just right! Fully capable of serving Him and loving others too!

So Peter went over the side of the boat and walked on the water toward Jesus. But when he saw the strong wind and the waves, he was terrified and began to sink.
MATTHEW 14:29–30 NLT

God, remove my focus from the world and what others might think of me. Thank You for creating me just the way I am. Help me to keep my eyes on You so that I can see myself just as You see me—Perfect! Just right! Capable of doing great things for You! Capable of serving others too! Amen.

DAY 111
Where's Your Playbook?

If you have ever played a sport, you probably had to look at a rule book or game plan written by your coach. You studied the rules and learned how to play the game before you actually competed against another team. You then practiced what you learned, hoping to come out a winner.

We all want to be good at following Jesus and doing His will for our lives. And the best way to know how to play on His team is to read His rule book, the Bible. We can try to live as Christians on our own, but it's so much better with His Word to guide us. He is our coach, and we need to understand how He wants us to play the game.

> *All Scripture is inspired by God and is useful to teach us what is true and to make us realize what is wrong in our lives. It corrects us when we are wrong and teaches us to do what is right. God uses it to prepare and equip his people to do every good work.*
>
> **2 TIMOTHY 3:16–17 NLT**

Jesus, thank You for being my coach. I know I can win in the game of life with Your encouraging guidebook. I will set aside time every day to read Your Word and then will give my very best effort to follow Your rules for life. I know it will guide me, play by play, to be the best at whatever You have planned for me. Amen.

DAY 112
God Said It, and He Meant It

Do you ever lie awake at night and worry that you've somehow disappointed God and He's turned away from you? Or maybe you worry that you never really surrendered your life to Him in the first place?

Even if you've grown up in a Christian home and you've been going to church for years and years, sometimes doubts can set in about whether or not your faith is real.

But God's Word is true. He said that when you turned to Him, He gave you a new identity. You are a new person in Christ. He doesn't play games with that. He is not a liar. He promises that He'll finish the work He started in you. You can trust Him.

He who began a good work in you will carry it on to completion until the day of Christ Jesus.

PHILIPPIANS 1:6 NIV

Dear God, thank You for coming into my heart and saving me. Please forgive me for doubting the finished work of Your salvation. Help me remember Your promises and trust that I am a new creation in You, and no one can take that away from me. Tonight I will go to sleep in peace. Amen.

DAY 113
My Life GPS

MORNING •

There are many decisions to be made in life. Wouldn't it be awesome to have a life GPS to figure it all out? It could tell you which paths to avoid, which turns to make.

God is our GPS. He sees the whole picture. He knows every detail of every life. His children are referred to as His "workmanship" in the Bible. You were made to love Him and to do good works that only you can do!

Don't get overwhelmed because you don't have all the answers yet. Stay close to Jesus. He will let you know His plan for your life, in His perfect timing.

> *For we are His workmanship, created in Christ Jesus for good works, which God prepared beforehand so that we would walk in them.*
> **EPHESIANS 2:10 NASB**

EVENING •

Dear Father, sometimes making a decision is overwhelming. How do I know I'm making the right choices for my life? How can I be sure I'm making You proud, God? I will stay close to You and listen for Your voice. You'll show me the way. Thank You for creating me and making me a special "workmanship." Help me to listen to You and to obey You so that I can do the works You have created me to do. In Jesus' name, amen.

DAY 114
The Favor Factor

MORNING •

Guess what? You have favor with the guy in charge—*God!* The Bible says that He has crowned your head with glory and honor and favor. He loves showering you with favor because He adores you.

You can walk in the favor of God all the time. Here's all you have to do. Start thanking God for His supernatural favor. Every morning before you head off to school, thank God that you have favor with your teachers, your principal, your coaches, your peers, your parents, and anyone else you might encounter. Then watch your life begin to change for the better. It's amazing, really. Once you start praising God for His supernatural favor, you'll begin to see more of it in your life. So start praying and praising, and enjoy the favor of God today!

> *Surely, Lord, you bless the righteous; you surround them with your favor as with a shield.*
>
> **PSALM 5:12 NIV**

EVENING •

Lord, it's strange to me when I think about having Your favor. You...the God who created the heavens and the earth...You adore ME?... Today, I will praise You, Lord. I will completely accept and enjoy Your favor. I can't wait to see all the blessings You have in store for my life. Thank You for Your favor, Lord. I love You. Amen.

DAY 115
A True Friend Will Tell You the Truth

MORNING •

When I think about one of my very best friends, one of the things I love is that she will always tell me the truth. If I am cranky and have a bad attitude, she may tell me that I need to trust God. When I need to hear something from the Bible to help me with my life, she is honest. That's one of the things I love about her: she tells me the truth in love.

Jesus is a best friend who will tell you the truth. His truth will protect you and guide you. He will never lie to you.

If you want a best friend who will tell you the truth and help you if you are going the wrong way, Jesus is this kind of friend. He loves you more than anyone can. Just open your heart to hear Him.

> *No longer do I call you servants, for the servant does not know what his master is doing; but I have called you friends, for all that I have heard from my Father I have made known to you.*
>
> **JOHN 15:15 ESV**

EVENING •

Lord, I am so very thankful to have a loving Friend like You. I know I can trust You to tell me the truth—even when it's hard for me to hear. Even when You need to tell me hard things, still You love me. And Your love never changes. Thank You that You want to help me in every area of my life. I know that You will never lead me in a way that will hurt me. There is no one more faithful than You. Amen.

DAY 116
Which Road Should I Take?

MORNING •

If you've ever been on a road trip, you know what it's like to follow a map. Sometimes we come to a fork in the road and don't know which way to go. If we don't pay attention to the map, we can get lost in a hurry!

Did you know that God has a spiritual road map for your life—the Bible? When you come to a fork in the road—and you don't know which way to go—His Word will give you answers. And remember, you can always pray and ask God to guide you if you're really feeling lost. He will! Just listen closely to His still, small voice. He wants to show you the correct road, one that will lead you to a place of safety and peace.

"I say this because I know what I am planning for you,"
says the LORD. "I have good plans for you, not plans to
hurt you. I will give you hope and a good future."
JEREMIAH 29:11 NCV

EVENING •

God, sometimes it's hard to know what to do. Having
choices can be confusing. I don't always know which road
to choose or which direction to go. When I feel mixed up
and lost, You always guide me. When I read Your Word and
pray for wisdom, I will always discover the right thing to do.
Thank You for helping me choose the right road! Amen.

DAY 117
Happiness vs. Joy

Most children have learned the popular song "If You're Happy and You Know It." Remember clapping your hands, stomping your feet, or nodding your head along with the song to show your happiness?

But what about times when you don't feel happy?

The great thing about being a child of God is that instead of just happiness, which is temporary, you have permanent joy in your heart. A relationship with Jesus Christ brings a peace that non-Christians simply don't have access to, no matter how hard they may look for it. It's a peace found only in Christ, and it comes with a bonus gift of joy!

Even on your most difficult days, spend some time in prayer or worshipping the Lord, and you will feel that deep-down joy well up in your heart. Try it!

But let all who take refuge in you rejoice; let them sing joyful praises forever. Spread your protection over them, that all who love your name may be filled with joy.

PSALM 5:11 NLT

Thank You, God, for planting joy deep down in my heart! Even though every day won't always be happy, I can always find joy—because I have You in my life. Please help me to reach out to others who don't know You... and who don't have this same kind of never-ending joy in their hearts. May others be pointed to You when they see my joy bubbling up, even in hard times. Amen.

DAY 118
A Loved Child of God

God made you, and He loves you unconditionally. And all humans are equal in His sight. He loves you just as much as He loves your friend, your mom, and your pastor. Nothing you do could make Him love you more. And nothing you do could make Him love you less. We are children of God because of what Jesus did for us on the cross.

When you start feeling down, remember how much God loves you. The Bible tells us that His love is unfailing! Psalm 13:5 says, "But I trust in your unfailing love; my heart rejoices in your salvation" (NIV). That's a good verse to memorize for those days when you're feeling bad about yourself. Never forget that you're a child of God and you're loved!

For you are all children of God through faith in Christ Jesus. And all who have been united with Christ in baptism have put on Christ, like putting on new clothes. There is no longer Jew or Gentile, slave or free, male and female. For you are all one in Christ Jesus.
GALATIANS 3:26–28 NLT

God, I can't describe how good it makes me feel when I think about how much You love me. You don't love me more or less than any other human being on earth. We're all special in Your eyes. But I often feel less than special. And I sometimes forget who I am. Help me to remember that I am Your child and that You love me more than anyone else ever will. I rejoice in You! Amen.

DAY 119
Dumpy Days

For every cheerful day you have, there's bound to be a dumpy one waiting just around the corner. A day when everything is boring, every*one* is annoying, and you feel like shouting, "Leave me alone!"

God knows all about those kinds of days. As the Father of many children, He's watched a lot of kids grow up. You're not the first to sulk over something trivial or to cry "just because." Thankfully, as God's child, you have a great advantage. You can climb into the lap of the Great Comforter and let it all out on His big shoulder.

The next time you're in a foul mood that you can't seem to snap out of, take some time to pray. Sneak away to a private place where you can talk to God, out loud, without being interrupted or overheard.

The Lord hath comforted his people.
ISAIAH 49:13 KJV

Lord, I'm so glad that You understand me even when I don't understand myself. Thank You for being willing to listen even when I'm having negative thoughts and emotions. I don't always have to be happy when I talk to You. Remind me of that when I'm feeling moody and sad, and help me cast my cares on You. I trust You will comfort me and make me feel better, Lord. Thank You. Amen.

DAY 120
Promises Kept

Do you ever find it hard to keep promises? Do you think most people do? What about God? Do you wonder about the promises He made to His children? Are you afraid that someday He won't be there for you? If so, reread the verse below. God keeps His promises *always*. He cannot break them any more than He can lie. He is God, and He never breaks His word. His promises are true for those who lived long ago, all the way up to the present, and even into the future. That means they are for you and your children and even your children's children! They are for everyone who believes in Him. Trust Him. Run to Him!

The believer replied, "Every promise of God proves true; he protects everyone who runs to him for help."
PROVERBS 30:5 MSG

Dear God, when I'm feeling worried, please help me to remember that You always keep Your promises. I can trust 100 percent that You will guide and protect me for all my life. Please help me to keep my promises, even when it's hard to do. And help me remember to run to You for help every time I need it. Amen.

DAY 121
Better Than Happy

Being a child of God has its perks. One of them is joy. We're talking full-out JOY. It's a joy that doesn't depend on everything going your way.

Being a Christian doesn't mean that your life will never have any challenges. In fact, Jesus made it clear that you can expect some troubles in this life. But you don't have to worry because He HAS overcome the world (John 16:33).

When things seem to be out of control, just know that God is at work in ways you can't see. You don't have to be happy about the troubles in your life, but trusting God can give you joy in spite of them.

In him our hearts rejoice, for we trust in his holy name.
PSALM 33:21 NIV

Dear God, thank You for the joy that comes from knowing You. Your kind of joy doesn't have anything to do with how well school is going (good or bad). . .whether I'm feeling alone or surrounded by friends. . .or whether I made the team or not. Sometimes my life doesn't go the way I'd like it to, but I know that I can trust You to help me through even the toughest times. Thank You that You are always with me. Your joy makes my life complete. Amen.

DAY 122
The Fingerprints of God

MORNING •

When you look into the mirror, what do you see? Messy hair, imperfect skin, big ears? . . .

Or, instead, do you see strands of hair numbered by God, a heart loved by the Savior, eyes to see His creation, and skin covered in the Father's fingerprints?

You're not only God's uniquely made child but created in His image (Genesis 1:27)!

God doesn't make mistakes. "God saw *all* that He had made, and behold, it was *very* good" (Genesis 1:31 NASB, emphasis added).

You're not a piece of trash to be thrown in the garbage. You're not a blunder or a mess-up. You're a child of the Most High God (Romans 8:15–16)! He loves you (John 3:16; Romans 5:8; Ephesians 2:4–5), and He has plans for you (Ephesians 2:10).

> *For You created my innermost parts;*
> *You wove me in my mother's womb.*
>
> **PSALM 139:13 NASB**

EVENING •

Lord, thank You for creating me as I am. I am Your child—a child of the Most High God! I am covered in Your fingerprints. And I can't imagine anything more won-derful than knowing I am perfectly made and loved by You. Thank You for loving me no matter how sinful I am or how ugly I may feel. Thanks for Your unending and magnificent love. In Jesus' name I pray. Amen.

DAY 123
Down in the Dumps

When you've scored poorly on a test, gotten into a fight with a friend, or disappointed a parent, it can be really hard to dig yourself out of the dumps. The world seems like it's been turned upside down, and everything and everyone is against you.

There is only one way out of this hole. God has given you the incredible ability to be joyful at all times. The key is to have faith in knowing you are His. God is watching over you, He will forgive your sins, and He has prepared a special place for you in heaven. What amazing things to be joyful about! If you trust God to do these things for you, He can help you climb out of the pit and view the day with fresh eyes and a happy heart.

Be full of joy always because you belong
to the Lord. Again I say, be full of joy!
PHILIPPIANS 4:4 NLV

God, sometimes I am deep down in the dumps. And it's so hard for me to see the light. When I feel like this, I need You so very much! Please show me Your light, Father. Remind me of all my blessings. Thank You for giving me so much to be joyful about. Help me to turn my eyes away from earthly troubles when they bring me down and to instead trust in You to rescue me. Amen.

DAY 124
What Makes You Stumble?

Did you know you can hurt yourself just as much by tripping on a stone as you can by trying to jump over a big rock? We often think that little stone can't bother us much. But the little stones are sometimes hidden and can be even more dangerous. When we're just walking along, not really watching our step, those little stones can really trip us up.

That's the way it is when we try to make good choices. We worry about the big stuff—the things we know for sure are not right for us. But if we don't pay attention to the "little" bad choices we make, pretty soon they will become mountains that block our view of God.

Always choose well in the little things, and the big decisions will be easier.

> *"Jeremiah, say to the people, 'This is what the Lord says: "When people fall down, don't they get up again? When they discover they're on the wrong road, don't they turn back?"'"*
> **JEREMIAH 8:4 NLT**

Dear Lord, so often I am focused on the big stones blocking my path, when instead I should be looking out for the little stones that can trip me up. When I need to make good choices for my life, help me to see the little stones as well as the big ones, Father. I want to make the right small decisions and be ready for the big ones too. Thank You for guiding me each step of the way. Amen.

DAY 125
In the Middle of the Mess

MORNING •

Sometimes life just isn't fair. Bad things can and do happen to good people. It started way back when Adam and Eve were tempted in the Garden of Eden. They introduced sin into the world and, from that point on, everything changed. God had a choice at that point. He could have said, "I've had enough of these people I created! I'm walking away!" But He chose a different route and stuck with us. Why? Because He loved us then, and He still loves us today.

So when bad stuff happens, God has already made His choice to stick with you; but you have to make the choice to stick with Him. Don't blame Him for what Satan has done to our world. Instead, choose to look for the ways He loves you. He's there somewhere. . .just reach out to Him.

> *Can anything ever separate us from Christ's love? Does it mean he no longer loves us if we have trouble or calamity, or are persecuted, or hungry, or destitute, or in danger, or threatened with death?*
> **ROMANS 8:35 NLT**

EVENING •

God, I don't understand why some things happen. I often ask myself questions like, "How in the world did this happen to me?" I've wondered why things ended up badly, even when I'm sure I did things right and made good choices. Remind me that life isn't fair all the time. Sometimes bad things happen, no matter what. I'm not always in control of how things turn out, but I promise to look for Your love in the middle of the messes, God. Amen.

DAY 126
Don't Believe the Bully

MORNING •

It's your choice whether or not you allow someone else to make you feel like you don't matter. A person might think he or she is better than you, but it won't really make a difference unless you actually start believing it for yourself.

Bullies like to act like they're better than everyone else. But remember this the next time you come across a bully: hurting people hurt people. Most times, a bully is just a kid (or even a grown-up) who has had a lot of hurts in life and who hasn't experienced the love of Jesus. You might not be the one to give them the help they need, but you can pray for them whenever they come to mind.

> *Out of my distress I called on the Lord; the Lord answered me and set me free. The Lord is on my side; I will not fear. What can man do to me?*
> **PSALM 118:5–6 ESV**

EVENING •

Dear God, please remind me that I don't have to give power to the bullies in the world. You alone speak the truth, Lord—and my worth comes from You. There is a bully in my life who really bothers me and makes everyone else feel bad. Please help. This person must be hurting, and I pray that the bully will come to know You as Savior. Amen.

DAY 127
My Lord Knows Me Better Than Myself

Did you ever long for a best friend who knew you so well that they could finish your thoughts or sentences? Someone who understood when you were sad, without you even having to say a word? Someone who would always be there to comfort you, no matter how badly you treated them? A friend like that is a treasure indeed.

You have a friend like that waiting for you. God knows everything about you. The good, the bad, and even the ugly. But you know what? He loves you, flaws and all. He won't ever turn His back on you; He'll always be there.

Even before there is a word on my tongue, behold, Lord, You know it all.
PSALM 139:4 NASB

God, thank You for being my best friend. Even when others fail me, You'll always be there—in the happy times, in the sad times, when I'm all alone, and when I'm surrounded by people. Remind me that I can always talk to You—about anything! You want to hear everything that's on my mind— every worry, every wish, every hope. . . You're never too busy for me. Thank You for being my Everything, Lord. Amen.

DAY 128
Take a Deep Breath!

MORNING •

What a terrible day! When you were drawing with your colored pencils in art class, three of them broke. You left your math homework at home. And–as if that wasn't enough–on the walk home from school your backpack strap snapped, sending your books sailing because you hadn't zipped it shut! Whew!

Take a deep breath. God made you. He wants to fill your heart with joy. He knows everyone will have a bad day from time to time. Just remember that He made you with power, love, and a sound mind. Then thank Him for it!

God made you in His image. And God doesn't make mistakes.

Though you have made me see troubles, many and bitter, you will restore my life again; from the depths of the earth you will again bring me up.
PSALM 71:20 NIV

EVENING •

Lord, when I get out of sorts because things aren't going my way, remind me to stop and take a deep breath. Remind me to focus less on my circumstances and the world around me and more on You. You will always love me. You will always fill my heart with Your joy. I'm so happy You made me. I know Your love is FOREVER. And Your guidance is important to me. Tomorrow is a new day, and I can start over then. Thank You for fresh starts! Amen.

DAY 129
Fake It till You Make It

Have you ever met a faker? They pretend to be one person, act like someone completely different, but deep down they're nothing like either of those people.

God wants nothing more from you than for you to be authentically, truly Christ-like. That doesn't mean you can be perfect; no one is. But it does mean that you strive for honoring Christ with your words and your actions. God can help you do that authentically.

If you want to be pure and righteous on the outside, you need to be pure and righteous on the inside. That's what it means to be true to yourself and honor God.

> *Create in me a clean heart, God, and*
> *renew a steadfast spirit within me.*
> **PSALM 51:10 NASB**

Dear God, I don't want to be a faker. You created me to be me and nothing else. And You created me perfectly—just the way You wanted! Whenever I'm tempted to act like someone I'm not—or do things that aren't honoring to You—please forgive me. I will look to Jesus as the perfect example of how I should live my life. Help me walk in Your truth today and always. Amen.

DAY 130
Love One Another

Jesus gave the disciples a command at His last supper with them. He told them to love one another. It sounds so simple; yet it isn't always an easy command to follow.

The same command holds true for us today: *love one another.* What does this look like in your life? Loving your parents includes treating them with respect and obeying them. Loving your brothers or sisters means putting them first and not always fighting for your own interests. Loving your classmates calls for going the extra mile. Treat others with kindness—*always.*

But what if someone doesn't treat you in a loving manner? What a great opportunity for your reaction to stand out! You will be known as a Christian when you show love, just as the Savior first loved you.

> *"So now I am giving you a new commandment: Love each other. Just as I have loved you, you should love each other. Your love for one another will prove to the world that you are my disciples."*
>
> **JOHN 13:34–35 NLT**

Jesus, You want me to love others, just the way You love them. This means I will be considerate, caring, kind, forgiving, and generous. And so much more! You gave the perfect example to follow. Help me to love others well—even those who are hard to love sometimes. I want to be loving, but often I fail. It's so hard to put others before myself. Help me, Lord. Amen.

DAY 131
Do You Feel Inadequate?

MORNING •

Has God placed a dream in your heart? When you think about your dream, do you feel excited? Or do you feel like you can't accomplish it? If you feel like you are unable, be encouraged! It's actually great that you know you can't do it all on your own because then you know that you have to lean on God to help you. Then, when you succeed, He will get the credit. This is why God likes to use people who can't do stuff in their own strength. He likes to give His strength to people who can't accomplish their dreams on their own.

"So do not fear, for I am with you; do not be dismayed, for I am your God. I will strengthen you and help you; I will uphold you with my righteous right hand."
ISAIAH 41:10 NIV

EVENING •

Lord, I love that You place dreams directly into my heart. They are gifts from You! When a dream I have seems hard, remind me to rely on You to make it happen. With Your help, I can fulfill Your plans for my life. I am so thankful that You give me strength to accomplish the dreams You have for me. I don't have to be perfect to do anything for You, Lord. I just need to give You control. I am excited about everything You and I can do together, God! Amen.

DAY 132
Ready and Waiting

MORNING •

Have you ever tried to get the attention of someone who has earbuds in their ears? You can yell and holler, but if they're busy listening to something else, they're just not going to hear you.

There are very few people we can name who will listen to us anytime.

But God isn't like that. He is ready to listen—all the time. At school, before an exam. On the bus, on the way home from school after a hard day. At 3:00 a.m., when you just can't sleep. The instruction we have is to not worry, but rather pray. You can run to a friend, to your mom, or to someone else for help, but first take it to God. He will hear you and will give you what you need.

> *Don't worry about anything; instead, pray*
> *about everything. Tell God what you need,*
> *and thank him for all he has done.*
> **PHILIPPIANS 4:6 NLT**

EVENING •

Dear heavenly Father, when I need help, remind me to come to You first. The good thing about talking to You, Lord, is that I have Your full attention every single minute. I don't need to compete with anyone or any-thing for Your attention. This is such a blessing to me! Thank You for listening to me right now. You're never too busy for me. You're never too distracted to notice me. Thank You for all Your many blessings. Amen.

DAY 133
Hello, God. . .Are You There?

Isn't it cool to know that God always answers when you call? In fact, He's waiting on your call right now! You don't even have to have a phone to talk to Him. All you have to do is just open up and share your heart. You don't need a special place or a special time. He's there, around the clock!

Not only does the Lord hear you, but He cares about what you're telling Him. He's on your side. So next time you really wish someone would listen to you, forget about calling a friend on the phone. Call on the best Friend of all, the One who's always there when you need Him. He can't wait to hear from you! C'mon, give Him a call! What are you waiting for?

The Lord is near to all who call on Him, to all who call on Him in truth. He will fill the desire of those who fear Him. He will also hear their cry and will save them.
PSALM 145:18–19 NLV

God, I'm so glad You hear my prayers! I never have to ask You to schedule time for me because You're always there and ready to listen. There is no one else in my life who's readily available like You are. And there's no one else who understands me like You do. Thank You for caring so much about me. I love You, Lord! Amen.

DAY 134
Courageous

What are you most afraid of? The first day of school? Being the new kid? Being the last one picked for the kickball team? Maybe you're nervous about a big test coming up. There are many things in this life that can make us feel anxious, that can make us want to pull the covers over our heads and never come out.

But God doesn't want us to feel afraid. When we place our trust in Him, He gives us courage. No matter what we may face, God wants to face it with us. He will never leave us alone, and if we ask Him to help us, He will. We just have to hold our heads high and trust Him.

> **Be strong, and let your heart take**
> **courage, all you who wait for the Lord!**
> **PSALM 31:24 ESV**

Dear Father, when I need help, I'll always come to You first. When I need wisdom, You'll provide it. When something is dangerous, You'll give me the protection I need to keep me safe. When I am afraid, You'll give me courage. Whatever I face, I am so thankful that I never have to do it alone. You will always be right beside me, no matter what. Amen.

DAY 135
Do You Really Love God?

These are some strong words in the book of 1 John. Basically, if you say you love God and act with hatred toward another boy or girl at school, or a bully, or a family member—*or anyone at all*—the Bible says you can't possibly love God. You may be angry at people, but to truly hate someone else is not possible for those who have Jesus in their heart.

Are you struggling to be nice to someone else? Ask God for help. Are you angry with a certain person pretty much all the time? Ask God to forgive you for your anger and help you to see that person just as He sees them.

If anyone boasts, "I love God," and goes right on hating his brother or sister, thinking nothing of it, he is a liar. If he won't love the person he can see, how can he love the God he can't see? The command we have from Christ is blunt: Loving God includes loving people. You've got to love both.

1 JOHN 4:20–21 MSG

God, I want others to see You through my words and actions—and that includes how I treat people. Please forgive me for my anger toward others. I don't want to hate people—I don't even want to dislike people. I want to see the best in them—just as You see them, Lord. But there are some people who really get on my nerves. Help me to be nicer. Show me how to act with kind- ness in my heart. Help me to be more like You. Amen.

DAY 136
Say What?

It seems totally weird to pray for someone who constantly hurts your feelings and enjoys being mean to you. Doesn't it? But that's exactly what Jesus says to do. In His Word, He says to pray for your enemies. He doesn't say you have to like it, but He does say you have to do it.

So the next time someone acts ugly toward you, don't fight back. Instead, pray for that person. You probably won't feel like praying at that very moment, but do it anyway. You may have to do it through gritted teeth; but if you'll do your part, God will do His. He may not change your enemy's actions, but He will change the way you feel about that person. So determine today to pray—especially for your enemies!

"Love your enemies, do good to those who hate you, bless those who curse you, pray for those who mistreat you."
LUKE 6:27–28 NIV

God, I don't have many enemies. But there are some people I really struggle with. . .they make life harder for me. And I don't like it one bit! Please help me to do better with my thoughts and feelings. I want to obey You, Lord. And You ask that I pray for my enemies. So, Father, I trust You'll help me to love my enemies the same way You do. Amen.

DAY 137
All Wrapped Up

There are many things in the world that make us feel frightened or angry. We might be mixed up and not know where to turn. All we really want is to feel better. So we search for someone or something to make that happen. Maybe it's a friend's voice on the phone, a hug from Mom, or your favorite music. . .whatever makes you feel safe and secure.

We need even more comfort when we are sad. When someone dies or a bad thing happens, God is ready to give us peace like a warm fuzzy blanket. He comforts us like no one or nothing else can. He wants His children to come to Him and snuggle up close.

The next time you need comfort, run to the heavenly Father and let Him wrap you up in His loving embrace.

"God blesses those who mourn, for they will be comforted."
MATTHEW 5:4 NLT

Dear God, thank You for all the things that bring me comfort: my soft, fluffy blanket, a glass of milk and warm chocolate chip cookies, a hug from my best friend. . .All these things make me feel better. But there are times when the only thing that will bring me comfort is a hug from You, Lord. Thank You for sending Your comfort just when I need it most. Help me to be a comfort to others too. Amen.

DAY 138
Dreaming of Paradise

What do you think heaven looks like? A fluffy place filled with harp-playing angels or a lush garden with flowers and water-falls? How about a golden city with pearly gates somewhere in the clouds? No matter how awesome you paint it, the real thing will be a million times better.

The human mind is limited to the things of this earth. . .and this life. God's imagination goes far beyond that. His creating power has no limits. So when the Bible says that heaven will be a paradise, you can be certain that it's something you don't want to miss out on.

God has promised heaven to those who love and serve Him. Are you ready to go there? Now would be a great time to search your heart and make sure.

> *"What no eye has seen, nor ear heard, nor the heart of man imagined, what God has prepared for those who love him."*
> **1 CORINTHIANS 2:9 ESV**

Lord, I don't know what heaven will be like, but it's sure fun to think about. I know it will be more awesome and wonderful than anything I could ever imagine in my brain. That is because You are so powerful and creative. . .and my human brain can't possibly understand all the fan-tastic things You'll have for us to enjoy in heaven. I know I want to spend eternity there. Guide me every day of my life, Lord, and prepare me to meet You someday. Amen.

DAY 139
Is Anyone There?

MORNING •

It can be so frustrating to not be able to reach someone. You call and they don't answer. You leave a message. You send a text. And you still can't reach them. So frustrating! Wouldn't it be nice if everyone were available exactly when we needed them?

With God, though, He's *always* available. Day or night. Twenty-four hours, every day of the year, He never takes a vacation. And you can rest assured that He always hears us. The Bible is full of verses that back that up. He made you, He cares about you. . .and the coolest part? He's just waiting for you to call out to Him. He wants to hear from you.

So next time you're struggling, call your heavenly Father. He'll *always* be there with a listening ear.

The Lord hears when I call to Him.
PSALM 4:3 NASB

EVENING •

God, sometimes I can't reach my friend, and I really, really need someone to talk to. It's so frustrating! When I can't reach anyone else, I always have You, Lord. Thank You for always being with me. Thank You for always being right here, waiting to answer my call. Thank You for always listening. And remind me to keep the communication lines open all day. Amen.

DAY 140
En Garde! (On Your Guard!)

MORNING •

Did you know that right now, in this very moment, you're in a fight? It's true! It's not a physical fight; it's spiritual (Ephesians 6:12). And to win, you need to be really good at using the sword of the Spirit—the Word of God (Ephesians 6:11, 17).

Of all the pieces of armor listed in Ephesians 6, only one is for fighting—the Word of God. But like any weapon, you have to know something about it to be able to use it. A Bible that sits on the shelf gathering dust is a useless weapon.

Reading God's Word daily is like practicing your fighting skills. As you hide His Word in your heart, you'll find yourself growing stronger in your faith. When the enemy tries to tempt you, you'll have no trouble holding him off because your sword of the Spirit will be ready. *En garde!*

> *I have hidden your word in my heart that I might not sin against you. . . . I delight in your decrees; I will not neglect your word.*
>
> **PSALM 119:11, 16 NIV**

EVENING •

Dear God, I am so thankful that You have given me Your Word as a powerful weapon. Help me to learn to use it effectively. I want to become an expert at using the sword of the Spirit. Help me to hide Your Word in my heart so I won't sin against You. The Bible offers all the wisdom, strength, and courage I need—for life! Amen.

DAY 141
A Whole Pile of Birthday Presents

Have you ever felt like nobody really understands you or even "sees" the real you? Everybody feels that way sometimes. When a friend takes the time to know who you are, it's better than a whole pile of birthday presents. God is that friend who "sees" you and "knows" you because He's the One who made you—the One who formed you.

God knows your happiest day and your darkest fear. The things that make you cry when you're all alone or the things that make you smile or laugh out loud. He knows your innermost secrets and your biggest dreams.

God not only understands you but He wants you to be the very best version of you. That takes seeing and knowing to a whole new level!

> *For you created my inmost being; you knit*
> *me together in my mother's womb.*
> **PSALM 139:13 NIV**

Lord, You see the real me. And I love that so much! No one will ever know me quite like You do. Thank You for caring about me so much that You know me inside and out! You know the best about me. . .and the very worst. And still, You love me! Thank You for loving me enough to help me become all that You created me to be. Amen.

DAY 142
A Sneak Peek

If you haven't noticed, the Bible is gigantic. There are a lot of numbers and hard-to-pronounce names. You might even be wondering if the Bible could in any way relate to your life.

God's Word may seem like a long, boring, and confusing book, but it really is God reaching out and speaking to you in your everyday language. In the pages of the Bible, the Creator of the universe allows you a sneak peek into His intimate inter-actions with humanity. He chose to give you a book that would help guide you and give you insight into His character. And best of all, you get to read about the life of His Son, Jesus, who walked the earth, healed the sick, embraced children, and loves you unconditionally.

So when the Bible begins to seem dull or unimportant, just remember that it is God desiring to comfort, teach, and connect with you through His words.

You are my hiding place and my shield; I hope in your word.
PSALM 119:114 ESV

God, Your Word is so BIG! Please remind me that even though it's super-gigantic, it's also full of Your special messages and love for me. I can learn so much from scripture, and I trust You will help me understand what it means. You will help me be guided by it. Thank You for giving me a sneak peek into Your character and promises. Please help me learn how to study and under-stand Your Word. . .and then obey what it says. Amen.

DAY 143
Even What You Don't Say

You might tell your best friend *most* of what is going on in your life, but there are probably things you don't mention. How do you tell your best friend about that shaky feeling you have—when you can't seem to pinpoint what is causing you to feel so out of place? How do you describe the fact that your day seems off and nothing feels secure, but on the surface everything looks just fine? Feelings are not always easy to talk about until you figure out where they are coming from.

God knows everything about you—including all your features and characteristics *and* what you can't say out loud. It's more than okay for you to sit down with Him and say, "Look God, I feel insecure and I don't know why. Can You show me?" Trust the One who made you to help you sort it out.

For God is greater than our worried hearts and
knows more about us than we do ourselves.
1 JOHN 3:20 MSG

God, thank You for understanding who I am. Even though I can't always explain how I feel or what I'm going through to my friends and family, I can always talk to You about it. Because You know. . .and You understand. I'm grateful I can come to You when I don't have answers. I trust You to help me sort it all out. Amen.

DAY 144
Don't Be Greedy, Help the Needy!

MORNING •

Jesus wants us to help other people who are in need. This is easy to forget because you probably don't see needy people on a daily basis.

And since it is so easy to forget about them, we get caught up in the things we want that we don't have. Having nice things is okay, but if they are the most important thing in your life, that's called greed. The Bible says in Luke 12:15, "Watch out! Be on your guard against all kinds of greed; life does not consist in an abundance of possessions" (NIV).

Christmas is a time where churches sponsor clothing and food drives, and that's wonderful. But those same people have needs all year long. Call your church and find out how you can help the needy in your community today.

Use your hands for good hard work, and then give generously to others in need.
EPHESIANS 4:28 NLT

EVENING •

Dear God, please help me to really see people—especially where there are needs I can fill. I am Your child, and You ask me to serve others. When I serve others, I honor You and then others notice You too! Please give me Your eyes to see the needs in my community. And show me all the ways I can help! Amen.

DAY 145
To Grow or Not to Grow?

MORNING •

Are there times when you get so overwhelmed that it seems like you can't keep on going? There's no easy way out. . . . You can't give the mouse a click to turn off the trouble and walk away from your problems.

Why does God allow you to go through hard things? Why doesn't He just stop the painful things from happening?

1 Peter 1:6–7 gives an answer: the Lord loves you, dear one. He is testing your faith, which is more precious than gold, so that it may result in praise at the revelation of Jesus.

You're not alone in the hard times (see 1 Peter 5:8–10; Matthew 28:20; 1 Corinthians 10:13). Trust Him. He knows what He's doing.

In this you greatly rejoice, even though now for a little while, if necessary, you have been distressed by various trials, so that the proof of your faith, being more precious than gold which perishes though tested by fire, may be found to result in praise, glory, and honor at the revelation of Jesus Christ.

1 PETER 1:6–7 NASB

EVENING •

God, thank You for difficulties and hard situations. I know that You're using them to help me grow. I really want to learn, Lord. And if the way to do that is by pushing through the hard times, then I'll trust You and "press on toward the goal for the prize" (Philippians 3:14 NASB). In Jesus' name I pray. Amen.

DAY 146
He Loves Me Anyway

You gather around the kitchen table with your family. Dad opens his Bible and reads the Ten Commandments. He reminds you to always obey God's rules. But you wonder, *What if I don't obey them? Will God stop loving me?*

That night, you go to your room. You read over the Ten Commandments again. You get on your knees and say your prayers. Then you snuggle up in bed, finding comfort in knowing and trusting that the heavenly Father loves you—*no matter what!*

You will always try your best to obey God's commandments, which is just what He wants you to do. But if you ever fail, He will love you anyway. And He'll gently guide you back to His embrace. Oh, how He loves you!

> ***Jesus replied, "Anyone who loves me will obey my teaching. My Father will love them, and we will come to them and make our home with them."***
> **JOHN 14:23 NIV**

God, thank You for loving me. Thank You for giving us a very clear list of rules to follow so we don't ever have to wonder about what's right and what's wrong. I want to follow Your rules for the rest of my life. No matter what, Your love is all-forgiving and Your Word is unfailing. And I am so thankful! Amen.

DAY 147
Who Knows You Best?

MORNING •

Are you ever amazed at how well your parents know you? They seem to know what you think or what you are about to say before the words leave your mouth. Well, God knows you even better. He made you—He even knew you before you were born! And when the unexpected happens, always remember that the same God who knows you so well is also going to take care of you. You are His child, and He will see you through everything that comes your way.

> *"And he pays even greater attention to you, down to the last detail—even numbering the hairs on your head! So don't be intimidated by all this bully talk. You're worth more than a million canaries."*
>
> LUKE 12:7 MSG

EVENING •

Dear God, please help me to always remember that You know everything that happens to me—good or bad. And You will always protect me and guide me. Please remind me that You know what is going to happen to me even before it ever does. And that You know how to help me when I don't know how to help myself. Thank You for always taking care of me, Father. Amen.

DAY 148
On His Mind

MORNING •

Is there a big event coming up or something exciting you've been planning for a while? There are always things going on, filling your mind with details, anticipation, and anxiety. Your thoughts are revealed in the words you say, and both show the condition of your heart.

That same is true for God. He has thoughts, and those thoughts come out through His words, and His thoughts and words reveal the condition of His heart. The cool thing is that God's thoughts are constantly about you and what's best for you. He is focused on protecting you, guiding you, providing for you . . .and loving you. He thinks about you all the time. And He talks about you too. In fact, the Bible is His Word to you!

> *What is man that You are mindful of him,*
> *and the son of man that You visit him?*
> **PSALM 8:4 NKJV**

EVENING •

Dear God, I think about You all the time. And I'm so thankful that You think about me too! Please help me to control my thoughts today. Let them be about You and Your goodness. Help me have the courage and strength to speak truth to others and to keep my heart turned toward You. Amen.

DAY 149
Forgiveness

MORNING •

One of the greatest things about God is that He knows all our flaws, and yet He loves us unconditionally. Yep, God loves you when you mess up or make a mistake. And there is nothing—*absolutely nothing!*—you can do to cause Him to stop loving you.

God sent His Son, Jesus, to die for us *while we were still sinners.* He didn't wait for us to clean up our act. He sent Jesus to pay the price for our sins. He knows us, and He loves us just the way we are.

God pours out His grace on you as He forgives your sins. Do you show grace to other people when they make mistakes? One way that others can see God in you is through forgiveness. Choose to forgive today!

> **But God showed his great love for us by sending Christ to die for us while we were still sinners.**
> **ROMANS 5:8 NLT**

EVENING •

God, I can't hide anything from You. You know my heart. You know my thoughts. You know everything there is to know about me. And the best news about that? You still love me! I don't have to change who I am to get Your love. Thank You for Your forgiveness. Help me to show that same kind of grace to others, Lord. Amen.

DAY 150
Honor Your Parents

Maybe your parents are totally great. On the other hand, maybe you feel like your parents are trying to rule your life. Or your mom and dad might fall somewhere in the middle.

The truth is that no parent is perfect. Parents are human just like you are. For the most part they are trying to help you become a mature young adult. Even though you might not like everything they say or do, you must remember that God has a reason for putting you together. He expects you to honor your parents—to respect and obey them.

When things go well, thank God. If you are struggling, turn your situation over to God. You might be surprised to discover that it's you who needs to change.

Above all, honor your parents, and enjoy God's blessing that follows.

> *Honour thy father and thy mother, as the Lord thy God hath commanded thee; that thy days may be prolonged, and that it may go well with thee, in the land which the Lord thy God giveth thee.*
>
> **DEUTERONOMY 5:16 KJV**

Heavenly Father, thank You for my parents. While I'm not perfect and they aren't either, You have set us in this family—together—for Your purpose. Help me to obey my parents and to show them honor. When I do, I know You will bless me. Thank You, Lord. Amen.

DAY 151
Live to Give!

Esther Kim and Kay Poe made national news in 2000—not for their great Tae Kwon Do skills, but for their strong friendship. Esther, then twenty, and Kay, then eighteen, had been best friends and competitors in Tae Kwon Do since they were very young. When the two buddies discovered they would have to fight each other for the last remaining spot on the 2000 U.S. Olympic team, they dreaded the match.

Then the unexpected happened. Kay dislocated her kneecap just before the finals and could hardly stand for the final match against her best friend. Moments before the two friends were supposed to compete, Esther forfeited the fight so that her best friend could claim the final spot on the Olympic team.

Esther may not have earned a spot on the Olympic team that year, but she gained recognition as a champion of love. Ask God to help you put others' needs above your own. Look for ways to be a better friend. Live the love!

"Love your neighbor as yourself."
LEVITICUS 19:18 NIV

God, Your Word tells us that love is not selfish or self-seeking, but...it's so hard to be selfless. I struggle with living that way. It's difficult to put others first and myself last. But with Your help, I can do it! Please help me to live to give, and help me to love my friends the way You love me. Amen.

DAY 152
Integrity and Truth

MORNING •

Since you were little, you've always been reminded to tell the truth, right? But did you know that telling the truth is not just about obedience?

Jesus is actually the source of all truth. And knowing Him—knowing about *real* truth—will set you free. When you know true freedom in Christ, you can live a life based on honesty and integrity. Integrity is knowing the right thing to do and doing it, even when nobody else is looking.

Mark Twain said, "Always tell the truth. That way, you don't have to remember what you said." When you make daily choices that honor God, such as being honest and trustworthy, you don't have to ever worry about being caught in a lie. And that's a freeing feeling!

Jesus said to the people who believed in him, "You are truly my disciples if you remain faithful to my teachings. And you will know the truth, and the truth will set you free."
JOHN 8:31–32 NLT

EVENING •

Jesus, You are the source of all truth. I am so thankful I have You to guide me in life—to show me good from bad, right from wrong. Help me to be faithful to Your Word. Thanks for teaching me what I need to know to be a good human being. Help me to make wise choices, even when nobody is looking. I know You are always looking, and I want to honor You with my life. Amen.

DAY 153
What to Wear

Do you ever worry about whether your clothes measure up to your friends' clothes or if your stuff is as cool as theirs?

If you do, that's normal. We all think about that stuff sometimes. And the great thing is, God understands how we feel. Most importantly, He wants to take care of us.

Whether it's through hand-me-downs, or bargain finds at a thrift store, or through parents who have the money to buy us brand-new things, God *loves* to take care of us. And He loves to see us smile because we feel good about ourselves.

Oh, He may not always give us every single thing we want. But He knows what we need, and He will provide it, if we just ask Him and trust Him with the results.

> *"And why do you worry about clothes? See how the flowers of the field grow. They do not labor or spin. Yet I tell you that not even Solomon in all his splendor was dressed like one of these."*
>
> **MATTHEW 6:28–29 NIV**

Dear Father, I know I have a lot of wants. And if I'm being truthful, most of my wants aren't very important to my well-being. And most of my wants aren't going to make me a happier kid either. I'm so thankful You see to it that I have everything I need. Help me to appreciate the things You provide every day. Amen.

DAY 154
Heavenly Language

A true child of God glorifies the Creator in every aspect of life. . . including the way he or she talks! The speech of the world is overflowing with four-letter words and off-colored humor. And the worst part is that bad language is contagious. The more you hear it, the more natural it may become for you to slip into the habit yourself.

While you can't entirely avoid hearing the world's language, you can limit what goes into your ears. Surround yourself with godly friends and influences. Choose your music carefully. Avoid television shows and movies that have bad language in them. And if you have friends who curse, ask them to try not doing so around you. Most of all, keep tight control of your own thoughts and speech. Remember that you represent God. . .and He is always listening!

Sound speech, that cannot be condemned.
TITUS 2:8 KJV

*Dear Father, the world is full of fun-sounding languages
. . .unique accents. . .interesting word pronunciations.
Words are so important, aren't they? When I speak, I
want others to know that I belong to You, Lord. I know
You don't want me to use bad language. Help me to
always keep my speech pure so I can honor You. Amen.*

DAY 155
Drop Anchor!

Sometimes life can be hard and confusing. You're not sure what direction to take, you're tired, you've lost hope that you'll ever see your way out of the darkness. School, youth group, sports, what you want to do with your life—it can all be overwhelming.

It's tough. But there is hope—in the Lord! Just as the anchor on a boat holds it steady, God is the anchor of your soul, and He's offering you *His* hope. And His hope is true and lasting. Allow Him to anchor you. Seek Him in everything you do, and He will guide you toward an even greater future.

So when you're lost, when you're tired and afraid, sometimes it's best to drop your anchor down and rest in Him. He's longing to take care of you.

***This hope we have as an anchor of the
soul, a hope both sure and reliable.***
HEBREWS 6:19 NASB

*Lord, sometimes I feel so lost. I'm confused about
what I should do. The choices and decisions I have
to make overwhelm me, and I'm not sure which way
to go. Please be my anchor. Hold me steady, Lord.
Thank You for Your hope. Help me to rest in You and
turn to You for all the decisions in my life. Amen.*

DAY 156
Streets of Gold, Really?

We are Christians because we choose to believe what God tells us. And He tells us that He is preparing a special place in heaven for us. If He said it, it's 100 percent true. All the details—including the streets of gold and pearly gates—really don't matter much. We can simply trust that heaven will be perfect because we know it's been created by a perfect God—the very same God who sent His Son, Jesus, to save us.

Think of how much God loved us—enough to make a beautiful home for us to live in forever. Everyone wants to know they will have an eternal home. And who wouldn't want to dwell in the most beautiful place we could possibly imagine?

Have you picked heaven as your eternal home? It's never too late. Jesus is waiting for you to say yes to heaven.

*The twelve gates were twelve pearls; each gate
was made from a single pearl. The street of the
city was of pure gold, transparent as glass.*
REVELATION 21:21 GNT

*Heavenly Father, what is heaven like? Are there really
streets made of gold and gates made of pearls? I can't
even imagine, but I believe You have made a home for me
there. I'm so grateful that You accept me as Your child and
that I get to spend eternity with You. I can't wait! Amen.*

DAY 157
God Is Always with Me

On occasion a small child or a pet will shadow someone they love. They follow close behind. It can be fun for a time, until the leader wants a little bit of freedom.

Sometimes we take the position of the leader in our relationship with God, with Him "along for the ride." When we want a taste of freedom, we try to dodge Him so that He can't see what we're doing. But He is *always* there.

Since God is our constant companion, it would work best for us to give Him the leader position and follow where He leads. He will never try to get away or "lose" us. He wants us to be following closely, maintaining a close relationship with Him.

I will be with you always, even until the end of the world.
MATTHEW 28:20 CEV

EVENING •

Dear Jesus, forgive me for trying to be the leader in our relationship. I should always be following You. I'm sorry. I fully give You the leader position. Wherever You lead, I will closely follow. You have promised to always be with me. No one else shows that kind of devotion. Thank You for loving me so much that You want to be with me—always! Amen.

DAY 158
Doing the Impossible

Good, hard work has always been valued. God wants us all to work hard at whatever He has given us to do. Hard work can seem daunting at times, but it is accomplished by taking it one step at a time.

Hard workers often become leaders. If you're shy, this may seem a little scary to you. But you're already a leader if you think about it! Aren't there other kids in your life who look up to you? Maybe a younger brother or sister. Or a neighbor.

Whatever you decide to do, work at it with all your heart. Other people are looking up to you. So don't cut corners. Don't be lazy. Work hard, and soon you'll be doing the impossible!

A hard worker has plenty of food, but a person who chases fantasies has no sense. . . . Work hard and become a leader; be lazy and become a slave.
PROVERBS 12:11, 24 NLT

God, I know You value good hard work. Please help me to accomplish the work I have ahead of me. I want to always work hard at whatever You have for me to do, Lord. I've never really thought of myself as a leader, but I guess I am! Help me to be a good one and a hard worker—and a great example for those who look up to me. Amen.

DAY 159
You Promised!

The last few times you promised you would do the dishes right after your favorite TV show, did you do it? Most of us would honestly say, "Well, sometimes I did, and sometimes I didn't."

Thankfully, when God makes a promise, it's not the same. The Bible is full of promises that He's kept and *still keeps* today. His track record is perfect. At times we may worry that He won't keep His promises; but chances are, He's just not going to keep a promise in the way we expect Him to. God always knows what's best, even when we don't.

So the next time it feels like God's not going to keep a promise, trust that He sees the bigger picture. He's there and working through all the details to give you only the best results!

"God is not a man, that He should lie."
NUMBERS 23:19 NKJV

God, I fail at keeping my promises all the time. Keeping promises can be hard! I am so thankful that You are the very best Promise Keeper. Everything You promise to do, You'll do—even if I have to wait for a while. Help me to be patient as I wait on You. I know I need to trust Your promises will happen in Your own perfect timing and perfect way. Amen.

DAY 160
Want to Hang Out with Me?

Have you ever had a friend say, "Hey, let's hang out together"? You make plans to do something, like go to the movies or have a sleepover, but then your friend ends up doing something else instead. Man, that can really hurt! Doesn't your friend want to spend time with you?

God isn't like that. The Bible promises us that He is standing next to us at all times. He never leaves us, no matter what! He's the best sort of friend!

Are you lonely today? Need someone to hang out with? Why not hang out with the King of kings and Lord of lords? He will wipe away your loneliness and remind you that you are loved. Best of all, He's already there, right beside you, waiting for you to say, "Hey, let's hang out together!"

> *You hem me in behind and before,*
> *and you lay your hand upon me.*
> **PSALM 139:5 NIV**

God, my friends and family members aren't always available when I'd like to spend time with them. I'm so glad You're never too busy to hang out with me. I get a little lonely sometimes, but You're the best friend in the world because You always say yes when I need someone to spend time with me. Thank You, Lord! Amen.

DAY 161
Watch Your Mouth

Your words have power. They have the power to build up or tear down, to bless or curse. The Bible says your words are so powerful they actually have the power of life and death (Proverbs 18:21).

Because words are so powerful, it's important to use them well. Some people (even Christians) who don't understand this lead empty, defeated lives because they are speaking all the wrong things. "I'll never get this right!" "My parents are the worst!" "My life is the pits!"

What are the right things? Whatever God's Word says. No matter what the situation, always make sure you find out what God's Word says about it. Then YOU say what GOD says. "I can do all things through Christ!" "The Lord cares for me because I trust Him." "By His stripes I am healed."

From the fruit of their lips people enjoy good things....
Those who guard their lips preserve their lives.
PROVERBS 13:2–3 NIV

Dear God, thank You for helping me to understand the power of my words. I don't always think about my words helping or hurting when I speak. But I know it's important! Help me to remember the power of my words—to think first, before I speak. Teach me to use my words well. Thank You! Amen.

DAY 162
Eternal Perspective

What in the world is an eternal perspective? Having an "eternal perspective" means that you realize all the work you do right now—your schoolwork, your chores at home, how you treat others—it *all* means something to God! And not just for right now—it means something for all eternity.

God is always with you and watching over you. He sees the choices you make. He sees inside your heart, and He knows and understands why you do certain things. When you remember this and realize that even doing your math homework can be pleasing to God, it changes how you do things! You're working for God and not for your teacher! You're taking out the trash for God and not just your parents!

Work willingly at whatever you do, as though you were working for the Lord rather than for people. Remember that the Lord will give you an inheritance as your reward, and that the Master you are serving is Christ.
COLOSSIANS 3:23–24 NLT

God, my work matters. . .not just to the obvious people. But it matters to You! This makes my work mean so much more. You know my heart, Lord. This means You already know how much I love You. But I will never stop telling You: I love You, Lord! Thanks for watching over me and guiding me in life. Help me to always remember that all I do is ultimately for You. Amen.

DAY 163
God's Design

Does God make mistakes? Do you think He was disappointed when He saw how you turned out? If you answer this question honestly, it gives a good insight into what you believe about God. . .and about yourself.

God made your body, and He designed your face exactly how He wanted it. He knew you before anyone else ever even saw you. He thinks you're perfect. It doesn't matter how much you weigh, how tall you are, or the kinds of clothes you wear. You are His beloved. And what's best is He knows your heart and loves you still.

Thank Him for making you a masterpiece, perfect in every way. Know that truth, and let it bathe you with confidence.

For you created my inmost being; you knit me together in my mother's womb. I praise you because I am fearfully and wonderfully made; your works are wonderful, I know that full well.
PSALM 139:13–14 NIV

Dear God, You never have—and never will—make a mistake. This means that Your plans to create me were 100 percent perfect. I trust You. I know You are so very good. If You love me in such a big way, I can surely love myself too! Please help me to love myself better so I can be a shining reflection of You to everyone around me. Amen.

DAY 164
My Guide

Is Jesus in your heart? If you have said *yes* to a relationship with Him, then the Bible tells us the Holy Spirit—the Spirit of God Himself—comes and lives inside of you (2 Corinthians 1:21–22) to guide you, to help you know right from wrong, and to encourage you every day of your life.

We all mess up. And without someone to guide us, we would be lost forever. Jesus says, "I am the way and the truth and the life. No one comes to the Father except through me" (John 14:6 NIV).

If you have never asked Jesus to come and be the center of your life, what's stopping you? You can talk to God anytime, anywhere. Even in the quietness of your own heart.

So I say, let the Holy Spirit guide your lives. Then you won't be doing what your sinful nature craves.
GALATIANS 5:16 NLT

Dear Jesus, I know I've messed up, and it's pretty clear that I need Your help. Please forgive me and come into my heart. Wash away my sins and make me new. Thank You for loving me so much that You gave up Your life to save me. Thank You for a fresh start. Thank You for being my guide. Amen.

DAY 165
He Knows You–and Loves You

MORNING •

As you lie down on a picnic blanket in the grass, you search the sky and are reminded that God knows you.

He was with you when you had a terrible fight with your best friend. He knew you would say you're sorry and ask for forgiveness. He was with you when you ice-skated all around the rink holding on to your dad's hand. Then He watched you try and try again until you were able to skate on your own.

God knows every little thing about you. . .your every thought. . . He knows the sins you have already committed and the sins of your future. And He loves you. He knows your heart.

And His arms will surround you in love and protection forever.

You have searched me, Lord, and you know me. You know when I sit and when I rise; you perceive my thoughts from afar. You discern my going out and my lying down; you are familiar with all my ways. Before a word is on my tongue you, Lord, know it completely.
PSALM 139:1–4 NIV

EVENING •

God, I'm so happy You know me. The color of my hair and eyes were Your design. You know how tall I will be when I grow up. You know all my likes and dislikes—every single one of them! You know my future. And I want to become everything You have planned for me, Lord. Thank You for letting me be me. Amen.

DAY 166
Does God Really Care?

You're so precious in the sight of God. Every move you make, every breath you take, every thought you think. . .He knows it all!

God's in absolute control. No matter what you're going through, God sees it. He knows your pain. He's got plans for you like you could never imagine. And He's *always* with you (Matthew 28:20). A flower goes dormant in the winter but comes back to life in the spring. It wasn't dead. . .just asleep as the Lord worked on it. And so it is with you. During those times of "winter," let Him carry you, and just rest in His strong and capable arms as He strengthens your heart and helps you grow.

> *We are afflicted in every way, but not crushed; perplexed, but not despairing; persecuted, but not abandoned; struck down, but not destroyed; always carrying around in the body the dying of Jesus, so that the life of Jesus may also be revealed in our body.*
> **2 CORINTHIANS 4:8–10 NASB**

Father, thank You for taking care of me. Thank You for knowing me—my thoughts, my fears, my dreams, my every-thing. . .every hurt and every pain, every tear that falls and every sickness, every laugh. . . I'm in total awe that You care so much about me. Thank You. In Jesus' name I pray. Amen.

DAY 167
Read the Instructions

Have you ever opened a brand-new board game and tossed aside the instructions? You find that you don't know how to set up the game, what the rules are, or most importantly, how to win! Soon you find yourself reading the instructions so that you can play the game correctly. It takes a little bit of time, but in the end it's worth it.

The Bible is God's instruction book for life. If you jump into life without reading scripture, you won't know God's will or His ways. You may start out on a wrong path. You won't receive the warnings that His Word contains for your good. And you certainly won't win in the Christian life.

Your heavenly Father has provided guidance and truth in the Bible. Take the time to read the instructions today!

All Scripture is inspired by God and is useful to teach us what is true and to make us realize what is wrong in our lives. It corrects us when we are wrong and teaches us to do what is right. God uses it to prepare and equip his people to do every good work.

2 TIMOTHY 3:16–17 NLT

Thank You, Lord, for giving me instructions for everyday living. Your Word includes everything I need to live a good, happy, healthy life! I know that a life without Your Word will be hard and confusing. So please create a love for scripture in me, Father. Help me to memorize the verses that I will need to recall throughout my life. Your Word brings hope, joy, peace, comfort. . .just what I need! Amen.

DAY 168
Obey? No Way!

Your mom asks you to clean your room before heading out to spend time with your friends, and you say, "Sure." But you don't get it done before you leave the house. You want to obey your mom but not enough to actually clean your room, right? If this sounds familiar, you may have an obedience problem.

Obedience is tough. But there's good news: If you're a Christian, God is constantly working on your heart so you'll want to obey Him. He will never give up on you. He doesn't keep reminding you of your disobedience. Instead, He just loves. The more you understand His love, the more you'll want to obey Him and others in your life. Ask God to help you, and remember today is a great day to obey!

> *For God is working in you, giving you the desire and the power to do what pleases him.*
> **PHILIPPIANS 2:13 NLT**

God, there are so many other things I'd rather do than chores. ANYTHING, really! But I know that obedience is important to You, Father. Please work on my heart. Help me to do better when it comes to obeying my parents. And help me to be more obedient to You. With Your help, I can do it! Amen.

DAY 169
God Loves Me

Are you ever afraid that you're not good enough for God's love? That maybe something you've done or something you've said will make Him stop loving you? Or maybe you are just unlovable?

The truth is, God doesn't ever stop loving because we are unlovable. In fact, His love is something we can count on and always trust to be there. If we do wrong, all we need to do is ask His forgiveness, and He will give it to us because He loves us. God will help us do better and make things right again for us if we turn to Him. Know that God loves you. . .and that He always will. You can count on it!

> *God's love, though, is ever and always, eternally present to all who fear him, making everything right for them and their children.*
> **PSALM 103:17 MSG**

Dear God, if I'm being completely honest, I'm not always a lovable human being. Sometimes I'm downright cranky and mean. It's such a relief to know that even when I'm behaving like that, You keep on loving me anyway. Thank You for loving me always, Lord. When I'm having a difficult day, please help me turn to You and feel all of Your love. Amen.

DAY 170
I'm Forgiven

No matter what you've done—God sent His Son to pay the price for your sins. You are forgiven.

Did you get that? If you have accepted His free gift of salvation, you are forgiven. For *everything*.

Even after you're saved, it's easy to mess up. But you are still forgiven! It's often harder to forgive ourselves than it is to understand that Almighty God loves and forgives us. So don't fall into that trap.

There will be days when you stand strong to temptation, and there will be days when you fail. But praise God, He is there, loving you, wanting to pick you up and dust you off. Confess your mistakes to Him and thank Him for His amazing grace. You are forgiven!

As for our offenses, You forgive them.

PSALM 65:3 NASB

Heavenly Father, I'm so sorry for all the times I've failed You. I'm sorry for my sin but so thankful for Your forgiveness. Please help me to stand strong today in the face of temptation, and help me to share Your forgiveness with someone else today. I love You, Lord. Amen.

DAY 171
A Thankful Heart

Bad days? We all have them. And you've been there with the haircut that didn't turn out like you wanted, the reprimand from your teacher for talking in class, and the bruised knees from your embarrassing trip over your chair in Sunday school.

We can't always control things that go wrong, but what we can control is our reaction to those things. So the next time you have a bad day, think about the wonderful things in your life—like your wonderful family, your cuddly pet, your best friend, your bedroom that's decorated just the way you like it. . . And you'll find yourself bouncing back fast from your sour mood.

And last but not least, thank God for all the good stuff in your life. He'll be happy to hear from you!

Always give thanks for all things to God the Father in the name of our Lord Jesus Christ.
EPHESIANS 5:20 NLV

God, I know bad days will happen. I just wish they didn't happen so often to me. Thank You for understanding how I feel. And when things don't quite go my way, instead of feeling sorry for myself, help me to think of everything that's good—there are a lot of wonderful things in this life of mine! Thank you for blessing me! You are so, so good! Amen.

DAY 172
You Have a History

Can you remember some really great seasons in your life? You got just what you wanted for your birthday. . . . You were invited to the best party of the year. . . . It was easy to see how God laid His hand on your life and blessed you magnificently.

If you think a little longer, you can also recall when things were downright awful. You flunked a class. . . . Maybe you broke your leg or lost your best friend. During those times, it wasn't as easy to see God's blessings.

When life gets tough, it pays to remember our history with the heavenly Father. By remembering the ways He has always protected and sent support, we can gain the courage to move through to the next great season in our lives—and we can feel grateful for what we have *right now*.

"Fear not, for I am with you; be not dismayed, for I am your God. I will strengthen you, yes, I will help you, I will uphold you with My righteous right hand."
ISAIAH 41:10 NKJV

God, You allow both wonderful seasons and hard seasons into my life. Please help me to be grateful for each one— because in each season, You shower me with blessings (even if I don't recognize them right away). Thank You for all You do for me—even if life does get a little tough at times. I trust that You have only good things planned for me. Amen.

DAY 173
Star Light, Star Bright

MORNING •

Have you ever looked at the night sky? If you live in the city, chances are you can't see very many stars. But if you get away from the streetlights of town and gaze at the same sky, you'll be amazed. Millions of stars, like scattered diamonds, shine in the heavens, brightening the darkness.

As God's child, you are like one of those twinkling stars. His light shines within you, visible to all who see. And each time you tell the truth. . .each time you show kindness to others. . .each time you obey God's Word, your light shines brighter. And just like the stars in the sky, you are most visible when surrounded by darkness.

Become blameless and pure, "children of God without fault in a warped and crooked generation." Then you will shine among them like stars in the sky.
PHILIPPIANS 2:15 NIV

EVENING •

Heavenly Father, I always want to stand up for what's right. I want to stand strong for You. Please help me to shine my light brightly for You. I want to be a glittering diamond in the night sky, lighting up the darkness. I want to be an example to others so they can come to know You too! Amen.

DAY 174
Rainbows and Promises

Remember the story of Noah? After a long time in a boat with a bunch of animals, God brought him and his family safely to land. The first thing they did was offer their praise to God for His goodness. And God placed a rainbow in the sky as a sign of His promise that He would never again flood the earth.

God's promises aren't just for long ago, though. He has made promises since then and will keep every single one. He will not break any of them. He promises to love us, protect us, guide us, and then take us to heaven to live with Him forever when our time on earth is done. What amazing promises!

We can always be certain that whatever He says, He will do. Remember that the next time you see a rainbow!

> *He will keep his agreement forever; he*
> *will keep his promises always.*
> **PSALM 105:8 NCV**

Dear Father, thank You for the many promises You have given to us in the Bible. I know that You will be faithful to keep Your word. Every time I see a rainbow in the sky, I think of Your amazing promises. Your promises are true. Your promises are forever. Help me to faithfully keep the promises I make too. In Jesus' name, amen.

DAY 175
What's So Scary?

There are lots of scary things in the world. Fear comes when we think there isn't anyone or anything to protect us. The Bible tells us that God is always near and that we can depend on Him to take care of us. The more we know what the Bible has to say, the more we will trust Him to rid our hearts and minds of fear.

The worst part of fear is that it can hold you back from becoming the kid God created you to be. It isn't part of His plan for you to be stopped in your tracks because you're feeling afraid and alone. He will help you fight the battle; all you need to do is ask for His protection and peace.

> *"I am leaving you with a gift—peace of mind and heart. And the peace I give is a gift the world cannot give. So don't be troubled or afraid."*
> **JOHN 14:27 NLT**

Dear Lord, I get scared sometimes and don't know what to do. I don't like being afraid, and I ask You to help me in those times. Please help me to clear my mind. I want to get to work on becoming who You created me to be. With You beside me, I have nothing to fear! Thank You that You are always with me and helping me to be me. Amen.

DAY 176
Hopeful

MORNING •

Let's face it. Some days are just rotten, and it seems like things will never get any better. It's a pretty crummy feeling to have no hope.

But with God, we always have hope for a better future! We can know, without any doubt, that things will get better for us. God loves us, and He has good things in store for us. We can dream. We can imagine. We can plan for the future. And we can do those things because of that one little word: *hope*.

No matter how bad things may seem, we can be certain there are good things coming our way. We can even talk to God about these things and tell Him our hopes and dreams. He loves us, and He wants to give us the secret desires of our hearts.

> *May the God of hope fill you with all joy and peace as you trust in him, so that you may overflow with hope by the power of the Holy Spirit.*
> **ROMANS 15:13 NIV**

EVENING •

Dear Father, thank You for giving me hope. When things seem hopeless, help me to trust in Your love for me. I will continue to dream. I will continue to imagine. I will always have hope in my heart—because I have You in my life. What a wonderful feeling! You always bring light into the darkness. Thank You, Lord. Amen.

DAY 177
Shine or Grumble?

You have a choice each day—to either shine for Jesus or grumble and complain. Every day of your life there will be plenty of things for you to complain about. There will also be many blessings to be thankful for. You can focus on blessings, or you can complain about problems. What kind of person do you want to be around? One who shines? Or one who grumbles?

God's Word tell us that "his divine power has given us everything we need for a godly life through our knowledge of him who called us by his own glory and goodness" (2 Peter 1:3 NIV). This means that when we accept Jesus as our Savior and choose to follow Him, God gives us everything we need to make good choices. . .to choose to shine!

Do all things without grumbling or disputing, that you may be blameless and innocent, children of God without blemish in the midst of a crooked and twisted generation, among whom you shine as lights in the world, holding fast to the word of life.

PHILIPPIANS 2:14–16 ESV

God, today I'm making a choice. I won't grumble and complain. Instead, I need Your help. Please help me to be someone who shines for You! There are lots of times it's easier to focus on the negative, but with Your help, Lord, I can focus wholly on my blessings and not my problems. Amen.

DAY 178
Count on It!

How many times have you used the words, "I promise!" Probably hundreds, right? We're always promising to do things. Sometimes we keep those promises, and sometimes we don't. Nothing makes you feel worse than having a friend or loved one break their promise to you.

God never has to say, "Oops! I said it, but I didn't really mean it!" You'll also never hear Him say, "Well, I told you I would do that, but then I changed my mind." See, with God, what He says is what He will do. In other words, He always keeps His promises! If you want to know more, read your Bible. It's loaded with great promises just for you!

Through His shining-greatness and perfect life, He has given us promises. These promises are of great worth and no amount of money can buy them.

2 PETER 1:4 NLV

Dear Lord, I feel like so many people have broken their promises to me! They say one thing and do another. I really dislike the way I feel when someone breaks a promise—sad, angry, disappointed. . . But, Father, I'm so glad You never go back on Your promises. Thanks for giving me Your Word—and keeping it! Amen.

DAY 179
Precious, Uncountable Thoughts

MORNING •

Who knows you? I mean *really* knows you? Who can you be yourself with? Who can you laugh with until you cry? But even in thinking about that person, there are certainly a few things they *don't* know about you—and probably a few things you would rather them *not* know about you.

There is a Friend who knows everything—*everything*—about you and loves you more than anyone else can. He not only made you but He knows all about you, and the number of His thoughts about you cannot even be counted!

You are precious to your Creator. There is nothing He does not know about you, yet despite any flaws, He wants you. He has big plans for you. And He loves you more than you can ever imagine!

> *How precious are your thoughts about me,*
> *O God. They cannot be numbered!*
> **PSALM 139:17 NLT**

EVENING •

> *Dear heavenly Father, thank You for creating me and*
> *for Your love for me. Some days I don't feel deserv-*
> *ing of Your love, but help me to remember that I*
> *don't have to do anything or be anything to earn it.*
> *I only need to be Yours. And that's it! Thank You for*
> *your precious thoughts of me that are too many to*
> *count! You mean everything to me, Lord. Amen.*

DAY 180
God Has a Plan

MORNING •

Do things ever seem to go wrong and just keep going wrong for you? You didn't get the part in the play or the spot on the team you wanted so badly. You couldn't go to the party you'd been looking forward to for weeks. You came down with a virus and missed too much school, and now your grades are suffering. Life's not always easy, but remember God has good plans for you. He will see you through the tough times and get you past any illness and disappointments. He has a plan for better days ahead, so trust Him. He knows the plans for your future, even if you don't.

> *"For I know the plans I have for you," declares the Lord, "plans to prosper you and not to harm you, plans to give you hope and a future."*
> **JEREMIAH 29:11 NIV**

EVENING •

Dear God, You never said life would be easy. But Your Word does promise that You have good plans for me. And I thank You for Your plans and Your promise! Your plan gives me hope and keeps me looking ahead to the future You have in store for me. Help me to remember that You do have a plan, even if I don't know what it is right now. Amen.

DAY 181
Heirs for All Eternity

A "covenant" is an agreement or promise made. In Genesis 15, God made His covenant with Abraham. Genesis 15:17–18 says that "a smoking oven and a flaming torch appeared which passed between these pieces. On that day the LORD made a covenant with Abram" (NASB). God sealed His covenant by passing between the halves of Abram's offering. Passing through the pieces was like saying, "Cross my heart, hope to die." God was telling Abraham that He'd die before He would break His covenant.

We're children of God through our faith; we've "received adoption" (Galatians 4:4–6). He's preparing a place for you in heaven and will fulfill His promise to you. He will *never* abandon you (2 Corinthians 4:8–18). God always keeps His promises, and He will never leave you to wander in this dark world alone.

If you belong to Christ, then you are Abraham's descendants, heirs according to promise.
GALATIANS 3:29 NASB

Lord, thank You so much for making me an heir through my faith in Your Son, Jesus. Help me to live freely, but not take my freedom for granted (Galatians 5:1, 13). Thank You for the forever home You're preparing in heaven for me. I look forward to eternal life with You, Father. In Jesus' holy and precious name, I pray. Amen.

DAY 182
Choosing Your Friends

Ever walked on a balance beam? It's tricky, isn't it? At first, young gymnasts require a coach to "spot" them as they try to keep their balance walking along the beam. Later, it becomes easier for them to stay focused and centered on their own.

Would it be easy to pull up a friend onto the balance beam to walk with you? No way! It would be next to impossible! And yet, how easily that friend could cause you to stumble and take a fall right off the beam. Just a tap of a finger might be all it would take.

The same is true in life. As you choose your friends, choose wisely. How easy it is to lose our way and be led down wrong paths by friends whose hearts do not belong to Christ.

> *The righteous choose their friends carefully,*
> *but the way of the wicked leads them astray.*
> **PROVERBS 12:26 NIV**

Lord, I know it's important to be kind and loving to all people. But remind me to choose my friends wisely. Help me to choose friends who love You as much as I do. These are the kind of friends who will walk beside me as I do my best to live my life for You, Lord. Thank You for Christian friends who encourage me to walk in Your ways. Amen.

DAY 183
Wonderful Things

Stores are loaded with wonderful things, aren't they? And it's all so tempting. Sometimes you want something so desperately that you convince yourself you *really need* it. . .that your life won't be as fun or meaningful without it. And so you buy it.

Sometimes you use what you've purchased and truly enjoy it. But many times it just ends up at the bottom of your drawer or stuffed into the back of your closet. And you sometimes even wonder why you bought it in the first place. Stuff goes from treasure to trash way too fast, and the thrill of buying has to be repeated over and over and over.

Fortunately, God cares more about you than to just give you everything you want. God gives you everything you need, and that promise won't ever fade or be forgotten at the bottom of a drawer!

And my God will meet all your needs according to the riches of his glory in Christ Jesus.
PHILIPPIANS 4:19 NIV

Lord, the world is filled with SO MUCH STUFF. And I admit, much of it looks really good to me. I'd like to have so many things. But do I really need all of it? Nope! Thank You for giving me everything I need, Father. You'll always see to it that I'm taken care of. And forgive me for sometimes being so busy asking You for more that I forget to thank You for what I already have. Amen.

DAY 184
You Call. . .He Answers

MORNING •

God hears you when you pray. Every single time.

God always answers too, even though it may not seem like it. Because God is more interested in your character than your comfort, the answer may not be the one you were hoping for. Sometimes the answer is "no." Sometimes the answer is "wait." And sometimes the answer is "yes," but you don't recognize it because it doesn't look the way you thought it would.

No matter how God chooses to answer your prayer, just know that He WILL. His ways are not our ways (Isaiah 55:8). You have to trust that He knows what is best. Just believe Him for the best because that's what He wants to give you. Anything is possible (Mark 9:23)!

I sought the Lord, and he answered me;
he delivered me from all my fears.
PSALM 34:4 NIV

EVENING •

Dear God, sometimes when I pray, I feel like my prayers
don't reach You. But no matter how I feel, I choose to
believe what Your Word says. When I call on You, You
will answer me and deliver me from all my fears. And it
doesn't make a difference whether I pray to You in the
morning or at night, silently or out loud. You ALWAYS
hear me! Thank You for being a God of answers. Amen.

DAY 185
It's Not My Problem!

MORNING •

We all have troubles from time to time. . . . How do you feel when you have troubles of your own? Lonely? Helpless? Afraid? Worried? You probably have at least one, if not all, of those feelings. Now imagine what you would do if you had no one to talk to. . .no one to help you through a tough time. Handling your problems all by yourself would make your troubles seem even bigger, wouldn't it?

Even though we may want to turn and run away from someone else's problems, we are called to follow God's example and reach out to help others in their time of need. Whether they need a listening ear. . .a shoulder to cry on. . .an extra set of hands to complete a big chore. . .we can pitch in and let God's light shine through us.

Help each other in troubles and problems.
This is the kind of law Christ asks us to obey.
GALATIANS 6:2 NLV

EVENING •

God, sometimes I just want to shout out, "It's not my problem! Why should I help? It has nothing to do with me!" But then I remember what You want me to do. Thank You for being a good example of reaching out to others in need. Remind me of what I feel like when I have problems of my own and it seems like no one wants to help or listen. Thank You, Lord, for being so wonderful! Amen.

DAY 186
Standing on the Promises

MORNING •

You lie in bed with your eyes wide open. You reflect on the day. . . .

It rained all afternoon. And just as the rain turned to a light sprinkle, you glanced out your bedroom window and spotted the most brilliant rainbow you'd ever seen. You ran outside to get a better look and saw that the rainbow spanned from one side of the sky to the other—a vibrant burst of color: red, orange, yellow, green, blue, indigo, and violet. A beautiful reminder of God's unfailing promises and amazing love for you!

> *Standing on the promises of Christ my King,*
> *Through eternal ages let His praises ring,*
> *Glory in the highest, I will shout and sing,*
> *Standing on the promises of God.*

Are you standing on His promises?

> ***My eyes stay open through the watches of the***
> ***night, that I may meditate on your promises.***
> **PSALM 119:148 NIV**

EVENING •

God, thank You for Your peace, rest, and love. Thank
You for the rainbow, a beautiful reminder of Your
love and promises to Your people. Your promises are
within my soul, Lord. I am standing on Your promises
today, tomorrow, and every day! Knowing Your prom-
ises are true, I feel strong and courageous. Amen.

DAY 187
Life Is Hard, but God Is Good

MORNING •

On very bad days, when you just want to give up because the world has thrown everything at you that it possibly can. . . remember that Christ suffered for you as well. That's one of the many ways our God is so amazing. He understands every hurt, every tear, every horrible event in your life because He's been there. He was publicly humiliated, battered, beaten, spat upon, and hung on a cross.

When you're in the middle of a trial, remind yourself to turn to Him. His comfort is the only comfort you'll ever need, and it is abundant. There's plenty of it for every day of your life.

For just as the sufferings of Christ are ours in abundance, so also our comfort is abundant through Christ.

2 CORINTHIANS 1:5 NASB

EVENING •

God, some days I really need a do-over. When everything seems to be going wrong, I need Your comfort. And it's so nice to know that You understand all the hurt and pain in my life. Thank You for Your sacrifice, and thank You for always being there for me. Help me to smile through the trials and keep my focus on You. Amen.

DAY 188
Fight the Urge to Fight!

Ever been so mad at one of your friends that you screamed ugly, hurtful things at them? Or how about your siblings? It can be especially hard to get along with your sisters and brothers because you spend so much time together. Sometimes you get sick of them, right? Fights happen.

But fighting, which is also known as "strife," is a very *serious* subject. James 3:16 tells us that where strife is, every evil work is also there. Being in constant strife is like inviting the devil into your home. It's like saying, "Yo, devil. Come on in and make yourself comfy. Oh, and bring all of your evil buddies along—like jealousy, fear, bitterness, and unforgiveness." Don't let strife camp out in your life. Instead, fight the urge to fight! You'll be so glad you did.

Do not repay anyone evil for evil. Be careful
to do what is right in the eyes of everyone.
ROMANS 12:17 NIV

God, help me to walk in love, not strife. I know I will get
angry at my friends and family sometimes. But I know You
can help me keep it under control. I don't want to fight,
God. I want to be a peacemaker. With You by my side, I
can stand up and tell the devil to get lost! With You by my
side, I can always do what's right. I love You, Lord. Amen.

DAY 189
Can You Hear Me?

MORNING •

At times, it can feel like God doesn't hear us when we talk to Him. We pray for a friend to pass a test, and by His miracle it happens. Then on another day, we pray for other friends in trouble and hear nothing. Is God so far away that He can't hear us? Or are we missing something?

Hearing God's voice isn't always easy. A lot of noise fills up our lives. If you need an answer, make sure you find some alone time and practice listening for His instruction. Most of all, be patient. . .because His answer comes in His timing—not ours.

> **But when you ask him, be sure**
> **that your faith is in God alone.**
> **JAMES 1:6 NLT**

EVENING •

God, I really need to hear Your voice today. Help
me tune out the noisy distractions of the world so I
can clearly hear You. I don't want anything to come
between us, God. I will find a quiet place where just
You and I can hang out for a while. And after we talk,
I will be patient as I wait for You to answer. Amen.

DAY 190
He Made Me

In this world we live in, it is sometimes hard to grasp the fact that our God made us. That He made us each unique, and that He knows everything about us. He knows our weaknesses and our strengths; He knows when we do wrong and when we do right. He knows everything that has happened and everything that will happen to us. And we owe Him *everything*. We should want to do His will always. But to be able to do His will, we need to know His commandments and follow them. He will help us. All we need to do is to pray for understanding.

Your hands have made me and fashioned me; give me understanding, that I may learn Your commandments.

PSALM 119:73 NKJV

Dear God, please help me to learn Your will and to understand it deep inside my heart so I can do the things You want me to do. I want to please You in all ways. It's the least I can do. You made me, You gave me life. . .You protect me and care for me. Help me to always remember that. Help me to know Your will, Father. Amen.

DAY 191
Temptation Nation

Temptation is everywhere. Temptation to do the wrong thing. Temptation to cheat on a test. Temptation from girls and boys at school—or even friends at church! When you choose to follow Jesus, the devil gets angry! The enemy will do whatever he can to try and trip you up!

So what's a kid who loves Jesus to do? Ephesians 6:10–11 gives us the answer: "Be strong in the Lord and in his mighty power. Put on the full armor of God, so that you can take your stand against the devil's schemes" (NIV).

Every morning, put on the full armor of God knowing that you are headed into battle. Remember, God is faithful, and He will always give you an escape! Be on the lookout!

> *No temptation has overtaken you that is not common to man. God is faithful, and he will not let you be tempted beyond your ability, but with the temptation he will also provide the way of escape, that you may be able to endure it.*
> **1 CORINTHIANS 10:13 ESV**

God, temptation is hard. And it's everywhere. Whatever I face, help me to be strong in You today! Cover me with Your power, and protect me from the devil's plans. Help me do the right thing and always stand up for what I believe in. Thank You for being a faithful God. Thank You for giving me a way out of every temptation that comes my way. Amen.

DAY 192
When Joy Is Hard

It's easy to feel joy when things are going right. When we make an A on a test, or get invited to sit with the cool kids at lunch. . . But what about when everything goes wrong?

The Bible tells us to rejoice, *even then*! That sounds crazy. But when we think about it, it's the hard times that build our character. It's the hard times that help us grow up and become mature. It's the hard times that teach us love, patience, and kindness.

Next time things seem to be going all wrong, take a moment and thank God. Let's remind ourselves that God must be doing something pretty special. And let's smile, knowing God's plans for us are always good, even when they don't seem good at the time.

Consider it pure joy, my brothers and sisters, whenever you face trials of many kinds, because you know that the testing of your faith produces perseverance. Let perseverance finish its work so that you may be mature and complete, not lacking anything.
JAMES 1:2–4 NIV

Dear Father, it's so wonderful when everything is going right in my world. But the reality is that the good times will sometimes be interrupted by hard times in life. When this happens, help me to be joyful. Help me to be thankful even when things aren't going my way. Thank You for caring about who I am tomorrow and not just about how I feel today. Amen.

DAY 193
God's Love for Me

It's rather easy to love someone who loves you back. It's the ones who have hurt or offended you who are the difficult ones to love.

But God loved us before we ever knew Him. He loved us when we knew Him but didn't love Him back. We hurt Him and offended Him, yet He kept on loving us.

Finally, the day came that we repented and told God that we chose to love Him. As God's children, we profess our love for Him, but we don't always show it. The Bible says that the person who really loves Him will obey Him.

"The person who has My commandments and keeps them is the one who [really] loves Me; and whoever [really] loves Me will be loved by My Father, and I will love him and reveal Myself to him [I will make Myself real to him]."
JOHN 14:21 AMP

God, why is loving other people so hard? I really do try, but some people are just super hard to love. They're mean and grouchy. They just aren't nice. Yet You ask me to love them anyway. And so I'll try my best—with Your help! I love You, Lord. I want to obey Your commands to show You that my love for You is real. Thank You for loving me when I'm not very lovable and for promising to ALWAYS love me. Amen.

DAY 194
Pure Joy!

Think about some things you'd like to have.... Pretty easy, right? Maybe you've been wanting a new pair of shoes. Or maybe you'd like to have a brand-new phone. We always have a ready list of "stuff" that would make us just a little happier, don't we?

But have you ever made a list—an A to Z, everything-that's-good-in-your-life list? From the simple to the big stuff, you have too many blessings to name!

While we often tend to think about all of the things we don't have, the fact is, every moment of the day, no matter where you look, you can find at least one item to thank God for—one blessing in your life. Now that's reason to celebrate...all day long!

Celebrate God all day, every day.
PHILIPPIANS 4:4 MSG

*God, help me to think about all the wonderful things
You have given for my enjoyment—not just "stuff," but
the things in my life that really matter. Like sunshine. My
favorite food. My friends. My room. You've blessed me
with so much that I could have an "I've-been-blessed"
celebration every day of the week! Thank You! Amen.*

DAY 195
Rejoice. . .Always?

MORNING •

Things happen in each of our lives that are terribly hard to deal with.

Jesus knows there are times when your heart hurts. He understands that you don't always feel like jumping for joy. But what He does want you to know is that He is always there. His wants your fellowship with Him through prayer to be constant. He calls you to trust Him to work good things from the bad in your life.

So even on your worst day, *pray* to God. *Thank Him* even for the hard times. Hard times lead you to the foot of the cross, which is a great place to be. *Rejoice* that you are not alone but that you belong to a heavenly Father who will lead you through every trial.

Rejoice always, pray without ceasing, in everything give thanks; for this is the will of God in Christ Jesus for you.
1 THESSALONIANS 5:16–18 NKJV

EVENING •

Father, sometimes very hard things happen to people.
Best friends move away, Pets die. Parents get divorced.
Yet Your Word says that we should rejoice and be thankful
in all things—and I know this means even the hard
things, Lord. I will do my very best to obey You, Lord.
I trust You to work ALL things together for good in
my life. I thank You, even in the hard times. Amen.

DAY 196
He Is Always with Me, Part One

MORNING •

The Lord God—your heavenly Father, the Beginning and the End, the Author and the Healer—is watching over *you!* He's your rock, your fortress, your deliverer, your refuge, your shield, your stronghold! His arms are stretched open wide ready to embrace you and shelter your soul.

Can you imagine that? Can you imagine God standing here with His arms wide? He is calling you, dear one (John 10:3)! Run into His arms. Take His outstretched hand, and don't let go! When the devil prowls around "like a roaring lion" (1 Peter 5:8), keep your eyes on your glorious Lord. He's your Savior. And He's always here.

> *The Lord is my rock and my fortress and my savior, my God, my rock, in whom I take refuge; my shield and the horn of my salvation, my stronghold.*
>
> **PSALM 18:2 NASB**

EVENING •

Lord, thank You for watching over me. Thank You for being my shelter, fortress, and shield. When the strong winds blow, when the water rises up high above me, when my enemies surround me, You're here to hold me tight and keep my heart at peace. And I am so thankful! I love You, Lord. Please help me to keep my eyes on You. In Jesus' name, I pray. Amen.

DAY 197
He Is Always with Me, Part Two

Did you know that the Spirit of God Himself dwells in you, and He'll never leave you? You were bought at a price, beloved child. The price of Jesus' blood on the cross. Through His death, we have the gift of eternal life.

Romans 8:15–16 says: "For you have not received a spirit of slavery leading to fear again, but you have received a spirit of adoption as sons and daughters by which we cry out, 'Abba! Father!' The Spirit Himself testifies with our spirit that we are children of God" (NASB).

God's our Father, and we're His children. He's here with us and in us. And just like a loving father, He guides and directs us through His Holy Spirit (John 14:16; John 16:13; Romans 8:26).

> ***Do you not know that you are a temple of
> God and that the Spirit of God dwells in you?***
> **1 CORINTHIANS 3:16 NASB**

*God, thank You for sending Jesus, the greatest gift
ever given. Because of Jesus, I am free. I am forgiven.
I will live in heaven forever! Thank You also for giving
me Your Holy Spirit. And thank You for Your Word that
gives me trustworthy guidance for life. Please help me
to keep my focus on You and never forget that You're
always with me. In Jesus' holy name, I pray. Amen.*

DAY 198
Bees and God's Plan for Me

Have you ever seen bees buzzing around beautiful flowers? The job the bees are doing is quite amazing.

When a bee visits a flower, yellow pollen rubs off on his tiny belly. Then he visits the next flower where the pollen drops into the flower. This is called "pollination." Without pollination from bees, many plants wouldn't have seeds, and therefore, they wouldn't grow fruit.

Isn't it incredible that God has given even the tiny bee an important job to do? It makes sense that if God has a plan for the tiny bee, He has a plan for you too. And even though the bee is small, what he does is not insignificant.

For we are God's handiwork, created in Christ Jesus to do good works, which God prepared in advance for us to do.
EPHESIANS 2:10 NIV

Lord, when I think about growing up and when I think about the future, sometimes it's scary. And sometimes I doubt that You have a plan for my life. But I know if You care about the tiny bee, You care about me. I trust that You will slowly reveal Your plan for me. In the meantime, I choose to walk with You each step of the way and trust You completely for what happens. Amen.

DAY 199
Forget about It!

When a friend hurts your feelings, it's likely you will be angry—maybe even a little sad. You might even hold on to your hurt feelings for a while.

No doubt about it, forgiving your friend will be hard. But this could be the perfect opportunity to reflect God's amazing love into the life of someone else—a way for your friend to see God through your actions. After all, God's Word gives us this bit of wisdom: "Dear children, let's not merely say that we love each other; let us show the truth by our actions" (1 John 3:18 NLT).

Talk to God and ask Him to take away your hurt feelings and then ask Him for His help in extending forgiveness to your friend. And after you forgive, forget about it. God will be delighted!

It's wise to be patient and show what
you are like by forgiving others.
PROVERBS 19:11 CEV

Heavenly Father, sometimes my emotions can be hard to manage—especially when I'm hurt by something my friends do or say. Friends shouldn't hurt each other! And forgiving others definitely isn't easy. But when I open my heart to Your Word and extend forgiveness, I know it makes You happy. And so I will do my very best to follow Your example and forgive! Amen.

DAY 200
Created for a Purpose

The world's view is that all life on this planet happened by accident. People who go along with that theory believe everything that happens is random chance. No plan. No order. No blessing. Can you imagine?

But the Bible says God made you for a special purpose. Nothing, good or bad, happens to you that God has not allowed. Even if something happens that seems bad at first, God can turn it around so that it is good for you in the end.

Knowing you have a purpose is like having a vision of where you're going. The Bible says that when "people can't see what God is doing, they stumble all over themselves" (Proverbs 29:18 MSG). But you won't stumble because you know God has a plan and a purpose. . .just for you.

Always do your work well for the Lord. You know that whatever you do for Him will not be wasted.
1 CORINTHIANS 15:58 NLV

Dear God, I am Yours. And You want to have a special relationship with me. You also have a specific job for me to do here on earth. I just have to be patient and trust You'll show me what that is. Thank You for creating me with a purpose in mind. Help me to understand what my purpose is and to be obedient to Your plans for my life. Amen.

DAY 201
God Will Forgive You—Always!

Have you ever messed up big-time and thought, *Uh-oh, now I've done it. I feel so bad about what I've done. I wonder if God will ever forgive me?*

Maybe you told a lie. Maybe you cheated on a test at school. Maybe you were mean to your best friend.

While all of us will occasionally make mistakes and fail to be "perfect," it's a comfort to know that God has promised in His Word to forgive us—*no matter what*. He loves each of us so much that there's nothing we could do to cause Him to turn His back on us—no matter how big or bad our sin may seem.

Need forgiveness from God? Simply ask, and you'll have it!

> *"Come now, let's settle this," says the Lord.*
> *"Though your sins are like scarlet, I will make*
> *them as white as snow. Though they are red like*
> *crimson, I will make them as white as wool."*
> **ISAIAH 1:18 NLT**

God, I feel so terrible when I mess up. I want to do better! I know I CAN do better! If I ever find myself doubting Your love for me, I will remember this: Your love is so perfect that when I tell You that I'm sorry, You'll always wrap Your arms around me and whisper, "I forgive you." You are so, so good to me, Lord. And I love You! Amen.

DAY 202
Do I Really Need it?

MORNING •

Our society is filled with things. Commercials, billboards, the mall. . .all of it telling you about the latest and greatest hot-ticket item. It's easy to get caught up in wanting things, even feeling like you *need* them.

But God doesn't want us caught up in this world and the stuff. He wants us to know that He's everything we need. And He will supply our needs.

God loves to bless us with extras all the time, but don't get greedy and caught up in things. This world is not your home, and in heaven you'll be surrounded by the Lord's treasures. So store up your treasure in heaven, and know that God will supply what you truly need.

And my God will supply all your needs according to His riches in glory in Christ Jesus.
PHILIPPIANS 4:19 NASB

EVENING •

God, I need Your help. Please turn my focus from myself to others. As I struggle with all my "wants," help me instead to focus on others' needs. How can I meet those needs today? How can I help? I know You'll give me ideas, Lord. Help me to be thankful for everything that I have and to remember that You will always supply my needs. Amen.

DAY 203
What about Me?!

You volunteer your free time at the local animal shelter. You donate new and used books, clothes, and toys to charity every year. And you regularly visit the retirement home and play games with lonely residents. To be honest, you're getting a little worn out from all this "doing good" stuff. You even find yourself wondering if it's worth all the effort.

If we focus on others instead of ourselves, we'll begin to see the effect of our good deeds. And God will have a hand in that. He sees what we're doing to make a difference in the lives of others; and He promises that we will experience something good because of it. Today, ask the Lord to give you the strength and energy you need to keep up the good work. And then wait and see what good things He brings your way!

***Let us not become weary in doing good, for at the
proper time we will reap a harvest if we do not give up.***
GALATIANS 6:9 NIV

*God, I'm so sorry that I sometimes get tired of doing nice
things for others. Please forgive me. Help me to notice all
the wonderful things that happen when I do something
good for someone else. And God? Thank You for noticing
my kindness, even when no one else does. Amen.*

DAY 204
Restore the Light

Do you ever wonder if maybe—just *maybe*—God has forgotten about you? Maybe you have a big problem at school or in your family and nothing seems to be getting better. . .even though you've been praying about it for a L-O-N-G time!

King David in the Bible felt just like this. And if most Christ-followers are honest, we've all felt the same way a time or two in our lives. But you know what? The truth is that God hasn't forgotten about you! God tells us in His Word that His ways are not our ways (Isaiah 55:8). His timing is perfect, and His plan for you is good. He is always working everything out for your good and His glory (Romans 8:28)—even when it doesn't seem like it. Check out Psalm 13 to see what David decides to do about his feelings!

> *O Lord, how long will you forget me? Forever?. . .*
> *Turn and answer me, O Lord my God! Restore*
> *the sparkle to my eyes, or I will die.*
>
> **PSALM 13:1, 3 NLT**

God, even when I feel all alone, I know You haven't forgotten me. I want to trust You. Please help my faith to grow so that I trust You even more. Please bring back the light to my eyes—the light that comes from my hope in You. When I have hope, my heart is full and my smile grows a little bigger. I am so glad I have You in my life, Lord! Amen.

DAY 205
Monsters under the Bed

MORNING •

When you were little, did you lay in bed at night with the covers tucked tightly around you? Did you worry that the boogeyman was going to come out from under your bed and get you? What did you do about it?

If you cried out to your parents for help, they likely told you to think about other things—pray, sing a song, or fill your mind with something silly.

When you're tempted to do wrong, think of that temptation as the monster under your bed. In order to resist it and turn from the sin, you need to fill your life and your mind with holy and righteous things that will distract you from the temptation of sin. Your enemy will throw temptation at you, but it's your job to resist it. When you do that, sin will flee.

Do not be overcome by evil, but overcome evil with good.
ROMANS 12:21 NIV

EVENING •

*Dear God, when temptation comes, help me to bring
to mind holy and righteous things. I need You, Lord.
Please help me to keep my mind from evil and focused
on Your holiness. Help me resist sin and temptation so I
can stay rooted in Your truth. Thank You, Lord. Amen.*

DAY 206
Call Yourself "Masterpiece"

Do you think of yourself as a masterpiece? God certainly does! He knows you are not ordinary or average—because He created you. You are an original. He designed you just as you are for a purpose. If you look at paintings that are considered masterpieces, you'll see that each one has its own prominent brushstrokes and color. No two are alike!

Today is a great day to start recognizing your value. Throw out those thoughts that say, *I'm just average. I'll never do anything special.* And instead, choose to tell yourself the truth. Every day, remind yourself, "I was made by the Artist who paints only masterpieces. His brushstrokes set me apart from everyone else. He filled my personality with original colors. I am special to Him!"

> *For we are God's masterpiece. He has created*
> *us anew in Christ Jesus, so we can do the*
> *good things he planned for us long ago.*
> **EPHESIANS 2:10 NLT**

God, I am a masterpiece! Thank You for creating me with such artistry! I am unique. I am valuable. I am set apart from every other person on earth. I am special. And I know it's 100 percent true because Your Word says so—and Your Word is reliable. Because I am Your child, I am able to do wonderful things for You and Your kingdom. I look forward to what You have planned for my life, Lord. Amen.

DAY 207
Being Strong

Has anyone ever told you to keep your chin up, hold your shoulders back, and be strong? That sounds like good advice. But sometimes it's hard to be strong. Sometimes we just want to cry, or throw a fit, or give in to peer pressure. Being strong isn't always easy.

But God says we don't have to be strong on our own. If we look to Him, He'll be strong for us. He'll give us strength for all sorts of things we may face in this life.

God's strength is unending, and He's never far away. For as long as we live, if we look to Him and ask Him for help, He will always, *always*, give us the strength we need.

Look to the Lord and his strength; seek his face always.
1 Chronicles 16:11 NIV

Dear Father, help me be strong when I need to be. You'll give me strength to be nice when others are mean. You'll give me strength to say no when someone tries to convince me to break the rules. You'll give me strength to share You with the world around me. Remind me that You are always there, giving me strength when I ask for help. Thank You, Lord. Amen.

DAY 208
God's Awesome Workmanship

MORNING •

What is the last thing you created? A science fair project? A painting? How difficult was it to make? Did it take a lot of time and effort?

With just His words, God created the sun and moon, stars and planets. He spoke into existence all animals and plant life. And for the grand finale, God created humanity.

Not too long ago, God crafted you. He caused you to develop in a very safe place until the day you were born. In those few months, He fashioned your body and began its functions. He made you unique, with the qualities that make you the person you are. If you ever question your worth, just think of the workmanship He displayed in creating you. He is intentional in what He creates, so you were made specifically, by the God of the universe. You are special!

Thank you for making me so wonderfully complex!
Your workmanship is marvelous—how well I know it.
PSALM 139:14 NLT

EVENING •

Dear God, You are the Master Creator. When I think of all You've created, I am in awe. You effortlessly spoke Adam into being. Then You created Eve to be his helper. You created everything on earth—including ME! Thank You for making me according to Your plan. Please help me to remember how special I am and how marvelous Your works are. In Your name, amen.

DAY 209
Can You Hear Me Now?

MORNING •

Did you know that God knows your voice? He really does! He knows exactly who you are when you pray; and not only does He hear you but He listens to *everything* you have to say. It's *all* important to Him!

Like our earthly parents, God has a special ear when it comes to listening for His children. He wants to hear from us anytime, anywhere, and for any reason. Your prayers matter to Him as though you were the only child He had.

There's no need to worry that He might not pay any attention to you, even if you don't always know what to say. Your prayers please God, and He listens. When He hears the cries of His children, He sends His love and protection.

> *The Lord has heard my plea;*
> *the Lord will answer my prayer.*
> **PSALM 6:9 NLT**

EVENING •

Dear Lord, it makes me so happy that You know my voice. When others are talking, You recognize which voice is mine. Thank You for hearing my prayers and really listening to everything I say. Remind me that You DO care about everything I care about. Help me to have more faith that You will answer my cries for help. After I've prayed, I will be still, Lord, and listen for Your voice. Amen.

DAY 210
God Has Made a Way

Have you ever been lost? Maybe your mom or dad made a wrong turn and you found yourselves lost in an unfamiliar city or neighborhood. But then the GPS gets you back on track.

Wouldn't it be crazy to turn off the GPS at that point? And yet, so many people do just that to Jesus every day. They tune Him out. They choose their own paths.

Long before you were born, God made a way for you. He sent His only Son, Jesus, to die on a cross for your sins. Jesus is the only way to the Father. To know God and to spend eternity with Him in heaven, you must know His Son.

If you're on a road that leads away from Jesus, turn around as soon as possible. God has made a way for you to come to Him.

Jesus said to him, "I am the way, the truth, and the life. No one comes to the Father except through Me."
JOHN 14:6 NKJV

Lord, I love You. Thank You for loving me first. Thank You for sending Your Son to save me. Come into my heart, Jesus, and forgive me of my sins. I want to follow You for the rest of my life. I know I can't find my way on my own. I need You! Amen.

DAY 211
Jump In! The Water Is Just Fine

MORNING •

Have you ever jumped into a swimming pool in the late spring? The water was so cold your teeth chattered. Even your goose bumps had goose bumps! But then an amazing thing happened—the water didn't feel cold anymore. . .because you got used to the temperature!

Do you know that sin is the same way? When you first enter the "sin pool," you'll immediately want to get out. But the longer you remain in the "sin pool," the easier it becomes to stay there.

Sin has a funny way of fooling you into thinking "it's okay" to sin a little, but the Bible says differently. So don't get used to sin. You have to choose between the world's way and God's way. Jump into God's way. C'mon in! The water is fine!

> *"But since you are like lukewarm water, neither hot nor cold, I will spit you out of my mouth!"*
> **REVELATION 3:16 NLT**

EVENING •

Lord, please help me to stand my ground when it comes to my beliefs. I want to be courageous for You. And I don't ever want to get used to sin. When it comes to You or the world, Lord, I choose YOU! Please help me to stand strong against the world. Your way is the very best way to live. Amen.

DAY 212
The Flip Side

Mark Twain said, "Keep away from people who try to belittle your ambitions. Small people always do that, but the really great ones make you feel that you too can become great." The flip side is just as important: Do what you can to make those around you feel they can become great! Be an encourager. Not just with your close friends. . .but treat *everyone* just like you want to be treated.

Jesus wants us to understand about the flip side. He talks a lot about not judging others when we have sin in our own life that needs to be dealt with first (see Matthew 7:1–5). He wants us to love and be considerate of others, even if we might disagree sometimes. Ask God to help you respond to others in a way that would make Him smile.

> *"Do to others whatever you would like them to do to you. This is the essence of all that is taught in the law and the prophets."*
> MATTHEW 7:12 NLT

God, please give me the courage to do the right thing. Help me think of others first and treat them like I would want to be treated. When I'm unsure, prompt me to ask myself the question: How would I want to be treated in this situation? You'll help steer me in the right direction. Thank You, Father! Amen.

DAY 213
Life Everlasting

MORNING •

Sometimes we get so caught up in this earthly life that we forget to think about the everlasting life we will one day have in heaven. Our eternal life is where our focus should be—even now!—and we should always be looking forward to that day when we meet Jesus face-to-face. God wanted us to have a life with Him so much that He gave His only Son, Jesus, to die that we might live! It should be on our mind every morning, every evening, all day long.

For God so loved the world that He gave His only begotten Son, that whoever believes in Him should not perish but have everlasting life.

JOHN 3:16 NKJV

EVENING •

Dear God, thank You for sending Your Son, Jesus—for loving us so much that we can accept Your gift of eternal life. . . the promise of life in heaven with You! Please help me keep my focus on the life that truly matters, the eternal life I will have someday because of Your amazing gift. Amen.

DAY 214
God's Garden

God's garden is the safest and happiest place to be. Plenty of sunshine and rain, along with constant protection, means that you have every chance to grow up healthy and beautiful. But God's ways of cultivating can also be uncomfortable at times, especially if you need a lot of pruning or tend to attract pests. You may be tempted to run wild rather than endure His methods of shaping you.

Plants left to themselves don't remain lovely for long. They are eventually choked by weeds, devoured by insects, or crushed by careless feet. You're far better off submitting to the hands of your wise and loving Creator than trying to develop on your own. Have patience, dear one. It may be a lot of work, but God's flowers always grow up wonderfully!

And the Lord God planted a garden.
GENESIS 2:8 KJV

Lord, You make all things beautiful. And I want to
grow up strong and healthy in Your garden. Help
me to be patient and give You all the control while
You make me into a blossom worthy of Your love.
I am thankful for You Lord. I love You. Amen.

DAY 215
Replace Judging with Loving

MORNING •

It's not easy to put yourself in someone else's shoes. And the Bible warns to be careful when you judge someone. When you judge someone without understanding their situation, you'll often be put in a very similar situation during your lifetime. That's what "the measure you use will be used on you" means. Sometimes God allows things like that to happen so that you can understand and forgive those toward which you harbor bitter feelings.

You just never really know someone else's situations. So pray for others and be careful how you judge them.

"For in the same way you judge others, you will be judged, and with the measure you use, it will be measured to you."
MATTHEW 7:2 NIV

EVENING •

Dear God, please help me not to judge others. I want to be a loving example of You to everyone I see each day. I don't want to avoid people just because I don't understand them, Lord. Please give me Your wisdom so I know how to act around others. With Your help, and with You by my side each step of the way, I can share You with everyone I meet. Amen.

DAY 216
Your Future's So Bright, You're Gonna Need Shades!

MORNING •

What are your plans for the rest of your life? Do you have it all figured out? Even if you don't have a plan, God does.

His plan for you was established long ago. He wants you to prosper and have a bright future. He's already given you all the gifts and talents you're going to need. But guess what? You can choose to go along with God's plan. . .or not. God isn't going to force you to follow His plan even though He knows it's the best one. The choice is yours.

As you plan your future, ask God to guide your choices. Let Him know that you want His plan to be *YOUR* plan for the future. Then you'll have it made in the shade!

> *"For I know the plans I have for you," declares*
> *the LORD, "plans to prosper you and not to harm*
> *you, plans to give you hope and a future."*
> **JEREMIAH 29:11 NIV**

EVENING •

Dear God, as I make choices about my future, I want to be
sure they are the right ones. Please guide me, and help me
to know the plans You have for me. I choose to go along
with Your plan, because Your plan is always the best plan.
And Your Word says if I give my plans to You, then my
plans will succeed (Proverbs 16:3). Thank You, Lord! Amen.

DAY 217
The Company You Keep

Are you influenced by your friends? Do their words, activities, and behaviors have an impact on you?

The truth is that God wants us to be part of the world around us. *But* we should be shaping the world, not letting the world shape us.

We can only impact the world when we strive to solely be "joined" or united with people who share our love for Jesus and our goal of pleasing Him with our lifestyle. If you feel that those types of people are difficult to find, pray that God would lead you to ones who will build you up, and with whom you can live as an example to others.

To stay in God's light, ask Him to give you wisdom in choosing your friends.

> *Do not be joined together with those who do*
> *not belong to Christ. How can that which is*
> *good get along with that which is bad? How can*
> *light be in the same place with darkness?*
> **2 CORINTHIANS 6:14 NLV**

Heavenly Father, I want to be a light in the world. So please help me to walk closely with You every day. And help me to choose my friends wisely. Lead me to others who will positively influence my words, my thoughts, and my actions. This world definitely needs more light! Thank You, Lord! Amen.

DAY 218
Cowardly Lion or Courageous Princess?

MORNING •

It's really hard to stand up and be strong and courageous, but God is calling you to do it for Him! You're God's warrior. You are a child of the King! And no matter how big or small you are, whether you are quiet or loud, God wants to use you in His divine plan. He's calling you to muster up courage, because you have it inside you!

Be courageous in every situation. You might be able to stand up for someone who's being bullied, or tell the truth—even when it's the unpopular thing to do—or audition for that part you thought you were too scared to try out for. . . The possibilities are endless when you draw on the courage of the Lord.

Therefore, being always of good courage, and knowing that while we are at home in the body we are absent from the Lord—for we walk by faith, not by sight—but we are of good courage.

2 CORINTHIANS 5:6–8 NASB

EVENING •

God, sometimes I'm so scared of trying something new or even doing what's right. Please help me to see that You have given me courage—I'm not like the Cowardly Lion who's fierce on the outside but timid on the inside. With You in my life, I don't have to be afraid. I can be a world-changer! Amen.

DAY 219
Hope Giver

MORNING •

It's seven p.m., and your dad still isn't home from work. You're beginning to worry. You look outside, and the rain is coming down so fast that water rushes down the street and the storm drain is overflowing. The street begins to look more river-like with every passing minute.

Mom notices that your worry is beginning to spiral out of control, and she reminds you of the Hope Giver, Jesus, who holds everything in the palm of His hand—even the raging storm outside. She reminds you that Jesus is only a prayer away and that He alone can calm your fears and the storm.

Another hour goes by. You notice the swing set has toppled over and the backyard looks like a swimming pool. But now instead of fear, you have hope in your heart—hope because of the Hope Giver!

Shortly after, you hear the garage door go up. Dad is safe and sound—praise God!

> *Do any of the worthless idols of the nations bring rain? Do the skies themselves send down showers? No, it is you, Lord our God. Therefore our hope is in you, for you are the one who does all this.*
> **JEREMIAH 14:22 NIV**

EVENING •

Lord, thank You for my family. And thank You for giving me hope, even in situations that seem hopeless! You are the one and only Hope Giver. When things are hard, I won't give up hope. I'll keep believing. I'll keep praying. I'll keep trusting You. Because You are so good! Amen.

DAY 220
God Understands

"Kali, let me see your math homework," said Courtney, sliding into her seat. Courtney glanced at the classroom door. "Hurry! Mr. Perez will be here any minute!"

Kali bit her lip. "I can't."

"Why not? You didn't do it either?"

"No. I did it. But I can't let you copy it. Don't you remember? We talked about this in Sunday school last week. Cheating is the same as stealing."

A guilty flush crept across Courtney's cheeks. "I know, but—Kali, I have to get this done. I'll get in big trouble if I miss another assignment. God understands that."

Kali considered for a moment. Then she looked her friend in the eye.

"Courtney, friends don't ask friends to disobey God. You and I both know it's wrong to cheat. *That's* what God understands."

Be ye doers of the word, and not hearers only.
JAMES 1:22 KJV

Dear Father, sometimes even my good friends try to convince me to do something I know I shouldn't. When this happens, please help me to be courageous. I never want to make excuses to sin against You, no matter what others do. And I never want to give others the ability to influence my actions. Give me boldness to stand up for what's right, even if those I have to stand up to are my friends. Amen.

DAY 221
Knock, Knock!

MORNING •

God tells us *not* to worry—*not* to be anxious—but to come to Him in prayer with thanksgiving. You can call on the name of the Lord with confidence—and thankfulness!—that He hears you.

What if you don't know the "right words to say"? Romans 8:26 says, "The Spirit also helps our weakness; for we do not know what to pray for as we should, but the Spirit Himself intercedes for us with groanings too deep for words" (NASB). You don't have to say long, eloquent words and phrases for God to hear and/or answer your prayer. All He asks is that you come to Him (Matthew 11:28). Today's verse says He even gives you the gift of peace that "will guard your hearts and minds in Christ Jesus" just for calling on Him.

> *Do not be anxious about anything, but in everything*
> *by prayer and pleading with thanksgiving let your*
> *requests be made known to God. And the peace*
> *of God, which surpasses all comprehension, will*
> *guard your hearts and minds in Christ Jesus.*
> **PHILIPPIANS 4:6–7 NASB**

EVENING •

Father, I'm so thankful that I can call out to You with the assurance that You hear me—and You will help me! It makes me feel so good to know that even when I don't know what to say, You help me find the words. You know what's on my mind and in my heart, Lord. Thank You for Your love and for giving me Your Holy Spirit. In Jesus' holy name. Amen.

DAY 222
My Future

Do you ever wonder what God has in store for your future? Will you be tall or short? Will you have a super-successful career? Will you stay in your hometown or move across the country—or across the world?

God has a beautiful plan for each of us. And His plan includes this: He wants us to be like Him. He doesn't want us to mess up our lives by leaving Him behind and becoming like the world.

We may not know the details of our future, but we can be assured about God's most important plan. He wants to make us beautiful in spirit. And He will do what He needs to do to bring about that plan.

> *Do not conform to the pattern of this world, but be transformed by the renewing of your mind. Then you will be able to test and approve what God's will is—his good, pleasing and perfect will.*
> **ROMANS 12:2 NIV**

Dear Father, thank You for making good plans for my future. I trust You have something very wonderful in store for me! Help me to fulfill Your plans by becoming more like You every day and less like the world. Even though I don't know what tomorrow will bring, I know without a doubt that You will be with me every step of the way. Amen.

DAY 223
My Strength Comes from God

Have you ever had a hard time standing up for what you know is right? Or saying no instead of going along with the crowd? Do you feel weak when you must make a decision to go against the crowd? Do you worry that your friends might desert you if you don't go along with them? Remember that God is with you in every situation—offering you His strength when you need to be strong, to help you stand up for what is right. Lean on Him. He will always give you the courage to do what is right.

"Don't panic. I'm with you. There's no need to fear for I'm your God. I'll give you strength. I'll help you. I'll hold you steady, keep a firm grip on you."
ISAIAH 41:10 MSG

Dear God, please give me the strength and courage to do what is right. Please help me to trust that You are always in my corner, keeping me strong and steady. Please help me to make decisions according to Your will and not go along with the crowd when I know I shouldn't. Please help me to encourage my friends to lean on You too. Amen.

DAY 224
A Mega Best Seller

MORNING •

Maybe thinking about reading the Bible makes you want to yawn. Maybe you think the Bible is just a book about ancient characters who don't have anything to do with you.

Bible folks may not have driven cars, or watched TV, or eaten pizza, or texted anyone, but their hearts were just the same as yours. They looked up at the same night stars and wondered if the God who made them was real, if He loved them as much as He claimed to, and if He had a plan for their lives.

God was faithful to those ancient people, just as He is faithful to you today. Not only can you learn from the people you meet in the Bible, but God's Word is also a mega best seller—and it's helpful for guidance in everything that matters most in life.

All Scripture is God-breathed and is useful for teaching, rebuking, correcting and training in righteousness.
2 TIMOTHY 3:16 NIV

EVENING •

Lord, I admit that sometimes I just don't "get" the Bible—and I don't always want to set aside time to read it. I'm sorry! Please give me the desire to read Your living Word so that I might grow stronger in my faith. There's so much to learn on every page. Help me to see the importance of the Bible. And help me to learn from all of the Bible people who really are not that different from me! Amen.

DAY 225
But You Promised!

The thing about promises is they are no good unless they're kept. God *always* keeps His promises, but sometimes we get tired of waiting for them to come true. We want God's promises on *our* time instead of trusting Him for His perfect timing. And in our selfishness, we run out of patience.

But we must remember that the best things come from God, and sometimes we need to be patient until He's ready to deliver on His promises. It means choosing what He wants for us instead of choosing what we think we should have and when. It's always better to wait for the best instead of settling for second best. God's way is perfect, and He will prove it!

God's way is perfect. All the Lord's promises prove true.
PSALM 18:30 NLT

Jesus, please help me to have patience. I want to wait patiently for all the good and wonderful promises You have for me. I believe You have only the best in store for me. You have made so many promises to me—and You've kept every single one! You will give me all good things, and all in Your good timing. Thank You for proving Yourself through Your promises, each and every day. Amen.

DAY 226
Make the Best of It

It's been said that the happiest people don't have the best of everything, they just *make* the best of everything! The Bible tells us that trouble is going to find us in this life. And that can be a bit discouraging if you think about it too much. But don't let it get you down! Jesus says, "I have told you these things, so that in me you may have peace. In this world you will have trouble. But take heart! I have overcome the world" (John 16:33 NIV).

Here's what you need to focus on instead: When you're facing difficult situations, Jesus Himself will come alongside you to help you through it. He will give you peace, and you will feel closer to God during hard the stuff (see Psalm 34:18)! Praise Him!

Dear brothers and sisters, when troubles of any kind come your way, consider it an opportunity for great joy. For you know that when your faith is tested, your endurance has a chance to grow.
JAMES 1:2–3 NLT

God, things don't always go my way, but I want to have a good attitude and be a good example in every situation. Please give me the strength to make the best of everything that I face in life. With You by my side, I can overcome discouragement—and I can be full of joy, no matter what! Thanks for being faithful to me and giving me peace. Help me trust You 24-7! Amen.

DAY 227
More Than Just Muscles

There's more to being strong than having big muscles. It takes strength to do the right thing. You need to be strong to stand up for a friend. When you have the strength to be loyal or to say no, you are showing strength in your character.

God has given you unique strengths so that you can overcome the challenges that come your way. It won't always be easy. Even strong people will have moments of weakness, but you have a partner and friend in God. He will always be there to hold your hand and strengthen your heart during the battles. By being strong in character, you are flexing *your* kind of muscles!

In your strength I can crush an army;
with my God I can scale any wall.
PSALM 18:29 NLT

God, I am strong! Please show me areas where I need to be stronger and where I can use my strengths more for You. I want to be able to fulfill the purpose You have for me. This means doing the right thing, standing up for the weak, and being an all-around good example for You, Lord. Thank You for giving me more than muscles! Thank You for giving me strength of character. Amen.

DAY 228
That You May Know

There are things you know in life—and things you don't. Truthfully, some things are just plain confusing. But you *can* find absolute truth in the pages of God's Word. One of those truths is that, as a believer in Jesus, when you die, you will go to heaven to live forever with God.

Unlike flipping a coin, your eternal life is not a wish or a chance. It is a promise, something to hold on to. It is certain. When writing the book of 1 John, the apostle did not say, "I write these things to you who believe in the name of the Son of God so that you may HOPE that you have eternal life." Nor did he write, ". . .that you PROBABLY will have eternal life." He wrote, inspired by God, ". . .that you may *KNOW* that you have eternal life " (emphasis added).

> *I write these things to you who believe in*
> *the name of the Son of God so that you*
> *may know that you have eternal life.*
> **1 JOHN 5:13 NIV**

Heavenly Father, there are so many things I don't know. And many more things that I just don't understand. And that's okay, because Your Word, the Bible, holds all the truth I need for living. In fact, it holds the most important truth there is. And it's this: I know I have eternal life through Jesus. Thank You for the gift of forever life with You in heaven, God. I love You! Amen.

DAY 229
On Earth, in Heaven

God has made a way for sinners to have a relationship with Him. He sent His Son, Jesus, to earth to take our punishment. He died for our sins, rather than require that we suffer for them ourselves, as we deserve.

Because He loves His followers so much, He has prepared a place for us to live with Him forever. This is a blessing we will experience, living with Him in a place where there will be happiness and joy forever.

Throughout the days that God has appointed for us to live on the earth, we are to live for the Lord. What we do here should be for the purpose of pointing others toward Him. And then, when our days here are done, we will be united with our Savior to begin our forever with Him.

"If I go and prepare a place for you, I will come back and take you to be with me that you also may be where I am."

JOHN 14:3 NIV

Dear Father, thank You for making a way for me to really know You. I can't imagine my life without You in it! Thank You for sending Jesus to die for my sins. Until I go to heaven with You, I know I need to be doing the work You have for me while I'm on earth. I'm really looking forward to being in heaven with You for eternity. I can't wait to see the place You've prepared for me! Amen.

DAY 230
Between Sundays

Sundays are special days to get together with other Christians to worship God and study the Bible, but it's the things we learn and the decisions we make during the week that make all the difference in life.

Jesus taught through stories how God's ways are important for everyday life—not just for Sundays. And much can be discovered through reading your Bible, but God also designed life so that we can learn from other Christians how we should react in different situations.

If you have Christian parents, watch them and ask them for advice. If you have not been blessed with Christian parents, ask a pastor or Sunday school teacher for help finding a mentor. Many Christian adults are happy to take time to help you learn God's ways.

> *Teach them to your children, talking about them when you sit at home and when you walk along the road, when you lie down and when you get up.*
> **DEUTERONOMY 11:19 NIV**

God, life doesn't have to be so hard all the time. Your ways help make things easier—even arguments with a brother or sister. . .bullying at school. . .struggles with my schoolwork. . .everything, really! Thank You for the good Christian influences You have placed in my life. I am grateful for each one of them. And I am ready and willing to learn all the lessons You have for me. Amen.

DAY 231
Hungry for Love

Just as your stomach gets hungry when it doesn't have food, your emotions can get hungry too. Just like your stomach craves food, you were made to crave love.

Some kids get so hungry for love from a parent, or someone else who is special in their lives, that they will do anything to get it, even if it means that they allow someone to hurt them.

When you are hungry for love, remember God loves you more than anyone can. Also remember that He created a "hole" in your heart that He wants to fill with Himself. He created you to give and receive love to and from others—but no matter how well others love you, there will always be an empty place inside you that can only be filled by Jesus.

But you, Lord, are a compassionate and gracious God, slow to anger, abounding in love and faithfulness.
PSALM 86:15 NIV

Lord Jesus, I want and need love. I thank You that You made me for love. Help me so that when I feel the need for love, I don't try to get it in ways that aren't good for me and don't glorify You. Help me to turn to You for the love that I need. You are the only one who can fill me up. I love You, Lord! Amen.

DAY 232
My Idol

TV shows hold contests to pick the best singer, survivalist, cook, designer, model, businessman, and even bride in the land. Every viewer judges them, looking for the very best qualities that stand out above all others. But the winners' moment of fame is often that—a *moment*—and soon we've forgotten their names.

An idol is anything in your life that is held up above God or that gets more of your attention than God.

God is firm when He tells us that we are to put nothing before Him. No person, nothing you own, no hobby or activity you enjoy should ever push God out of first place in your life. Each day be sure to check what you are giving first place and work to keep God at the top of the list.

Little children, keep yourselves from idols.
1 JOHN 5:21 KJV

God, please help me to recognize the things that are or could become idols in my life. Help me to keep You in first place every single day. I want You to be the first friend I call, the last person I talk to at night, my most prized possession. You are everything to me, Lord. Nothing compares to You! Amen.

DAY 233
He's Got Your Back

Sometimes life can be scary. Almost every day you face tough decisions, encounter fears, or take on new challenges. Whether it's presenting a project in front of your class or standing up to a bully, life requires you to have courage to get through most days.

But you can't possibly face all of life's intimidating moments on your own. The good news is that God offers His strength if you will ask for it. He will provide you with the courage you need when you can no longer face life alone. If you wake up *every* morning knowing that God will take care of you in *every* circumstance, there will be nothing to fear. The meanest bully, the hardest test, the roughest day—none of it can separate you from His love and protection. He's got your back.

"In the world you will have tribulation.
But take heart; I have overcome the world."
JOHN 16:33 ESV

Father, because of You, I never have to face anything in life alone. You are always with me, day and night. Thank You for watching over me and giving me strength when I ask for it. Help me not to be afraid or anxious when life throws new and difficult things my way. I trust You to take care of me in every circumstance, both good and bad, so I never need to worry or be afraid. Thank You. Amen.

DAY 234
Attitude Is Everything

Attitude is so important. In fact, it's much more important than many things—including your education, the amount of money in your bank account, whether you fail or succeed, what others think of you, your talents and skills. . . And the good news about attitude is you get to choose. You can make a choice every single day how you're going to face the day, and this means you're the only one in control of your attitude.

What a great reminder to all of us! *No matter what happens to you*, you are always in charge of your attitude. The Bible wants our attitudes to be like Jesus. He was humble, He put others above Himself, and He was obedient to God (Philippians 2:7).

Not looking to your own interests but each of you to the interests of the others. In your relationships with one another, have the same mindset as Christ Jesus.
PHILIPPIANS 2:4–5 NIV

Dear God, I struggle with my attitude sometimes, especially when something doesn't go my way or I'm just having a bad day. I can be grumpy and mean, and I really don't want to be that way, Lord. I want to be full of joy. I want others to enjoy being around me because I have a good attitude. Please change my attitude to be more like Yours. Help me to be humble and be a servant to You and others. Amen.

DAY 235
Does God Give Homework?

Ever had a goldfish? At first, it's the perfect pet. It swims happily around in its little bowl, not a care in the world. That is, until the water gets cloudy and the fish gets hungry. Hungry little fish don't last very long, especially in dirty water.

The same is true for your spiritual walk. The Word of God is like fish food for your soul, and your spirit cannot grow in relationship with God in cloudy water. Each day, you need to sprinkle fresh food into your life by reading the Bible and thinking about what it says. When you apply it, you'll get answers for your questions and help for your struggles.

And though the world may be cloudy and dirty, when you shine the light of Christ into the space around you, it will clear up just like fresh water for your fish.

> *Such things were written in the Scriptures*
> *long ago to teach us. And the Scriptures*
> *give us hope and encouragement as we wait*
> *patiently for God's promises to be fulfilled.*
> **ROMANS 15:4 NLT**

Dear God, living a good life is possible when I obey Your Word, make time to talk to You every day, and read my Bible. Help me set aside time to do these things every day of the week. And when I do read Your Word, please help me understand what it says so I can apply it to my life. Spending time with You is what my soul needs to be happy and healthy. And there's no one else I'd rather spend time with than You, Lord. Amen.

DAY 236
Two Commands

Flip through the first five books of the Bible, and you'll find list after list of rules and regulations for God's chosen people, the tribe of Israel. The Ten Commandments are just the beginning. Within the pages of Old Testament law, God's people received instructions on every part of their lives, like how to settle arguments, offer sacrifices, farm the land, and even prepare food to eat. Most of the laws started with the words *do* or *do not*.

Jesus came to free God's people from all these rules. His message was simple to understand: love God and love others. And Jesus came to earth to offer freedom through His sacrifice on the cross.

Thank God for His love today, and share that love with someone else. Then you'll be living out Christ's commandments to the fullest.

Jesus said, " 'Love the Lord your God with all your passion and prayer and intelligence.' This is the most important, the first on any list. But there is a second to set alongside it: 'Love others as well as you love yourself.'
MATTHEW 22:37–40 MSG

God, thank You for sending Your Son, Jesus, to set me free from lists and lists of rules. You ask for love above all. Love really is the most important thing—not rules and requirements. When people are too focused on rules, they often take their eyes off You. Please help me to love You and love others well. Help me to keep my focus on You. Amen.

DAY 237
The God of Hope

Let's face it. Stuff happens. Life is full of surprises, and not all of them are good. Things happen that you had nothing to do with, didn't cause, and certainly didn't plan on. And sometimes those things can make your life miserable. You're disappointed and confused and don't know what to do.

Being a Christian doesn't always shield you from bad situations. The difference between you and the nonbeliever is that when bad stuff happens, you have hope. Everything is possible with God. Nothing is too hard for Him. As you grab hold of that truth and learn to trust Him, you'll find yourself overflowing with hope, joy, and peace. The Bible says not to worry about anything, but pray about everything. Tell God what you need. He'll do the rest (Philippians 4:6–7).

May the God of hope fill you with all joy and peace
as you trust in him, so that you may overflow
with hope by the power of the Holy Spirit.
ROMANS 15:13 NIV

Dear God, just because I have You in my heart doesn't mean I'll be shielded from everything bad. But when bad things do happen, it's so good to know that You are the God of the impossible. I put all my hope and trust in You. I know that You are always the answer to any problem I have. Nothing is too difficult for You. Thank You for the peace and joy I have in You, no matter what's going on in my life. Amen.

DAY 238
Choose Your Own Adventure

You make a ton of choices every day. What to wear, what to eat, how much to study, what to watch, what to read. . . All day long you are faced with choices. Some are easy to make, and some much more difficult. But every choice you make influences what happens next.

Have you ever read a "choose your own adventure" book? They give you the option to make choices throughout the book with an outcome of several different endings. Each choice affects the ending. The same is true for us.

If you decide to follow after God and you try to make choices that honor Him, then you'll be seeking after God's will in your life and headed down the right path. What a great adventure!

> *I am offering you life or death, blessings or curses. Now, choose life! Then you and your children may live. To choose life is to love the Lord your God, obey him, and stay close to him.*
> **DEUTERONOMY 30:19–20 NCV**

Dear God, I have to make so many choices every single day—some are little choices, others are super big. . .and it can be overwhelming sometimes. But with You by my side, making choices doesn't have to be so hard. Please help me to make good choices. I want to live my life for You. Thanks for this great adventure You've given me! Amen.

DAY 239
What's Your Attitude?

MORNING •

Our level of strength is dependent on many things—including food, rest, water, exercise, and a positive attitude. A positive attitude is super important—especially for our inner strength. We can be physically fit and strong outside but weak and tired on the inside.

Negative attitudes will drain our inner strength because negative thinking blocks the wonderful things God wants to share with you. Your attitudes and thoughts can put up a wall between you and God's amazing power.

But there's good news! You can tear down that wall by opening your heart to positive attitudes, and God can then add strength, joy, and peace to your life. It takes practice to turn off the negative thinking, but you can do it with God's help. Just remember He is always there, waiting to give you the strength you need.

I pray that from his glorious, unlimited resources he will empower you with inner strength through his Spirit.
EPHESIANS 3:16 NLT

EVENING •

Heavenly Father, it's strange how some days I feel strong and other days I feel weak. When I don't feel strong, it's easy for me to have a negative attitude toward life. Forgive me for giving in to negative thoughts and attitudes. I know that You want me to be positive as well as a blessing to others. Thank You for giving me Your power and strength to do ALL things. Amen.

DAY 240
God Listens

Sometimes we wonder if God is listening to our prayers. But the Bible tells us that God does listen. He loves us, and He cares about what we have to say.

Psalm 66:18, though, tells us that if we have "cherished sin" in our hearts, God may not listen. That means that if we are doing something against God, and we're not sorry, and we plan to keep doing that particular sin, God may not listen to what we have to say until we get that issue right. We must constantly go to God and say, "God, I love You, and I want to please You. I'm sorry for the things I do that hurt You. Help me not to do those things anymore."

As long as God knows we're trying to please Him, He listens. He hears us. And He delights in giving us the desires of our hearts.

But God has surely listened and has heard my prayer.

PSALM 66:19 NIV

Dear Father, I really do want to please You every day. And I want to make good choices that honor You. I'm sorry for the times I've sinned. Help me to stay away from sin, Lord. I need Your help. I know You hear me. Thank You for being such a good listener. It's nice to know that You are always there for me. And You're ALWAYS listening. Amen.

DAY 241
He Is Strong

You probably know the song "Jesus Loves Me" very well. But have you thought about the words, *"We are weak, but He is strong"*?

At certain times in life, you may feel particularly weak. You simply are not strong enough to do the task that is before you. Maybe you need to apologize to someone, but it's so hard to do. Perhaps you are experiencing some problems in your family that are just too big for you to handle.

There is good news. You don't have to be the strong one. The Bible tells us in 2 Chronicles that God is *always* looking for His children who are in need of strength. He wants to be your strength. Call on Him. Tell God where you are weak and ask Him to be strong in your place.

> *"For the eyes of the LORD range throughout*
> *the earth to strengthen those whose*
> *hearts are fully committed to him."*
> **2 CHRONICLES 16:9 NIV**

God, there are days when I just feel like I can't do things—especially when I'm facing a big problem and feel like I can't handle it all on my own. I am weak, Lord. But how wonderful to know that You are strong! And if I ask, You will give me all the strength I need—today, tomorrow, and in the future. When I can't, You CAN! Thank You, Father. Amen.

DAY 242
God's Got This!

Have you ever had to prepare for something really big? Like trying out for a team. . .or running for student council. . .or giving a presentation? You try not to panic. Your brain runs down a mental checklist over and over and over. You practice and practice—until you've done all you know to do. Still, you can't help but wonder, *What was I thinking when I decided to do this?*

It's time to trust the Lord! He knows how you feel! He planned your life journey to include experiences where you will do your best to prepare, without an immediate guarantee you'll get the results you want. In these moments, you need to force yourself to depend on Him to take you the rest of the way. Let go, then celebrate and say, "God's got this!"

> *Those who listen to instruction will prosper;*
> *those who trust the Lord will be joyful.*
> **PROVERBS 16:20 NLT**

God, today I will depend only on You. I want to give You everything that is troubling me. I am nervous, and I want You to take it! I am stressed out, and I want You to take that too! All of those negative thoughts—I give them ALL to You, Lord! I want to smile with the satisfaction of knowing You've got this—and You've got me too! Thanks for being with me today and always. Amen.

DAY 243
Jesus Knows Me—I Am His!

God gave man free will—the ability to choose right or wrong (Genesis 3). You can *choose* to follow His ways and standards, or you can *choose* to rebel against them (see 1 John 2:15–17).

He chose you (John 15:16), and if you accepted Jesus as your Savior, you answered His call. Does this mean you should continue with a life of sin? Should you live like the world lives? No way! God knows who you are, what you want to do, how you spend your time. . .and everything else! He wants you to get to know Him as well. Just like best friends spend time together and get to know one another more and more, so is your relationship with God. You will grow in your knowledge of Him, His love, and His ways as you spend time with Him.

> *"I am the good shepherd, and I know*
> *My own, and My own know Me."*
> **JOHN 10:14 NASB**

Lord, when I asked You into my heart, You made me a new creation! Help me to appreciate Your calling more and more. I know I'm Yours. Help me not to listen to the temptations of this world but to our voice and Your voice alone. You gave me free will—the ability to choose for myself—and I want to make choices that will honor You for the rest of my life. I love You, Lord. In Jesus' name I pray. Amen.

DAY 244
Give Me Peace

MORNING •

Being sick is the worst! You've been in bed for days. Your body aches all over. You toss and turn. You finally give up all hope of sleep and turn on the bedside lamp and attempt to read a book. But then your mind begins to wander: you start thinking about the mountain of homework you'll have to make up once you return to school. You bury your head in your pillow, feeling completely defeated. But then you remember. . .

You get out of bed and fall to your knees to pray. You call out to God to give you the rest and peace that you really could use right about now. You then snuggle back under the covers, and it doesn't take long for you to doze off. Peace, peace, peace.

I love the Lord, for he heard my voice; he heard
my cry for mercy. Because he turned his ear
to me, I will call on him as long as I live.
PSALM 116:1–2 NIV

EVENING •

God, some days are just the pits—especially days
when I don't feel well and can't get anything done.
Those kinds of days stress me out and make it hard
to rest. But I am thankful that You bring me peace,
Lord. You can calm my stressed-out mind. And You
can give me the rest my body needs to get well. I
know You hear my prayers. Help me not to forget You
are always here for me. Thank You, Lord. Amen.

DAY 245
Saying Grace

Are you afraid to say a prayer of thanks for your food in public? Don't be embarrassed if you are. Sometimes it feels like everyone is watching you. . . .

It's always uncomfortable to feel like an oddball. Unless all of your friends are Christians who also pray for their food, you may feel a little uncomfortable doing so. But saying grace before meals is not just a family-around-the-dinner-table thing. And thanking God in public opens the door for you to witness to your unbelieving friends.

Don't be shy about asking God to bless your food. Depending on what they're serving in the lunch line that day, you just might need it!

I will praise him among the multitude.

PSALM 109:30 KJV

Dear God, thank You for all my blessings, including the food that I eat. I'm sorry for worrying about what other people might think if they see me praying in public. I want to be courageous when it comes to my relationship with You, Lord. Give me courage to praise You publicly, even if others think I'm weird. Because it really only matters what You think of me. Amen.

DAY 246
Protection from Danger

Danger is a topic taught from a young age. Moms advise their children, "Don't run with scissors!" And, "Don't stick anything into electrical outlets!" And, "If it starts to thunder, come inside immediately!"

Kids are taught to stay away from strangers because of "stranger danger." They are advised to choose the right friends because the wrong ones could influence them to make decisions that could lead them into danger.

God has offered Himself as a safe place in times of danger. He is like a place of safety in a storm. When His child looks for a place to run and hide, God opens His arms wide and provides a comfortable place to wait out the storm.

This I declare about the LORD: He alone is my refuge, my place of safety; he is my God, and I trust him.
PSALM 91:2 NLT

Dear Father, thank You for being a safe place for me. Help me to remember to come to You when I face a difficult situation, rather than trying to make it through on my own. You will always guide me and steer me in the right direction. You want what's best for me. You want to help me, and I trust You. Thank You for caring about me so much, Father! In Jesus' name, amen.

DAY 247
Adored

To "adore" something means you not only love it, but you can't bear the idea of being away from it! You're devoted to it. You can't give it up, no matter what!

Did you realize that God adores you? He's crazy about you, and nothing you do can change the way He feels! He won't give you up, no matter what! In fact, He cares so much about you that He doesn't like to be away from you, even for a few minutes. He hopes you feel the same way about Him.

The next time you start to wonder if anyone loves you, remember that God not only loves you. . .He adores you.

***And I am convinced that nothing can
ever separate us from God's love.***
ROMANS 8:38 NLT

*Lord, it's tough to admit this, but I don't always feel loved.
Sometimes I wonder if people love me. And if I'm being
completely honest, I've even wondered at times if You love
me. But Your Word assures me over and over that You do.
And Your Word is 100 percent truth! Remind me of this
every day, Lord. I know that You adore me, even when
I mess up. I'm so relieved! Thank You for that. Amen.*

DAY 248
My Protector

On days when you are afraid and feel the need for protection—from the bully in class, from all the bad things you hear on the news, or horrible things that happen in your school or in your hometown—remember that you have a Protector. Every day and always, you have God. He protects you from every kind of evil. And if you let Him, God will even protect you from yourself and the things you might do—the wrong choices you might make that would bring you harm. Remember, He is always there. Turn to Him instead of thinking you can protect yourself. With Him by your side, you have nothing to fear!

You protect me with salvation-armor; you hold me up with a firm hand, caress me with your gentle ways.
PSALM 18:35 MSG

Dear God, thank You for always watching over me, always knowing what will happen even before I do. Please guide and direct me daily. Help me know what to do when I am afraid or when I am about to do the wrong thing. Help me to be quiet and listen for Your guidance and fully trust that You protect me from all things. Thank You for being my protector. Amen.

DAY 249
An Unopened Love Letter

Beethoven was a famous musician who wrote beautiful music. He never got married but loved a woman, and a lot of smart people have spent years trying to figure out who she was. When Beethoven was forty-two years old, he wrote a love letter to this woman that no one knew. "Oh, why must one be separated from her who is so dear?" he wrote. "However much you love me—my love for you is even greater. . . ."

After he died, someone found the letter in Beethoven's desk. It wasn't stamped or addressed. Some people wonder if Beethoven's special lady ever knew how he felt because of this secret, unopened note.

I can't imagine not opening a love letter, can you? God has given you a love letter. It's called the Bible. It is God's story of longing for and desiring relationship with the people He made. It's the main way you can hear Him speak to you.

> *Jesus answered, "It is written: 'Man shall not live on bread alone, but on every word that comes from the mouth of God.'"*
> **MATTHEW 4:4 NIV**

Lord, I can't imagine not opening a love letter from someone who cares about me. I want to know You better. Help me to spend time getting to know You through Your love letter to me. The Bible brings light to my life. It helps me know what to do. It's the most beautiful love letter ever written. I will make time to read the Bible every day, Father. Through it, I will hear You speak to me. Amen.

DAY 250
The Best Kind of Friends

If you have a pure heart and your motives are good, then you never have to watch your back. You don't have to worry about what other people may be saying about you or what they might think of you. The way you live your life is between you and God. If you are living a God-honoring life, you don't have to worry about the kind of friends you'll attract. Because the best kind of friends are those who want to honor God like that too.

But did you know that Jesus had people upset with Him all the time? That's a good reminder to us all that we can't please everybody. Even Jesus didn't do that. He doesn't want us to please everyone—just Him! God doesn't want you to be a people-pleaser; He wants you to be a Jesus-pleaser!

***One who loves a pure heart and who speaks
with grace will have the king for a friend.***
PROVERBS 22:11 NIV

*God, help me to do my best to please You—because
when I please You, that's really all that matters. I don't
ever need to worry about what other people think
or say about me. Help me to attract the best kind of
friends. I know that if I seek You every day, You will help
me find the people who should be part of my circle.
And our friendships will bring honor to You. Amen.*

DAY 251
Beautiful Creation

MORNING •

Have you ever wondered what God looks like? The Bible says that humans are created in His own image. Maybe that means He has characteristics like a body with arms to hold His children and legs to walk beside them. Maybe God has a face to show emotion, eyes to portray warmth, and a mouth to smile brightly.

God made us in His image because He wants us to identify closely to Him. Of all the living things He created in the beginning of time, He loved us the most and showed that love by placing a little bit of Himself in the way we look.

God looks at each of us and sees the beauty of His creation. No matter what you like or dislike about yourself, your heavenly Father sees the beauty of heaven in you.

Man is made in God's image and reflects God's glory.
1 CORINTHIANS 11:7 NLT

EVENING •

God, I sometimes wonder what You look like. I imagine that if I saw You, I'd be drawn to You. . .I'd want to be near You, because I'd sense Your loving-kindness and Your goodness. It thrills my heart to know that You love me so much that You created me in Your perfect image! Help me to see myself the way You see me, Lord. Amen.

DAY 252
Life's Not Fair

MORNING •

Life isn't always fair; in fact, it seldom is. Jesus teaches us to place little importance on worldly, material things, and instead to set our eyes on the spiritual things that bring us eternal rewards.

There is no gain to feeding the flesh while the spirit starves. In other words, it doesn't help you at all if you take care of your body but let your heart go to waste.

God cares just as much for the starving child as He does for you. He weeps for those who hurt and aches for those who need. He created each of us, and He will provide according to our greatest needs. Today, ask God where He can use you to help those who are suffering. Perhaps letting you bless others was part of His plan all along.

Who shows no partiality to princes and
does not favor the rich over the poor,
for they are all the work of his hands?
JOB 34:19 NIV

EVENING •

Lord, why do some kids have it so easy and others
have it really hard? It doesn't seem fair that there are
super-rich people and super-poor people. It breaks
my heart to know that some people are suffering.
Show me where I can help others who are in need,
Lord. Please help me see where You can use me to
make a difference. I want to be a blessing! Amen.

DAY 253
I Am Not Alone

Sometimes when you have worked hard to do the right thing, everyone around abandons you and you find yourself very alone. It makes those choices even more difficult because nobody wants to be alone.

But the Lord understands those feelings all too well. One week, the crowds adored and praised Him. The next week, the crowds screamed for His death in hatred and ugliness.

Just remember that you are never. . .*never* alone. As a child of the King, He promises to never leave you. And the more you communicate with Him, the closer you will feel to Him.

So don't give up. Don't give in. Even if the world turns its back on you, remember that you have the God of the Universe with you wherever you go.

The Lord is near to all who call on Him.
PSALM 145:18 NASB

Lord, sometimes I feel like no one cares about me and they don't want to hear about what I'm going through. It's hard when I feel alone, but I know that You under-stand better than anyone else. Help me continue to make the right decisions. Thank You for sticking with me through thick and thin. I won't give up, Lord! Amen.

DAY 254
Always There

Many of us have been told that God is everywhere and that He's always with us. That sounds nice, but when we feel afraid or alone, it can be difficult to believe He's really right there. After all, we can't see Him. We can't touch Him. We can't hear Him speaking out loud to us.

Although we can't physically touch God, we can feel His presence. He loves us, and when we ask Him to live in us, He gladly accepts the invitation. He has promised never to leave us, never to turn His back on us. And though He doesn't talk out loud to us, if we listen, we can hear Him speaking to us in our thoughts. And we can always hear His words by reading the Bible.

***Don't you know that you yourselves are God's temple
and that God's Spirit dwells in your midst?***
1 CORINTHIANS 3:16 NIV

Dear Father, thank You for always keeping Your promises, no matter what. I know You are always with me. When I feel Your presence, and even when I don't, You're there! I am never alone—not for one second! Help me to dedicate time each day to talk with You and share what's on my heart. And then help me to listen for Your voice. Amen.

DAY 255
Simple Gossip

We've all said something about somebody else that we wish we wouldn't have said. Gossip is a very common thing, and even church people don't see it as a very big deal sometimes. But it really is a big deal. Gossip hurts people!

It's been said that if you have to glance at the door to see if anyone is coming before saying something, you probably shouldn't be saying it! This is a hard lesson to learn and an even harder action to put into practice, especially if all your friends do it too.

It's important to remember that simple gossip is simply sinful. It hurts others, it ruins friendship, and it is never harmless.

It is foolish to belittle one's neighbor; a sensible person keeps quiet. A gossip goes around telling secrets, but those who are trustworthy can keep a confidence.
PROVERBS 11:12–13 NLT

Dear God, please forgive me when I have gossiped. There are times when I've said something and immediately regretted it. Some things should not be said. Gossip hurts people, Father, and it ruins friendships. I want to avoid gossip, Lord. I know You want me to do—and say—the right things. Please help me in this area, Father. Amen.

DAY 256
Fear Not

MORNING •

Not all fear is the same. Sometimes fear is healthy—like being afraid to break the law or fearing God. Those are the kinds of fears that keep you safe and help you lead a happy, productive life.

But sometimes fear can stop you from doing the things you need to do and can get in the way of the blessing God has for you. Being afraid to stand up for yourself, talk in front of a classroom full of people, defend your beliefs, or reveal that hidden talent are fears that can keep you from fulfilling your destiny.

The good news is you don't have to be afraid. God is with you. You are His child, and He will never leave you or forsake you. Just trust Him.

> *"Be strong and courageous. Do not be afraid or terrified because of them, for the LORD your God goes with you; he will never leave you nor forsake you."*
> **DEUTERONOMY 31:6 NIV**

EVENING •

Dear God, Your Word says that You have not given me a spirit of fear. I choose to believe Your Word. I will not allow fear to keep me from doing the things that You want me to do and rob me of blessings. Please help me to recognize the good kind of fear and the bad kind. Either way, I will not fear. And instead, I will trust You to take care of me in every situation. Amen.

DAY 257
Construction, Not Demolition

MORNING •

Little kids love to build a tower of blocks or sculpt a sandcastle only to gleefully stomp it to the ground. Destruction seems to be an instinct for humans.

God knows that our sinful nature gets pleasure out of seeing other people stomped to the ground. Even when we know what it's like to be on the receiving end of insults and mean words, sometimes we take pleasure in adding to the destruction of others by piling on words that are hurtful and mean spirited.

The heavenly Father doesn't want to see His children destroy one another with words. His plan is encouragement. With every sincere, kind word, God adds another building block to the life of His child. And with every block of encouragement, we are made stronger to stand up to any destructive, stomping words that come our way.

> *Encourage each other and build each other
> up, just as you are already doing.*
> **1 THESSALONIANS 5:11 NLT**

EVENING •

Heavenly Father, words are so powerful. They can heal, and they can destroy. Help me to only speak encouraging words that build others up. Show me where I can add building blocks of encouragement to my friends and family, Lord. When I build up others, I'm made stronger too. Thank You. Amen.

DAY 258
What Season Is It?

Imagine you're in a "springtime" season of life. Everything is "blooming." You've got great friendships; you're growing in the Lord. . .basically everything is going well. Then summer comes. Everything is sunny and in full bloom. You're in a great relationship with your parents and getting along well with your brothers and sisters.

Next comes fall. Maybe you notice that some of your friendships are coming to an end, or perhaps there are other changes in your life. Things are winding down. After fall comes winter. If you're in a winter season, maybe nothing seems to be working out. Perhaps you're lonely or disconnected—having a hard time with your prayer life.

No matter what season you're in, remember. . .that season will come to an end, and another will soon begin.

> *There is a time for everything, and a season*
> *for every activity under the heavens.*
> **ECCLESIASTES 3:1 NIV**

Dear heavenly Father, Your Word tells us that
everything has its season. Remind me that no matter
what season I'm in, a new season is just around the
corner. And through it all, You are there to hold me close
and give me strength and encouragement for whatever
each season brings my way. In winter, spring, summer,
fall. . .I will trust You through all of life's seasons! Amen.

DAY 259
No One Understands Me

Does it seem like no one understands you? Your parents, siblings, teachers, and friends may come close at times, but they're only human. Only a personal relationship with Christ can meet the need every human being has to be known and understood.

Jesus left heaven for earth. While He was fully God, He was also fully human. He experienced emotions, such as disappointment and loss. Scripture tells us He wept. Yes, even Jesus cried. He felt angry. He was tempted. He was betrayed by those closest to Him. At times, Jesus was exhausted and needed rest.

You never need to wonder where that someone is who "gets" you. Jesus gets you!

For this reason he had to be made like them, fully human in every way, in order that he might become a merciful and faithful high priest in service to God, and that he might make atonement for the sins of the people.

HEBREWS 2:17 NIV

Heavenly Father, no human being will ever be able to fill the Jesus-shaped spot in my heart. Only You can do that. I am so thankful that You want a close relationship with me. I can always turn to you when no one else seems to understand me. Thank You, Lord Jesus, for understanding me when I am not even sure I understand myself sometimes! I love You. Amen.

DAY 260
I Really Need That

There is a pretty big difference between needs and wants. And God is the only one who knows what you need. He longs to give you all your wants, but He also knows when and how you should get them. You may want the wrong things at the wrong time. He knows exactly what to give you and when.

If we give the desires of our hearts to the Lord, He can help us discover what is most important. He wants to be at the top of our wish list. We need Him first. And our relationship with Him is the key to happiness. After that, all the other things in our lives will come out in the right order of importance.

> *Seek your happiness in the Lord, and he*
> *will give you your heart's desire.*
> **PSALM 37:4 GNT**

Dear Lord, help me to recognize the difference between my wants and needs. I want to put You first on my list of wants. When I do ask You for things, Lord, remind me to ask myself if I really have a need or if I just want more stuff. Help me remember that You want to give me the desires of my heart. Thank You for providing for all my needs every single day. Amen.

DAY 261
Dream Big!

MORNING •

How often do you daydream about what you're going to do with the rest of your life? Maybe you've thought about being a teacher. What about a doctor or a scientist? Perhaps even the president of the United States? Before you think none of those are possible for you, you need to understand that your dreams are no accident. God has placed them inside your heart as part of His plan for you. With all He has in store for you, other options will never measure up. If things don't look so magnificent at the moment, you can rest assured that He is positioning you for bigger and better things to come.

> ***Now all glory to God, who is able, through his mighty power at work within us, to accomplish infinitely more than we might ask or think.***
> **EPHESIANS 3:20 NLT**

EVENING •

God, I'm so excited that You have my customized future ready and waiting. And I know that You have extraordinary blessings in store for me! Before I move ahead and begin making decisions for my life, I will ask You about it first. When I talk to You first, You'll show me the direction I should go. Help me stay on the path to Your best for me. I know Your plans are the best plans. Amen.

DAY 262
God Is Always Awake

Stress and worry and fear are common in kids just like you. But it doesn't have to be that way! God wants you to trust Him and leave your life and your worries in His mighty hands.

If something is bothering you, just talk to God about it. Anytime, day or night. He is always awake! The Bible says that He never sleeps, He never takes a nap, and He's never looking the other way. He is always watching over you.

When you do talk to God about your worries and fears, a truly miraculous thing happens: He gives you His peace that will guard your heart and your mind (Philippians 4:6–7)! We can't even understand how that happens, but it really does. Give it a try, and give your worries to God. He's always awake.

My help comes from the LORD, who made heaven and earth! He will not let you stumble; the one who watches over you will not slumber. Indeed, he who watches over Israel never slumbers or sleeps. The LORD himself watches over you!

PSALM 121:2–5 NLT

God, I love You so much. Thank You for not falling asleep while I'm talking to You. I'm so glad You're truly interested in everything I have to say. Thanks for not being bored by my problems. The world needs more listeners like You! I will give all my worries and cares to You today. What a relief to not have to carry them on my own. Please show me Your peace. Amen.

DAY 263
Joy in Trusting God

MORNING •

Do you ever find that you've put your trust in the wrong things? That you've trusted your friends more than God? That you look to your best friend to give you advice and even care more about that than what your parents or even God thinks? Have you felt you've gone in the wrong direction because you aren't fully trusting God? You aren't very joyful on those days, are you? Remember that God made you and knows what is best for you *always*. Your friends don't always act in your best interest, but He does. Put your full trust in Him and feel the joy!

> *But let all those rejoice who put their trust in You; let them ever shout for joy, because You defend them; let those also who love Your name be joyful in You.*
> **PSALM 5:11 NKJV**

EVENING •

Dear God, sometimes I've put my trust in the wrong things. . .and I'm so sorry! I should always trust You most! Please help me trust You alone to guide me in the decisions I need to make each day. I will look to You always, knowing that You are always there to defend me, to give me direction, to get me through each day so that I can be joyful again. You will always act in my very best interest. Thank You, Lord! Amen.

DAY 264
Rescue Squad

MORNING •

It's true that God protects you from many horrible dangers and catastrophes every day. In fact, we'll never know in this life just how many near misses we had when He spared us from injury . . .or worse. It's good to pray for and expect God's protection because He promised it to us.

But far better than saving us from a painful experience is that God saves us from sin. Sin carries the promise of eternal devastation—far worse than anything we could experience here on this earth. God offers the blood of Jesus as our rescue from sin.

If you haven't already, ask Jesus to forgive you for your sins and cleanse you with His blood. Once you do that, it's a done deal— you're rescued—and you can trust that He is with you always.

> *The Lord says, "I will rescue those who love me.*
> *I will protect those who trust in my name."*
> **PSALM 91:14 NLT**

EVENING •

Dear God, thank You for all the physical dangers
You've protected me from through the years. I'm
sure there are many times You've protected me and I
wasn't even aware of it. I'm most thankful that You've
offered a way that I can be saved from my sins. Please
forgive me for my sin and rescue me with the gift of
eternal life. I want to walk with You today and forever!
Thank You for being the best Protector, Lord. Amen.

DAY 265
When the Going Gets Tough. . .

God was a shield to David and gave him strength. But first, David *trusted* Him.

What does it mean to trust God? You lay down your "own understanding" and "acknowledge" that He has always been, is, and always will be the supreme God of all creation (Proverbs 3:5–6).

When you rely on God's strength and not your own, God's able to take control. He says to you, "I will give you rest. Take My yoke upon you and learn from Me" (Matthew 11:28–29 NASB). He has offered to take our burdens. Why insist on keeping them when His arms are reaching down to lift your heavy load? He will give you the strength to persevere. Just trust Him. He's "a very ready help in trouble" (Psalm 46:1 NASB).

The Lord is my strength and my shield; my heart trusts in Him, and I am helped; therefore my heart triumphs, and with my song I shall thank Him.
PSALM 28:7 NASB

Lord, I can't do hard things on my own. I need You. I surrender everything and give You complete control of my life. I trust You, Lord God. I don't ever have to worry when I can't find the strength to deal with my problems—because I have You! Please give me the strength to "press on toward the goal for the prize" (Philippians 3:14 NASB). In Jesus' precious and holy name, I pray. Amen.

DAY 266
Tick, Tick, Tick

MORNING •

Have you ever noticed how quickly time slips by when you're online? Techie gadgets are so cool! But they can also be dangerous. They're famous for sneaking off with the important hours that you should have spent doing something else. And once that time is gone, there is no way to get it back.

Popular apps come and go, but God's Word is forever. Set aside some time each day to read the Bible. It's where you'll find answers to your questions and the keys to your future. Ask God to remind you when it's time to turn off your gadgets and do something more worthwhile. Remember that He has great plans for your life, and He wants you to get started on them!

> *Making the best use of the time,*
> *because the days are evil.*
> **EPHESIANS 5:16 ESV**

EVENING •

Father in heaven, I don't want to ignore Your Word. The Bible is so much more than just a book full of big words in small print. . .it's Your love letter to me! Help me to be careful with the time I spend online, and tap on my shoulder if I start to get careless. I need You to guide me. I need Your direction so I spend my time on things that matter most in my life. Thank You! Amen.

DAY 267
Marsupials in the Dark

I once owned two sugar gliders named Sassie and Stubbie. These cute, tiny, nocturnal marsupials looked like squirrels, weighed only four ounces, and spent their days sleeping in my pockets.

When I wanted to play with them at night, I had to quietly enter their dark playroom, close the door, then stand still and wait. In less than fifteen seconds, they found me in the dark. Both of them always ran up my legs and sat on my shoulders. I was their human tree! Because they could see in the dark, we had a relationship.

Just like Sassie and Stubbie could see me in the dark, God can see you and me all the time too. When you feel like you are walking in the dark and God isn't with you, remember He is always there.

"Never will I leave you; never will I forsake you."
HEBREWS 13:5 NIV

Lord Jesus, thank You for Your Word that promises You will never leave me nor forsake me. Even though I don't always feel like You are with me, I trust that You are because You say so. I am never alone. I lean on what You say and not on how I feel. My feelings aren't always reliable. . .but Your Word is truth! Amen.

DAY 268
Let Go!

MORNING •

Have you ever picked up some candy at the store that you *just had to have* and not paid for it? Have you ever cheated on a test? What about taking money from your mom's purse without asking? You don't have to be told any one of these actions is wrong. You know it in your heart! But did you own up to your mistakes?

The good news is that God forgives you. He knows your heart. All you need to do is ask, and He will forgive any wrong that you've done.

Every day is a chance for a fresh, new start: another opportunity to do the right thing and make good choices. Now is the time to let go of the past and begin a new day full of God's wonderful blessings.

> *The other guests began to say among themselves,*
> *"Who is this who even forgives sins?"*
> **LUKE 7:49 NIV**

EVENING •

God, I am so thankful to be Your child. You are such a wonderful, caring Father. No one forgives like You do. You forgive the teeny-tiny sins and the super-big mess-ups—and everything in between. Please help me to learn to forgive myself as You have forgiven me. Thank You for giving me the ability to make my own choices—but help me to always choose what will honor You, Lord. Amen.

DAY 269
The Great Blue Ocean

MORNING •

Have you ever wondered if God loves you? Everyone has asked that question at some point in their lives. Even your Sunday school teachers. . .even the writers of these devotions. That question is as common as ketchup on french fries and purrs from a kitten.

The nation of Israel had that same question too, and God's answer was simple: *"I have loved you,"* says the Lord. And that is His answer to us today. His affection for us—for *you*—is as big and unfathomable as the great blue ocean. And yet His love is as tender and close as a mother's kiss on a baby's forehead.

God's kindness will never fail. It's new every morning like the dew on your lawn and the rising of the sun. God's love is sure, and His faithfulness is forever.

> *Because of the Lord's great love we are not consumed, for his compassions never fail. They are new every morning; great is your faithfulness.*
> **LAMENTATIONS 3:22–23 NIV**

EVENING •

God, do You love me? And if You do, how much do You love me? Your Word answers these questions that sometimes pop into my brain. Yes, You love me. And You love me so much that it can't even be measured. Your love never stops for me—even when I'm not very faithful to You. . .even when I forget to talk to You. I'm so glad You love me and watch over me. Thank You for Your love and faithfulness. Amen.

DAY 270
Promises, Promises

MORNING •

People break promises all the time. Sometimes a promise gets broken because a person just doesn't want to keep it. Other times people want to keep their promises, but circumstances prevent them from fulfilling their word. Either way, it hurts.

God always, *always*, keeps His promises. He's not like human beings, who forget or mess up or can't control their circumstances. If God says He'll do something, He means it. And He'll do it!

We can't take advantage of God's promises, though, unless we know what they are. That's why it's important to read the Bible and learn what He has said. When we find ourselves in need of God's help, we can remind Him of His promises, and we can be certain He will keep them.

> *"God is not human, that he should lie, not a human being, that he should change his mind. Does he speak and then not act? Does he promise and not fulfill?"*
> **NUMBERS 23:19 NIV**

EVENING •

Dear Father, You are more reliable than any human being. It's sad that promises get broken and that people fail to follow through on their word. But the good news is that You're a good Father who keeps every promise You make. Thank You for keeping Your promises. Help me to learn more about Your promises as I spend time in Your Word, the Bible, every day. Amen.

DAY 271
Heartbreak Hotel

At one time or another we all get our feelings hurt. But sometimes the hurt is so bad you think you just might die from it. It might be because of something a friend did or something your parents said. It could be betrayal or worse. Whatever it is—it can leave you heartbroken.

In some people a broken heart can lead to bitterness, anger, and depression. But you don't have to go there. You're a child of God. He sees everything, and He knows just how you feel. You can choose to turn all that hurt over to Him. It might be hard at first. You might have to let it go again and again—especially in the beginning. But if you let Him, God will mend your heart and give you back your joy.

The Lord is close to the brokenhearted and
saves those who are crushed in spirit.
PSALM 34:18 NIV

Dear God, You know about every time I've been hurt
in the past—and You know every hurt and broken
heart I'll experience in the future. Because I don't
want to get caught in a trap of anger and bitterness,
I choose to let it all go. Please heal my broken heart
today. Help me release all my hurts to You so I can live
a life of joy and freedom. Thank You, Lord. Amen.

DAY 272
Fully Understood

MORNING •

Ever wonder if anybody understands you? Do they "get it"?

Jesus Christ understands everything about every one of His creations. He knows how you feel on the best of your best days and on the worst of your worst days. And usually it's hardest to find someone who understands us in the difficult times.

Jesus faced rough times on earth. His earthly parents didn't always understand His mission. His close friend betrayed Him. Another friend lied and said he never knew Jesus to keep himself out of trouble. And finally, society turned against Him and killed Him.

He knows what it's like to not be understood, but He truly understands all about us. Trust that He "gets it."

This High Priest of ours understands our weaknesses, for he faced all of the same testings we do, yet he did not sin.
HEBREWS 4:15 NLT

EVENING •

Dear Jesus, people don't always understand me or what I'm going through. Thank You for understanding everything about me and loving me anyway. Even on my worst of days, You are there, full of understanding. You know what makes me laugh. You know what makes me cry. You know ALL about me, and You get me even when no one else does. You are the greatest of friends! Amen.

DAY 273
More than Ordinary

Do you ever feel like you're too ordinary to do great things? Well, there's great news for you: God loves to use ordinary people to do extraordinary things.

Look at Peter. He was just a fisherman, but God called him "the rock upon which I'll build my church." What about Mary? She was just a teenager, yet God chose her to give birth to Jesus. How about David? He was the little guy in the family. When his brothers went to war, he had to stay home and watch the sheep. Still, God called him to defeat the giant Goliath.

Know this: if you're feeling very ordinary, then you're the perfect person to do extraordinary things!

> *"And I tell you that you are Peter, and on this rock I will build my church, and the gates of Hades will not overcome it."*
> **MATTHEW 16:18 NIV**

God, sometimes I don't feel like I'm enough. I feel like I'm not talented enough. I'm not smart enough. I'm not special enough. Just not "enough" to do something really great.

But You have very good news for very average people, Lord. You used ordinary people throughout history to do amazing things for You. And today, You make us capable of doing very extraordinary things too. Help me to see myself as You see me—capable of wonderful things! Amen.

DAY 274
A Crown for His Child

Choices, choices, choices. Sometimes you are faced with really difficult ones. In your heart, you know what is right, but all your friends want you to go the wrong direction.

Because we live in a sin-filled world, the choices we have to make get harder every day. The world around us doesn't care about God or His commandments. It wants to be free to do whatever it pleases.

The Bible reminds us that this life is going to be hard. We're going to have lots of temptations and lots of trials. But by making the right choices—following God's guidelines for our lives—the rewards will be immeasurable.

Blessed is the one who perseveres under trial because, having stood the test, that person will receive the crown of life that the Lord has promised to those who love him.
JAMES 1:12 NIV

God, help me to guard my mind and my heart so that I can do the right thing today. As Your child, I'm a child of the King! Remind me of this every time I have to make a choice. I always want to follow Your guidelines for living my best life. I want to follow You closely today, tomorrow, and in the future. It will be amazing to receive a crown in heaven from You someday! Amen.

DAY 275
Don't Be Afraid

Fear can creep up on any of us. But when we allow fear to have a firm grip on us, we aren't trusting God the way He wants us to.

The next time you're really afraid of something, repeat these verses to yourself and let them sink into your heart:

"I am leaving you with a gift—peace of mind and heart. And the peace I give is a gift the world cannot give. So don't be troubled or afraid" (John 14:27 NLT).

"This is my command—be strong and courageous! Do not be afraid or discouraged. For the LORD your God is with you wherever you go" (Joshua 1:9 NLT).

When I am afraid, I put my trust in you.
PSALM 56:3 NIV

Dear God, I don't need to be afraid of anything—not even a dark and stormy night. When I do begin to feel afraid, help me to be still and feel Your love inside my heart. Please help me to remember that You are always with me and that I can talk to You about anything—good or bad—that's on my mind. Please give me Your peace. Give me Your comfort, Lord. Amen.

DAY 276
A Real Happily Ever After

Don't you just love a happy ending? God does! That's why He's got the perfect happily ever after planned out for you. It's all going to take place in a land far, far away. . .a place called heaven. In that regal place, you'll walk in streets of gold, live in a mansion, and dine with the King! It's true!

How do you get to this amazing place? It's really simple. Just place your trust in Jesus, God's Son. He gave His life for you so that you could one day spend eternity with Him. Talk about a happy ending!

Whoever believes in the Son has eternal life.

JOHN 3:36 NRSV

*God, I believe You sent Your Son, Jesus, to die for my sins.
I ask Him to come into my heart and wash me clean.
Because of what He did on the cross, I know that I can
live forever with You in heaven. I can't wait to see
what heaven will be like. I know it will be amazing!
Thank You, Lord, for happy endings! Amen.*

DAY 277
Fruits of the Spirit

MORNING •

The mark of a true Christian is that Jesus can be seen in every area of that person's life. There are certain traits that help identify a child of God. Love, joy, patience, and kindness are just a few. Do you believe that your friends would know by your love of others, your patience, and your kindness that you are a follower of Christ?

Take a look at your actions and your attitudes and make sure that they line up with the fruits of a true Christian. Jesus asks His children to be like Him in the way they deal with others. In fact, it's our treatment of others that sets us apart in the world. Jesus modeled perfect sacrifice and love for others. We need to share that love with those around us.

But the fruit of the Spirit is love, joy, peace, forbearance, kindness, goodness, faithfulness, gentleness and self-control. Against such things there is no law.
GALATIANS 5:22–23 NIV

EVENING •

Dear heavenly Father, what would my friends have to say about me as a person? Would they describe me as a kid who follows You closely? Or would they be surprised to learn I'm a Christian? Please help me take a good, honest look at myself as I consider whether I'm being a true representative of You. Help me to be a good example of Your love. Amen.

DAY 278
God Is in Control

MORNING •

This world can be a scary place. Reports you see on the evening news or things you hear your parents discussing may sometimes frighten you. Ever since sin entered the world in the Garden of Eden, it has been less than ideal. That's a fact.

But the good news is that God is in control. Even the worst or scariest circumstances are never too big for God. There is always hope with our heavenly Father.

The Bible promises that one day there will be no more tears and no more trials. In heaven, there will be no scary news reports and there will be no more pain. Until then, rest in the knowledge that God has commanded angels to watch over you. Lay your head on your pillow at night in peace.

> *In peace I will lie down and sleep, for you alone, O LORD, will keep me safe.*
> **PSALM 4:8 NLT**

EVENING •

God, life isn't always as it should be, and sometimes I feel afraid. But what is meant for evil in the world, You are able to use for good. . .and I'm so thankful! Thank You for Your promise that You will never leave me. You are my safety, Father. Nothing can reach me without going through You first. I trust that You are in control of absolutely everything. Amen.

DAY 279
I Love That!

The word *love* is used for just about anything, isn't it? We use it to describe all kinds of feelings or to express how much we enjoy something.

But is *love* really the right word to use for everything? It could be we use it too much. If *love* really describes so many things, what word should we use for much deeper emotions and attachments? It's silly to use the same word for our affinity for cake as we do for the deep feelings we have for our parents. But it's the only word we know that fits.

That said, how can we even begin to understand the greatness of God's love? The only way is to know who lives behind the word: God IS love. It's more than just a feeling He has for us; it's a state of being.

But God, being rich in mercy, because of His great love with which He loved us, even when we were dead in our wrongdoings, made us alive together with Christ.
EPHESIANS 2:4–5 NASB

Thank You, God, for Your great love for me. I can't always comprehend it, but I know Your love is the best kind. You are my Father and Creator. And Your love is bigger than I could ever imagine. Help me to love others with a deeper love and to show them that You ARE love. Help me to know You better, Lord. Amen.

DAY 280
The Spirit of Intelligence

Age is not a boundary or a limitation on God. So if He gives you something to say or gives you understanding, don't allow Satan to deceive you into feeling that you are too young to be taken seriously.

There are many areas of ministry that are great for young people to get involved in. Leading or mentoring those in younger grades, serving on planning committees for special events, offering testimonies or prayers at youth events, etc. The best thing you can do for the body of Christ, though, is to have a heart that desires to bring others to a saving knowledge of Jesus. Invite others to church and youth events and learn enough about the Gospel of Christ so that it becomes easy for you to share it with others.

> *"I thought, 'Those who are older should speak,*
> *for wisdom comes with age.' But there is a*
> *spirit within people, the breath of the Almighty*
> *within them, that makes them intelligent."*
>
> **JOB 32:7–8 NLT**

God, even though I'm young, I can still make a difference in the world. I can get involved in my community and my church. Please show me where You'd have me volunteer my time and energy, Lord. Thank You for choosing me to make a difference for You. I want to introduce everyone I know to You, Father. I love You. Amen.

DAY 281
Be Content and Trust God

MORNING •

People react to change in one of three ways. Some people are really nervous about every new situation, while others are too full of their own plans to accept what God has for them. And then there are some who are as happy to trust God in the difficult times as they are to rely on Him in the pleasant periods of life.

Has God given you something difficult to face? Don't be nervous and jittery about your circumstances, waiting for a chance to go a different way. And don't be so full of your own plans that you can't trust God. Learn to be content with His plan. God loves you, and He knows best. Trust Him in all things, and stand strong in the face of change or struggle.

"I will make you strong if you quietly trust me."
ISAIAH 30:15 CEV

EVENING •

God, sometimes You allow hard things to happen in my life. And while it's not fun for me, I can trust that You will provide me the strength and courage to get through them. Even though end results aren't always clear at the beginning of a difficulty I am facing, I will trust You. I will accept that You always know what's best. Because You really do, Lord! Thank You! Amen.

DAY 282
The Hope of His Calling

You are a child of God. You are called (2 Timothy 1:9; John 10:3; 1 Thessalonians 4:7)—with hope!

What are you called to? You're called to prayer (Philippians 4:6–7). You're called to walk by faith (Galatians 2:20; 2 Corinthians 5:7). You're called to live with the fruit of the Spirit (Galatians 5:22–25). You're called to love the Lord with all your heart, mind, and soul (Matthew 22:37). And you're called to study His Word (Psalm 119:105; Matthew 7:24–25; 2 Timothy 2:15).

God's Word is our Guidebook—our Life Manual. Everything we need to know about how God has called us to live is inside, waiting to be discovered! It is by *knowing* His hopeful calling and His Word that you will blossom into the young man or woman He has called you to be.

I pray that the eyes of your heart may be enlightened, so that you will know what is the hope of His calling, what are the riches of the glory of His inheritance in the saints, and what is the boundless greatness of His power toward us who believe.
EPHESIANS 1:18–19 NASB

Lord, thank You for calling me. Thank You for choosing me. I know that I am and always will be Yours—and for that I have hope that lasts forever! Please help me to study Your Word diligently. Remind me to have a conversation with You every single day of the week. I want to grow closer to You every moment. In Jesus' name, I pray. Amen.

DAY 283
Hope: An Anchor for the Soul

MORNING •

For a lot of people, a hope is a wish. It's kind of like cotton candy; it's just a bunch of fluff. But the hope that God describes in the Bible is certain. . .it's a solid anchor for your soul.

Have you ever seen a boat with an anchor? When the waves start rolling, the fishermen throw the anchor over the edge into the water to steady the boat. That's what God's hope is. It's like an anchor to steady you when life is hard. Hebrews 6:19 describes this hope: "We have this hope as an anchor for the soul, firm and secure" (NIV).

Just like an anchor holds a boat steady when the waves are rolling, God's hope holds your thoughts and your emotions steady when life is difficult. All you have to do is believe and trust God.

Be strong and take heart, all you who hope in the Lord.
PSALM 31:24 NIV

EVENING •

Lord Jesus, because of You, I have hope. And I am so glad that hoping in You holds me steady when things get tough! I am glad that You are always my anchor and that You will never leave me. With You by my side, I can be steady even in the biggest storms of life. I believe in You. I trust You, Lord, with every-thing in my life. You are an amazing Father! Amen.

DAY 284
Worry Doesn't Help

MORNING •

Here are some Bible verses to think about the next time you start to worry:

> *"Look at the ravens. They don't plant or harvest or store food in barns, for God feeds them. And you are far more valuable to him than any birds! Can all your worries add a single moment to your life? And if worry can't accomplish a little thing like that, what's the use of worrying over bigger things?"*
>
> LUKE 12:24–26 NLT

God doesn't want you to worry about having the best clothes or the most expensive smartphone. You don't have to be afraid of what's going to happen to you this summer or who your friends will be next year. The Bible says that worry won't change a thing, so trust God instead.

> *Jesus said, "That is why I tell you not to worry about everyday life—whether you have enough food to eat or enough clothes to wear. For life is more than food, and your body more than clothing."*
>
> LUKE 12:22–23 NLT

EVENING •

> *Dear God, Your Word has a lot to say about worry and fear. It says "Don't!" Don't worry; don't be afraid! And I want to obey Your Word, Father. Forgive me for all the times I worry. I want to trust that You're in control. Please give me Your peace no matter what's happening in the world. Thank You! Amen.*

DAY 285
Oops!

Do you ever wish you had a time machine that could transport you back in time? Back to that moment when you did or said something you shouldn't have?

Life is full of mistakes. It's part of being human! But being a child of God means fixing those mistakes as soon as possible. How? By being humble. By telling the person you hurt or upset that you're sorry.

God loves it when you humble yourself in prayer and ask for His forgiveness. Your parents may be upset by your goof, but they'll appreciate your apology. Your hurt friend will feel a lot better when she hears you say you're sorry.

Don't putter around in the garage, trying to figure out how to build a time machine. Take the humble route. It works every time.

Pride ends in humiliation, while humility brings honor.
PROVERBS 29:23 NLT

God, I'm human and I sometimes make mistakes. When I do something wrong, I feel so terrible about it. And I know You're disappointed in me too. I'm so sorry, Lord! Please help me to always make things right as soon as possible. When I mess up, I will always ask for Your forgiveness. And I'll apologize to the people I've hurt too. I always want to make things better, Father. Thank You for Your help. Amen.

DAY 286
A Plan for Me?

Are you a planner who likes to be in control of what happens? Or do you prefer to let other people do the planning?

If you're a planner and like to be in control, do you realize that someone bigger than you and wiser than you might direct you off your planned path? As a Christ-follower, that has to be okay with you. Remember that no matter how independent you are and confident you are that your way is the right way, you can't see the future.

Trust in God's wisdom and know that He really does care for you and wants the very best for you. Knowing that's true and knowing that He sees all things, does that make it easier for you to let go of your own will and trust Him fully?

> *"I know what I'm doing. I have it all planned out—plans to take care of you, not abandon you, plans to give you the future you hope for."*
> **JEREMIAH 29:11 MSG**

Father, I trust You fully. I trust You with my whole heart.
I give up my own will and surrender control to You.
I trust that You will direct me to what's best for me.
Thank You for loving me enough to have a plan for me.
Remind me that my plans aren't always the best plans.
When my plans don't align with Yours, I need to let You
take control of my life. . .and of my future. Amen.

DAY 287
Pretty Special

Do you ever wonder how God keeps all his children straight? How can He possibly remember all our names? How can He remember details about our personalities, or what we need, or what makes us laugh or cry?

But the truth is God does remember all those things. While we humans may forget a name or forget someone's birthday, God *never* forgets. He loves us. We belong to Him, and because of that, He takes a deep interest in everything about our lives.

The reason He loves us so much is because we are important to Him. And if the God of the universe says we're important, we can believe it's true.

"Fear not, for I have redeemed you; I have called you by name, you are mine."
ISAIAH 43:1 ESV

Dear Father, thank You for knowing me, for calling me by name, and for thinking I'm special. Help me to remember who I am in You. When I feel forgotten, remind me of this: You, the God of the universe, the King of kings and Lord of lords, call me by name! That makes me feel really special! Help me make others feel special too. Amen.

DAY 288
D-I-S-C-I-P-L-I-N-E

MORNING •

"Discipline"—how we dislike the word. When your parents discipline you, they are taking the time to correct your behavior. Maybe you were supposed to clean up your room days ago, but didn't. Now it's time to pay the piper. You can't spend the night with your best friend, and you've got to stay in there all day, doing what you neglected earlier. Maybe you were rude (or mean) to your little brother, and now you have to do extra chores (fold the clothes or wash the dishes).

Here's the truth: If your parents didn't love you, they wouldn't discipline you. If they didn't give you boundaries, you wouldn't know the difference between right and wrong. And believe it or not, when they use those words: "I'm doing this for your own good!"—they really are!

> **The Lord disciplines those he loves,**
> **as a father the son he delights in.**
> **PROVERBS 3:12 NIV**

EVENING •

God, in the moment, discipline doesn't feel good at all. I really don't like it! But when I think about what I'd be like without discipline, that's even worse! I need boundaries in my life to help me grow into the person You created me to be, Lord. Discipline from You...discipline from my parents...it all comes from a place of love. It really is what's best for me. Thank You for loving me enough to discipline me when I need it. Amen.

DAY 289
Rainbow Hues

It's the variety of human emotions that make you who you are!
Cheery yellow, daring orange, fiery red, sensible brown. . .hue
after hue of personality make up the person that is uniquely you.

Ever had a blue day or felt a twinge of envious green? No
human would be complete without them. The trick is keeping
all of those emotions—good and bad—in check. Have fiery red
and melancholy blue mixed to create a gloomy purplish mood?
Or maybe that twinge of green has blossomed into full-blown
emerald jealousy. Tell your Creator! He understands you like
no one can and knows exactly how to brighten a dark, unbe-
coming mood.

Pray about your feelings. Remember that as God's child, you
have the power to rule over them instead of letting them rule you!

O lord, thou hast searched me, and known me.
PSALM 139:1 KJV

Dear God my Creator, thank You for emotions—both
good and bad. Help me to recognize when my emo-
tions are getting out of control. You know how I feel
and why. Teach me to control my feelings before they
cause me to act in a way that doesn't bring honor to
You. You can brighten even my darkest mood, Lord.
Thank You for bringing joy into my life. Amen.

DAY 290
It's Tough to Lose Someone You Love

MORNING •

When someone you love dies, it hurts—a lot. Death can separate you from people you care about. You can't touch them or hear their voice. You can't call them on the phone or make plans to meet next weekend. All you have left are memories.

Because you are a believer, death has no hold on you (1 Corinthians 15:55). When Jesus died and rose again, He defeated death once and for all. The Bible says that when a believer leaves this life, they go to be with the Lord (2 Corinthians 5:8). Even though you may be separated from someone you love, it won't be forever. You'll see them again in heaven. Now that's a comforting thought!

Brothers and sisters, we do not want you to be uninformed about those who sleep in death, so that you do not grieve like the rest of mankind, who have no hope. For we believe that Jesus died and rose again, and so we believe that God will bring with Jesus those who have fallen asleep in him.

1 THESSALONIANS 4:13–14 NIV

EVENING •

Dear God, my heart hurts when I think of the people I love who have died. It hurts to know I can't see them anytime I want. I'm SO glad I have hope in You. Death doesn't separate us forever. I'm thankful I will see my loved ones again because of what Jesus did on the cross. Thank You for defeating death for me and those I love. Amen.

DAY 291
Choosing the Right Thing

MORNING •

Choices. . . Which one? Where? When? So many questions await decisions.

Some decisions are simple and can be made rather quickly. Others take some time to pray and think through. It's during those times that we need to seek the Lord, making choices that aren't determined by our own wants. At times our first thought is, *What should I do?* But making decisions in light of what Christ wants for us can be more difficult. It may mean sacrificing something or dying to our own desires. It's no longer, *What should I do?* but, *Lord, what do You want me to do?*

All decisions—large or small—should be made in order to bring our heavenly Father the praise He deserves.

> *Whatever you do [no matter what it is] in word or deed, do everything in the name of the Lord Jesus [and in dependence on Him], giving thanks to God the Father through Him.*
>
> **COLOSSIANS 3:17 AMP**

EVENING •

Dear Father, it's important to take time when I have a big decision to make. Help me to seek Your guidance as I make decisions. I should be asking, "What would You have me do, Lord?" And then I need to be patient as I wait for Your answer. Please make me willing to do whatever You ask me to do, so that Your name is praised as a result of my choices. In Jesus' name, amen.

DAY 292
The King, My Protector

When bad things happen to good people, it's hard to understand. But as a child of God, you are sealed in Him. That doesn't mean that nothing bad will ever happen to you, but it does mean that your King—the Lord God—loves you so much that you can never be snatched out of His hand.

You can have confidence that nothing in this world can keep you from God. Nothing in this world can separate you from God. And nothing—absolutely *nothing*—can take away your eternal life in Him. Your future—your eternity—is protected.

> *Neither death nor life, neither angels nor demons,*
> *neither the present nor the future, nor any powers,*
> *neither height nor depth, nor anything else in*
> *all creation, will be able to separate us from the*
> *love of God that is in Christ Jesus our Lord.*
> ROMANS 8:38–39 NIV

God, sometimes bad things happen—even to very good people who obey You. It's hard to understand. But I am thankful that nothing can separate me from Your love. You love me so much that I can't even begin to understand how BIG Your love is. Help me not to be afraid even when things are really bad, but instead trust in You...no matter the circumstances. You are my King, You are my Protector. Amen.

DAY 293
Secret Service Man

If you've ever watched the president of the United States on TV, you've probably noticed the men in the background dressed in black. These are his bodyguards, and they're called the Secret Service. They always travel with the president and stick very, very close, in case anyone tries to harm him in any way. If that happens, these trained protectors jump into action to make sure the president stays safe!

Did you know that God is the ultimate Secret Service Man? He's always on your side, protecting you from the enemy. You don't always see how He protects you, but He does! He keeps you safe as you go back and forth to school. He protects you from harm as you sleep at night. He sends His angels to watch over you and He guards your steps everywhere you go. Why? Because He loves you!

Deliver me from my enemies, O my God; protect me from those who rise up against me.
PSALM 59:1 NRSV

Thank You, Lord, for making me Your kid. I am so thankful for that. I'm grateful that You protect me from harm. I feel like I have my very own personal bodyguard, always looking out for me to keep me from bad things. You are the best protector in the world. I know You're watching over me 24-7 to make sure I'm safe and sound. Amen!

DAY 294
You've Got Talent!

Do you remember the parable of the talents in Matthew 25? A man was going on a long journey, so he called his servants together and gave them money. To one he gave five talents; to another he gave two; and to another he gave one. Then he left. The man with the five talents gained five more. The man with two talents gained two more. But the man with one talent dug a hole and buried it. When the master returned, he was pleased with the men who had doubled his money. But he was upset with the man who had hidden his talent.

If we hide our talents, we're no better than the servant who buried his talent. Don't let fear or laziness keep you from shining for God. Remember, God gave you those talents, and He will gladly help you develop them and use them for His purposes.

Just think—you don't need a thing, you've got it all! All God's gifts are right in front of you as you wait expectantly for our Master Jesus to arrive on the scene for the Finale. And not only that, but God himself is right alongside to keep you steady and on track until things are all wrapped up by Jesus. God, who got you started in this spiritual adventure, shares with us the life of his Son and our Master Jesus. He will never give up on you. Never forget that.
1 CORINTHIANS 1:7–9 MSG

Thank You, God, for giving me special talents unique to only me. Help me to use my talents well. Show me how and where I can share them to further Your Kingdom, Lord. Amen.

DAY 295
A Grand Adventure

MORNING •

Making plans can be a lot of fun. Like calling up your friends to meet you for coffee, or getting a group together to go to a basketball game at school, or organizing a sleepover, or just creating some fun time to hang out and chat. God likes to be in the middle of all your dreaming and planning for the future.

In fact, God has a design for your whole life, just like a beautiful picture. He wants the best for you—a one-of-a-kind grand adventure—better than you could ever imagine for yourself. He wants to help you make the most of your talents and keep you close to Him. What a good, good God!

> *"For I know the plans I have for you," declares the Lord, "plans to prosper you and not to harm you, plans to give you hope and a future."*
> **JEREMIAH 29:11 NIV**

EVENING •

Thank You, Jesus, that You are always with me. I am so glad that You have a perfect design for my life. Help me to see it clearly so my steps will be always in the right direction. I will quiet my heart and listen for Your voice, Lord. I want to hear Your whispers of hope. I want to hear Your words as You guide me into the wonderful adventure You have planned for me. Speak, Lord, I am listening! Amen.

DAY 296
Promise Keeper

Remember the flood in the story of Noah's ark? And then. . .the rainbow! God put it in the sky as a promise to Himself and to all humankind that He would never again flood the earth to destroy all of life.

When you see a rainbow in the sky, think about God's promise. His brushstrokes of color are like whispers from heaven.

God keeps His promises. You can rest assured He will never again flood the whole earth as He did in Noah's day. And if He keeps that promise, wouldn't it make sense that our God would keep all His promises?

Your heavenly Father promises to never leave you. He promises that He has great plans for you—plans for a future, for hope, and never to harm you. Trust Him. He's a promise keeper!

"I have set my rainbow in the clouds, and it will be the sign of the covenant between me and the earth."
GENESIS 9:13 NIV

Heavenly Father, I love it when I see a rainbow in the sky. You are such a magnificent artist! Each rainbow I see reminds me of You and Your amazing promise. You are the very best Promise Keeper. I can trust every word in the Bible because each one comes from You! Help me never to doubt Your Word, Lord. Amen.

DAY 297
The Force of the Flow

Courage can be like the faucet you use when you wash your face in the morning. The more you turn the valve, the more forceful the water flows; and in the case of courage, the knob needs three turns for maximum flow. Turn one is a willingness to stand up to any negative self-talk going on in your mind. Don't let your inner conversations tell you your situation is hopeless. Turn your courage up another notch by recognizing God will never leave you alone in any situation. He is a big God who is standing beside you! He doesn't believe in hopeless! Turn three on your valve of courage is believing God has a specific plan for your life, no matter what is happening today. He wants you to succeed!

"Be strong and courageous. Do not be afraid or terrified because of them, for the LORD your God goes with you; he will never leave you nor forsake you."

DEUTERONOMY 31:6 NIV

God, help me to be brave and strong. I know You are with me through everything—the good and the bad stuff. I know I'm never alone. You are beside me every moment, showing me the way to succeed. You alone give me the courage I need to face the future. With You, all things are possible! Amen.

DAY 298
Christ's Ambassadors

MORNING •

Do you know what an ambassador is? In this instance, Dictionary
.com defines it as an authorized messenger or representative.
When we accept Jesus us our Savior, we become one of God's
messengers—an Ambassador for Christ!

It's a very important job to tell—and show—others about
what God has done in our lives. Because of the great love that
Jesus showed for us on the cross, God is not counting our sins
against us! We're free from guilt! Free from shame! And free to
live a life of joy for all eternity!

That's worth telling the whole world about, right? That's our
main purpose here on earth: to be Christ's ambassador!

*For God was in Christ, reconciling the world to
himself, no longer counting people's sins against
them. And he gave us this wonderful message of
reconciliation. So we are Christ's ambassadors;
God is making his appeal through us. We speak
for Christ when we plead, "Come back to God!"*
2 CORINTHIANS 5:19–20 NLT

EVENING •

*Dear Jesus, thank You for not counting my sins
against me. Thank You for Your great love. I want to
be an ambassador—a messenger—for You. This is a
super-important job. . .and I am so glad You're trusting me to do it! Give me the courage to share Your message of love and hope with the people who need to
hear it. I am so thankful that I'm all Yours! Amen.*

DAY 299
How Can I Make Someone Love Me?

Have you ever asked, "How can I make someone love me?" The problem is that *nothing* can make people love you. Here's why: true love starts in the heart of the one who loves, not in the heart of the one who receives the love. This means true love is not earned. It's freely given, like a gift.

This is wonderful because it means that you don't have to be perfect or beautiful, rich or smart to get true love. This is how God loves. He loves us even though we aren't perfect. Even if you are stubborn, mean, impatient, or unkind, God will never stop loving you.

What a relief, huh? You can't earn God's love, and He will never stop loving you. He chose to love you, not because of who you are, but because of who He is.

We love because he first loved us.
1 JOHN 4:19 NIV

Lord, the world tells us that there are things that can earn love—being good-looking, being popular, being smart or rich... But none of this is true. I am so thankful that there is nothing I can do to earn Your love. You love me because of who You are—not because of anything I am or anything I do. I am so grateful that You will never stop loving me. Help me to love You the way I am loved by You, Lord. Amen.

DAY 300
My Testimony

Why are you a Christian?

The world wants to know your answer, and it's important to think about your answer before you're asked the question. When someone opens the door for you to share your testimony, talk about your faith in three minutes:

Minute one: Talk about what your life was like and what struggles you had before you accepted Christ.

Minute two: Share your story of how you became a Christian and what steps you took to come to that point.

Minute three: Tell about how your life has changed since beginning a relationship with Jesus and the hope you have in spending eternity with Him in heaven.

Your testimony is an amazing recollection of a miracle God performed in you, His child.

Always be prepared to give an answer to everyone who asks you to give the reason for the hope that you have. But do this with gentleness and respect.

1 PETER 3:15 NIV

Dear heavenly Father, please help me to know just what to say when someone asks me about my faith. It's important that I can put it into words. Give me the right words to say, Lord. My story is special and unique, and it has power to touch the lives of others. Help me to use it to bring others to You. Thank You! Amen.

DAY 301
The Seedling Principle

Our heavenly Father is the Master Gardener of all creation. Have you ever watched a flower grow? What does a seedling do to spring forth its beautiful flower?

Jesus said that unless a seed dies, it remains alone. But if it dies, it bears much fruit (see also Romans 5:3–4).

"Walk in a manner worthy of the Lord, to please Him in all respects, bearing fruit in every good work and increasing in the knowledge of God" (Colossians 1:10 NASB).

We must give up our selfish desires if we want to bear fruit for Christ. God's asking you to surrender *everything* so He may give you *opportunities* to grow.

Think about it: How can we learn patience if we never have to wait? How can we learn to trust God if we never surrender?

Remember, God's given you everything you need: His everlasting love.

> *"Truly, truly I say to you, unless a grain of*
> *wheat falls into the earth and dies, it remains*
> *alone; but if it dies, it bears much fruit."*
> JOHN 12:24 NASB

Lord, thank You for your creation that tells us so much about the wonderful God You are. I trust You. Help me to die to my selfish wants and to grow in You. The desire of my heart is to follow You no matter what. As I grow in my faith, I want to become more like You every day. Please help me to walk with You and not let go. Thank You for giving me everything I'll ever need in this life. In Jesus' name I pray. Amen.

DAY 302
What a Glorious Day!

MORNING •

You miss your loved ones who have passed away. They were special to you. But if they know Jesus, they're now in heaven!

You walk around remembering the good times you had with your family who are no longer here on earth. There were so many! But then you think about all the things they will miss—holiday celebrations, birthday parties, family get-togethers—and your heart feels crushed, like you'll never feel joy again.

But then God reminds you that He offers the gift of eternal life—and you've already accepted that wonderful gift. And someday your loved ones will greet you in heaven. What a glorious day that will be!

"And everyone who has left houses or brothers
or sisters or father or mother or wife or children
or fields for my sake will receive a hundred
times as much and will inherit eternal life."

MATTHEW 19:29 NIV

EVENING •

God, I am so thankful that death isn't the end for those
who know You and who have accepted You into their
hearts. Thank You for offering me eternal life. Thank You
for preparing a forever home for me in heaven. Take care
of my loved ones until I get to heaven. What an exciting
day it will be when I see my loved ones again! Amen.

DAY 303
I Can Do It!

The Bible tells a story about Moses sending spies into the Promised Land. The chosen men came back with reports of giants living in the land. They were afraid that the giants would kill everyone if they tried to take the land God had promised them. They said they felt like grasshoppers next to the giant inhabitants. If only they had compared the giants to God instead, they could have seen how easy it would have been to win—God was on their side, after all!

God is on your side too; and He will provide all the courage you need if only you will believe. He will go with you into every scary situation. When you feel discouraged, remember how big God is compared to whatever it is you have to accomplish. With God, you can do anything—even slay giants!

*"This is my command—be strong and courageous!
Do not be afraid or discouraged. For the LORD
your God is with you wherever you go."*
JOSHUA 1:9 NLT

Heavenly Father, I sometimes wonder how I'll ever accomplish everything You have for me to do. Negative thoughts and fears hold me back. Big jobs can be super scary. . .and when I see all the "giants" in the land, sometimes I fail to believe Your promises. Help me to trust that I can have courage because You are beside me in everything I do. Help me to see that nothing—not even a giant—is too big for You, Lord. Amen.

DAY 304
On My Side

It doesn't matter who we are or what we've done, we can never claim nobody loves us. Because God loves each of us deeply, and He's always on our side. Even when it feels like the world is against us, God is always, *always*, for us.

When friends are mean, we can remind ourselves of this verse: *The Lord is on my side.*

When we get in trouble for something we didn't do, we can remember: *The Lord is on my side.*

When we fail a test or spill lunch in our laps or get chosen last for the kickball team, we need to tell ourselves: *The Lord is on my side.* No matter what happens, we can always be assured that God loves us *with all His heart*, and He will never leave us. He's rooting for us. He's on our side.

> ***The Lord is on my side; I will not fear.***
> ***What can man do to me?***
> **PSALM 118:6 ESV**

Dear Father, I've felt unlovable at times. But this feeling is so untrue—I'm never beyond love because of You and Your promises. When I feel like people don't love me and the whole world is against me, remind me of this unchanging truth: You love me so much that it's beyond my imagination. Thank You for loving me, Lord. Thank You for always being on my side. Amen.

DAY 305
Oh, Happy Day!

What makes you happy? New clothes, shoes, video games? Some people treasure time with friends or going somewhere special. Do those things really make you happy, or are they simply things you enjoy?

Everything mentioned in that list is temporary. It will pass away. If your happiness is dependent on any of those things or anything else that's temporary, it too will pass away. True happiness means being joyful and satisfied with whatever your circumstances are. It means that no matter what you have or what you get to do, you still have a smile on your face because your happiness comes from something permanent.

God wants to be the source of your joy. When you love God, your life is filled with so much joy that you don't even chase after those things you once did.

> *"Until now you have asked nothing in my name.*
> *Ask, and you will receive, that your joy may be full."*
> **JOHN 16:24 ESV**

Lord, sometimes I'm not happy unless I have more things. I wish I didn't feel that way. I want to change that about myself. Will You help me find my joy in You alone? Help me to spend more time with You and read more of Your Word. The more I know You, the more I'll find my complete joy in You. I'll understand that I don't need things to be happy. Thank You for providing everything I need to be truly joyful. Amen.

DAY 306
A Ticket to Heaven

Getting in to see a movie is pretty easy. You just buy a ticket, show it to the ticket taker, select a seat, and enjoy. Without that ticket, though, the ticket taker would have to turn you away from the movie. That ticket proves that you are worthy to enter the movie because you have paid the price for admission.

So it is with heaven. We need a ticket to enter heaven, and the price for that ticket must be paid. At the gates of heaven, we must present our ticket and show that we are worthy to enter. And there is only one way into heaven, one ticket, and that is through Jesus Christ. He has already bought your ticket and has freely offered it to you. You only need to receive it.

> *"God loved the world so much that he gave his one and only Son so that whoever believes in him may not be lost, but have eternal life."*
> **JOHN 3:16 NCV**

Dear heavenly Father, there's only one way to get a ticket to heaven: through Jesus! Being good won't get me into heaven. Money won't get me into heaven. Nothing but my acceptance of Jesus' gift on the cross will get me into heaven. Thank You for sending Jesus to provide a way for my entrance into heaven, God. I want You to live in my heart. I want to live with You forever in heaven someday, Father. Amen.

DAY 307
The Security of God's Love

When you were very young, perhaps you had a special stuffed animal or blanket that you just carried with you wherever you went. Many children are attached to something soft and cuddly that brings them a feeling of security.

Now that you are growing older, you realize that while a stuffed animal is a cute "friend," it really doesn't provide security. True security only comes through a personal relationship with Jesus. God's Word promises that He will never leave you. Check out the list in Romans 8! Nothing today or in your future, no distance, no power, nothing heavenly or demonic, nothing in the world can separate you from the love of God!

When you feel alone, remember that you always have God. He loves you with an everlasting love.

For I am convinced that neither death nor life, neither angels nor demons, neither the present nor the future, nor any powers, neither height nor depth, nor anything else in all creation, will be able to separate us from the love of God that is in Christ Jesus our Lord.

ROMANS 8:38–39 NIV

Lord, it's nice to have something in life that makes me feel safe and secure. But truthfully there's no "thing" that can really do that for me. But the good news is that YOU are all I need to feel secure. If You're in my life, I'm safe and cared for! I am so thankful that nothing can ever come between us. Remind me on my hardest days that You are always with me. Amen.

DAY 308
The Right Friends

It's hard to find good friends. But remember that God is always with you, and He gives you clear direction so you can pick the right friends to hang out with.

The Bible tells us not to be friends with angry people or those with a hot temper. That doesn't mean that you should be rude to people and start ignoring them. It just means you shouldn't spend a lot of time with angry people or friends who have a really short temper. If you do, it can start to rub off on you.

You can tell a lot about a person by how they treat other people and how they talk about them. Pay close attention to how your friends talk about other people when they aren't around. It says a lot about them!

> *Don't befriend angry people or associate*
> *with hot-tempered people, or you will learn*
> *to be like them and endanger your soul.*
> **PROVERBS 22:24–25 NLT**

God, thank You for always being with me and helping me make wise decisions about my friends. Please provide me with friends who want to honor You. These are the kinds of friends You want for me, Father. Help me steer clear of angry, hot-tempered people. I know that after a while, I will become more like the friends I choose to spend time with. And who wouldn't want to hang out with and become more like friends who love You? Amen.

DAY 309
What's Love Got to Do with It?

What does it really mean to love others? Does it mean feeling all warm and fuzzy about people you don't even like? The truth is you can treat someone kindly, refuse to get angry and bitter, and treat someone with respect even if you don't like them very much. By doing this, you show the love of God. The world has a different view of love, but God's definition is the one that counts.

The world says you only have to love those who love you back. God says there is a more excellent way. God says love everyone. It's not always easy, but how else will the world know that we are His? What's love got to do with it? Just everything.

Love is patient, love is kind. It does not envy, it does not boast, it is not proud. It does not dishonor others, it is not self-seeking, it is not easily angered, it keeps no record of wrongs.

1 CORINTHIANS 13:4–5 NIV

Dear God, thank You for Your love for me. Help me to love others in a way that shows them who You are. Sometimes it's hard to love people who hurt me or make me angry. Help me to better understand Your definition of love and not accept the world's definition. Help me to love even people I don't like very much, so that I can be the kind of example You want me to be. Amen.

DAY 310
Pray Anyway

Daniel was a man with a lot of great stories to tell. It all started when he was a boy—maybe not a lot older than you are right now. The powerful Babylonians captured Jerusalem, and Daniel was taken captive, but he wasn't treated poorly. The king could tell Daniel was very wise, so Daniel received an excellent education and royal treatment.

Daniel determined to stay true to God, and he continued to remain faithful throughout his life. He knew that he would be tossed to the lions if he bowed to any but proud King Darius. But even in the face of that threat, Daniel openly prayed to God.

When you face teasing or rules saying you can't pray, be like Daniel and pray anyway. Stand true to God.

Now when Daniel knew that the writing was signed, he went into his house; and his windows being open. . .he kneeled upon his knees three times a day, and prayed, and gave thanks before his God, as he did aforetime.
DANIEL 6:10 KJV

Father God, thank You for the gift of prayer. I love that I can talk to You anytime—day or night—about anything. You are always ready to hear what I have to say, even when no one else wants to listen to me. Remind me of how important prayer is in my life. I don't want to imagine what my life would be like if I couldn't talk to You every day. May I always have the courage to stay true to You. No matter what, I will pray anyway! Amen.

DAY 311
The Path to Take

MORNING •

With so many choices and directions you could take in your life, it can be difficult to know which path to choose.

That's why it's so important to go to the Lord for direction. Not only in prayer but by reading your Bible.

We have the awesome privilege of having God's Word as our guide. We can read it in book form, on our computers, even on our iPods or phones! Filled with stories of triumphs and failures, God's Word is exactly what we need to help us through each day. No matter the obstacle.

Why not make a commitment to read more of the Bible—it will guide you and show you the path to take.

In all your ways acknowledge Him,
and He shall direct your paths.
PROVERBS 3:6 NKJV

EVENING •

Father, I want to know You better, and I need Your help in choosing the correct path for my life. Please give me the desire to study Your Word more, and show me exactly what I need to do each day. I want to grow and learn everything You want me to know, Father. What You want for me really matters—and it's super important for me to obey. Amen.

DAY 312
Letting It Go

It's pretty easy to think it's no big deal when you get caught "borrowing" your sister's tablet without asking. She'll get over it, right? But when we really mess up, the consequences can be severe. We can lose trust and respect with family and friends. And we begin to have feelings of guilt and shame. We need to remember what God told us to do in these moments.

He wants us to honestly admit our sins to Him. He won't erase the consequences, because they usually help us remember not to make the same poor decision again, but He also doesn't want us to walk around forever feeling guilty or ashamed. Confess to Him, and let it go. We can't go back in time, but we can *always* have a fresh start with God.

If we confess our sins, he is faithful and just and will forgive us our sins and purify us from all unrighteousness.
1 JOHN 1:9 NIV

Dear God, thank You for understanding that I will mess up from time to time. I wish I would always make good choices. But the reality is that I'm human, and I will sometimes make mistakes. Although I can't take my actions back, I'm sorry for my sins. And I choose to do my very best today. Take all my shame and my guilt, Lord. Thank You for Your forgiveness. Amen.

DAY 313
Stressful Thoughts

Your life can be pretty stressful at times, right? What can you do about it? These verses in Philippians have an answer.

First, you pray! Tell God how you feel and what you need. Then thank Him for how He has always been there for you! The Bible says that doing that will give you a peace in your heart that you can't possibly understand.

Next, you change the way you think! Listen to the rest of the paragraph: "Fix your thoughts on what is true, and honorable, and right, and pure, and lovely, and admirable. Think about things that are excellent and worthy of praise" (Philippians 4:8 NLT).

Whenever stress starts to bother you, pray! And then fill your mind with good things instead!

Don't worry about anything; instead, pray about everything. Tell God what you need, and thank him for all he has done. Then you will experience God's peace, which exceeds anything we can understand. His peace will guard your hearts and minds as you live in Christ Jesus.
PHILIPPIANS 4:6–7 NLT

Dear God, Your Word tells me not to worry about anything! Wow! Is that even possible? I want to obey You in everything, so if the Bible says it, I want to do it! Instead of worrying, I will talk to You. You will provide all the answers to my problems, God. Thank You for good answers when I'm unsure of what to do. When I'm stressed, I will talk to You about it! Thank You for listening and caring, Lord. Amen.

DAY 314
Making Time for God's Word

Trying to juggle your daily activities can be frustrating. And if you don't currently read the Bible every day, adding one more thing to your schedule may seem nearly impossible.

But what better thing to do than read God's Word? He tells His followers that we can know what's right simply by reading the Bible! Sounds easy, doesn't it?

And it is! The more time we spend with God in His Word, the more we will become like Him. And that is the Christian's goal—to become more like our heavenly Father.

Start small. Read five minutes a day, and then increase your time as you go. You'll benefit by growing closer to Jesus.

All Scripture is inspired by God and is useful to teach us what is true and to make us realize what is wrong in our lives. It corrects us when we are wrong and teaches us to do what is right.

2 TIMOTHY 3:16 NLT

Dear Lord, I want to become more like You every day. I can do that by spending more time in Your Word. The Bible will help me to grow into the person You created me to be. Help me to make time to read the Bible daily. Lord, I want to know You better, and I want to learn to do what is right. There is nothing better I can do with my day than spend time with You and Your Word. Amen.

DAY 315
The Praying Stance

MORNING •

Sometimes when we start to pray, we find we have bad feelings about someone. When this happens, we need to think deeply about it.

If you are carrying a grudge against someone because you think he treated you badly, forgive him and then let it go. If you are angry at a friend because she didn't do what you wanted her to or even because she's mad at you, forgive her and then let it go. If you don't like someone because she doesn't like you, ask God to forgive you and to help you love her anyway. And then let it go.

If you want God to forgive you, you need to forgive others. So when you pray, forgive and then let it go. You'll feel better about things, and so will God!

"And when you stand praying, if you hold anything against anyone, forgive them, so that your Father in heaven may forgive you your sins."
MARK 11:25 NIV

EVENING •

Dear God, I don't want to have bad feelings about other people. It makes me feel terrible on the inside! And I don't like it! I want to love others just as You've asked me to, Lord. And even though it's not easy, I know I can do it with Your help. Please help me to forgive others who have hurt me. And then help me to let it go! I want to be a loving example to others every day of my life, Father. Amen.

DAY 316
20/20 Vision

MORNING •

Do you have perfect vision? Or is your eyesight a little fuzzy and in need of some help from a pair of glasses? Glasses or no glasses, God's Word tells us to fix our eyes on Jesus. That's the only way we are clearly able see how to live a godly life every day.

When our eyes are fixed on Jesus, we're able to see the good in every situation. We're able to see what needs fixing in our own life. We're able to see the truth. . .clearly! Where are your eyes fixed? Do you often see the negative side of things? Are you looking at the waves instead of the One who calms the storms? Fix your eyes on Jesus and ask Him to clear up your "heavenly vision!"

> *Fixing our eyes on Jesus,*
> *the pioneer and perfecter of faith.*
> **HEBREWS 12:2 NIV**

EVENING •

Jesus, sometimes my vision is a little fuzzy, and I don't see things quite as clearly as I should. When this happens, I need Your help—I want to see things from Your perspective. Please help me to see things clearly—through the truth of Your Word, the Bible— just as You would have me see them, Lord. I want to keep my eyes on You every day of my life! Amen.

DAY 317
Your Inner Umpire

Have you ever watched a basketball game? A referee—the man in a black-and-white striped shirt—stops the game when the ball goes out of bounds and blows a whistle when a player breaks a rule.

The Bible says that peace from God is like an umpire in your heart. If you listen to this peace that comes from God, it will show you the way to go. It's God's gift to help guide you.

Colossians 3:15 says to let peace rule in your heart just like a referee rules a basketball game. Let peace have its way. When peace shows you the way to go, don't ignore it. You'll never be sorry—and you'll stay out of trouble.

Let the peace of Christ rule in your hearts.
COLOSSIANS 3:15 NIV

Dear Jesus, I need Your peace in my heart today, so I know which way to go and which choices to make. Sometimes it's hard to know what is right and what is wrong. Help me to know Your Word better. When I know and understand Your Word, the best choices are easier to make. When I follow the Bible, I can be kept from harm and avoid negative consequences in my life. Thank You for being my Guide. Amen.

DAY 318
Outrun Your Shadow

MORNING •

The influence you have on others is much like your shadow. No matter how hard you try, you can't escape it. You are accountable for what your words and actions lead others to think about Jesus. Your behavior has a direct impact on the thoughts and the salvation of the people around you.

What kind of influence do you have? Are you kind, honest, and faithful? Do you live in a way that would cause unsaved people to want to know Jesus?

Kids of the Kingdom should influence other Kingdom dwellers to live for Jesus too. Do you have that kind of influence?

Being out under the bright sun gives you a good, sharp shadow. Living close to the Son of God helps you build a good, strong Christian influence.

> ***But as he who called you is holy, you
> also be holy in all your conduct.***
> **1 PETER 1:15 ESV**

EVENING •

*God, I know that the influence I have on others cannot
be avoided any more than I can run away from my
shadow on a sunny day. So it's super important for
me to always be kind, honest, and faithful. If others
can see how good life is with You in it, then they'll want
to know You too! Please help me to impact others so
they want to live for You, Lord. Give me the courage
and strength I need to be Your faithful child. Amen.*

DAY 319
Something Special

When I was twelve years old, I was convinced that I had been born with no talent. I thought perhaps God had forgotten to add that special something into my DNA. I didn't feel like there was anything special about me. I wasn't even sure what my dreams were. I felt like a dull weed in a garden full of colorful flowers.

If you have ever felt this way, know that God has not forgotten you. Your future may seem cloudy right now, but God has a specific and wonderful plan just for you! He doesn't want you to compare yourself to anyone else because He created you to be a unique individual. He gave you a special set of talents that you can use for His glory. You have a future full of hope and promise!

*And we know that in all things God works
for the good of those who love him, who have
been called according to his purpose.*

ROMANS 8:28 NIV

God, I'm sorry for ever wondering if You gave me any talents and dreams. You created me, and You made me special! I am one of a kind. Please help me not to compare myself to others. When I'm feeling plain or ordinary, help me to remember that You created me for a purpose—a wonderful purpose!—and You are in control. Thank You for being so good to me, God. Amen.

DAY 320
Breakfast of Champions

As a child of God, you face a lot of challenges. Choosing between right and wrong, fighting temptation, and dealing with difficult people all take spiritual muscles. The best way to build those muscles is with a steady diet of God's Word. Reading the Bible is like giving your soul a big stack of pancakes. It provides the spiritual energy you need to make it through the day.

Start your morning with God. Instead of reading the back of the cereal box, read a few passages from the Bible. Then take a moment to pray and ask God to help you with whatever you might face. That's the breakfast of a champion! And what an amazing difference a well-fed soul can make.

Man doth not live by bread only, but by every word that proceedeth out of the mouth of the Lord.
DEUTERONOMY 8:3 KJV

God, I don't ever wake up and forget to eat a good breakfast. So please don't let me forget to feed my soul every morning too! Time with You each morning guarantees that a very good day will be in store for me. Time in prayer and with Your Word, the Bible, makes for a great start to my day. Remind me to begin each day feeding my soul with Your Word. Amen.

DAY 321
New Things!

Next week is your first day at a new school. The school has lockers that look way too complicated, a brand-new teacher for each class, and hundreds of students (and you don't even know one of them!). You feel like running away—going back to the old school and old friends you knew so well. Your stomach is full of butterflies.

God will give you courage to look forward! Face the day with Him by your side. Before you leave the house, read a Bible verse and say a prayer to calm your worries and fears. Then keep the peace God provides with you throughout the day.

New experiences will bring new friends, brand-new adventures, and many blessings. Reach for the door of opportunity God has provided. You just never know where it might lead.

Joshua said to them, "Do not be afraid; do not be discouraged. Be strong and courageous. This is what the LORD will do to all the enemies you are going to fight."
JOSHUA 10:25 NIV

Lord, new things are always scary for me. Sometimes I just want to run and hide and never come out! When I'm nervous, Lord, give me courage. With You beside me, I can face anything. . .nothing is impossible when You're with me. Father, I ask that You would give me courage in everything I do today and in the future. Calm my nerves. Allow the butterflies in my stomach to settle. Thank You. Amen.

DAY 322
Hidden Treasures

Imagine a map of a deserted island, one that would lead you to the greatest buried treasure ever found. You follow the map until you come across a chest filled with priceless gold coins. What would you do with all that money?

The Bible says that the kingdom of heaven is like a treasure hidden in a field. It is a thing of great value. When you come into a relationship with Jesus, you've discovered the greatest treasure of all—one that will lead you all the way to heaven one day. The Christian life is a priceless gift, one you can't take for granted.

And guess what! God wants you to share that gift with others. Leave clear directions for others to follow so that they too will one day discover this awesome treasure!

"The kingdom of heaven is like treasure hidden in a field. When a man found it, he hid it again, and then in his joy went and sold all he had and bought that field."
MATTHEW 13:44 NIV

Dear heavenly Father, sometimes it's fun to think about what I might do if I found buried treasure. Would I buy something really nice for myself? Would I treat my friends to ice cream and a day at the water park? Would I help Mom or Dad pay the bills? Would I help someone in need? What would You have me do with the many blessings You've given me, Lord? That's really the most important question to ask. I want to share the treasure of heaven with others! Amen.

DAY 323
I Have Overcome

God has provided many ways to help us overcome our fears. Here are a few helpful "Courage Boosters" He has supplied:

One: Remember He promises to be with you—no matter what (Matthew 28:20; Psalm 23:4)!

Two: Pray. God's always ready to hear your voice. He *encourages* us to speak to Him! "Do not be anxious about anything, but in everything by prayer. . .let your requests be made known to God. And the peace of God, which surpasses all comprehension, will guard your hearts and minds in Christ Jesus" (Philippians 4:6–7 NASB; see also Matthew 11:28 and 1 Thessalonians 5:17).

Three: "Take. . .the sword of the Spirit, which is the word of God" (Ephesians 6:17 NASB). We can memorize and study God's Word. It's your Life Manual.

> *"These things I have spoken to you so that in Me you*
> *may have peace. In the world you have tribulation,*
> *but take courage; I have overcome the world."*
> **JOHN 16:33 NASB**

Lord, I need Your strength and courage to overcome
my fears. Help me to take up the sword of the Spirit,
the Bible—I want to read it and memorize it, Lord.
Knowing what the Bible says will help me in every-
day life. It will help me make good choices and remind
me of Your love and goodness. Thank You for giving
me strength to resist temptation. I need You today
and every day, Lord. In Jesus' name, I pray. Amen.

DAY 324
Make a Wish

MORNING •

Make a wish when you blow out the candles. Wish upon a falling star. Wish when you throw a coin into the fountain. Make a wish with a wishbone. Do you see a pattern here? A wish requires an object attached to it. If we pray to God, is it okay to make a wish. . .or is that the same thing as a prayer?

A wish is like tossing a need out into the universe, expecting some angelic force will grab it and do something about it. Prayer is speaking directly to God and asking Him to meet a need or provide a want.

When we trust that God will do good for us and we surrender our needs to Him, we are trusting in His promises.

For in this hope we were saved. Now hope that is seen is not hope. For who hopes for what he sees? But if we hope for what we do not see, we wait for it with patience.
ROMANS 8:24–25 ESV

EVENING •

Dear God, I trust in Your unfailing Word and know You'll supply all my needs. I don't want to wish into an empty vacuum hoping that someone hears me—not when I have You, my best Friend, only a heartbeat away. Wishes have nothing to support them, Father. So help me to always know and recognize the difference between a wish and a prayer. Thank You for always hearing me, Lord. Amen.

DAY 325
You Want Me to Love WHO?

Love each other. It doesn't sound so hard, does it? Love your family, love your friends, love that nice lady at church who gives out peppermints. . .that's pretty easy. But what about that guy in math class who keeps cheating off your papers even though you've asked him to stop? And what about the girl in phys ed class who makes nasty remarks about everyone—including you? Do you have to love those people too?

Jesus makes it pretty clear that loving others isn't an option. He has commanded us to love *everyone*, even our enemies. By loving this way, the world will know that we belong to Him. Love makes all the difference.

"As the Father has loved me, so have I loved you. . . . If you keep my commands, you will remain in my love. . . . I have told you this so that my joy may be in you and that your joy may be complete. My command is this: Love each other as I have loved you."

JOHN 15:9–12 NIV

Dear God, thank You for Your love for me. You loved me even when I was still a sinner. Because I love You, I want to be obedient to Your commands. Please let Your love work in me so that even the people I don't like will see You in my words and actions. Remind me that loving others is important to You, Lord. If You ask me to do something, I will do it. . .even if it's not easy! Amen.

DAY 326
My Eternal Shepherd

Sheep can be ornery creatures. They smell bad. They bite. They like to wander off.

Just like human beings. And humans need a shepherd—someone to lead and protect them—just as much as those wooly beasts do.

Isn't it cool that you have a Shepherd? He's always there to guide, direct, discipline, and protect you.

Your Shepherd has offered you eternal life! And it's free! He paid for it by dying on the cross for your sins. He sacrificed Himself so you could have the opportunity to spend forever with Him.

Once you've said yes to God, you're eternally part of His family. Isn't that wonderful? Is there someone you could share this with today—someone else who needs to know the Shepherd? Someone who needs the gift of eternal life?

"My sheep hear My voice, and I know them, and they follow Me. And I give them eternal life, and they shall never perish; neither shall anyone snatch them out of My hand."
JOHN 10:27–28 NKJV

God, thank You for sending Your Son Jesus to die for me—and every single human being! Thank You for the gift of eternal life. I am so glad I said yes to You, Lord! Thank You for knowing me and loving me. Nothing can take me away from You. I am Yours forever! Please help me to have the courage to share my faith with someone else today, so they might have a chance to spend eternity with You too. Amen.

DAY 327
Keep Going

Everyone struggles with having a bad attitude sometimes. It may seem impossible to improve your attitude once you start feeling upset, but God says there's another way.

Pray. Choose to be joyful. Find ways to be thankful for what's happening in your life. This is what God wants His children to do every day, no matter how difficult life is.

You may have to start out small. When you feel like your attitude is slipping, take a moment to pray and ask God to help change your outlook. Thank Him for something that is important to you. Then practice joy.

God doesn't want you to go through life with a sour attitude. Choose today to live with the outlook of Christ, and He'll give you the strength to make it through.

Always be joyful. Never stop praying. Be thankful in all circumstances, for this is God's will for you who belong to Christ Jesus.
1 THESSALONIANS 5:16–18 NLT

Father God, when life is tough, it's so hard for me to have a good attitude. Please give me guidance to get through it: to be joyful, to keep praying, to give thanks. Remind me that there's always something to be thankful for in my life. You have given me so many blessings that I can't count all of them. I trust You, Father, to help pull me out of the dumps. Amen.

DAY 328
Kindness Matters

When you say something nice to another person, you have no idea how God will use that to brighten their life! So use your words for good and not harm. Here are some verses to remember about kindness:

"Therefore, as God's chosen people, holy and dearly loved, clothe yourselves with compassion, kindness, humility, gentleness and patience" (Colossians 3:12 NIV).

"Love is patient, love is kind. It does not envy, it does not boast, it is not proud. It does not dishonor others, it is not self-seeking, it is not easily angered, it keeps no record of wrongs" (1 Corinthians 13:4–5 NIV).

"Your kindness will reward you, but your cruelty will destroy you" (Proverbs 11:17 NLT).

Get rid of all bitterness, rage, anger, harsh words, and slander, as well as all types of evil behavior. Instead, be kind to each other, tenderhearted, forgiving one another, just as God through Christ has forgiven you.
EPHESIANS 4:31–32 NLT

Dear God, my words impact others. I can use them for good or for bad. If I want to be a loving example for You, Lord, I will use my words to lift others up. I will choose to be kind. I know how important kindness is to You, Father. Please forgive me for the times when I've acted out of anger instead of being kind. Help me to love others better. Amen.

DAY 329
Understand. . .or Misunderstand?

MORNING •

Having someone misunderstand your words is tough! Lots of friendships end because one person gets upset over something the other one said. Sad, right?

Thankfully, God never misunderstands you. He never takes your words the wrong way or makes a big deal out of things that aren't a big deal. In fact, He knows what you're really thinking, even before you say a word! God also knows what you're going to say. . .and why. That's because He can see inside your heart and knows why you're feeling the way you do about things. He not only sees but He truly understands.

So, no misunderstandings with Him. Not ever!

O Lord, You have looked through me and have known me. You know when I sit down and when I get up. You understand my thoughts from far away.

PSALM 139:1–2 NLV

EVENING •

Lord, as long as human beings interact, they will have misunderstandings. Sometimes I take someone's words the wrong way; other times, the roles are reversed. But You never misunderstand me, Father. I'm so glad You always understand what I think and say. I don't always say all the right things, but You know my heart. Thank You for taking the time to really get to know me and to care about what I'm thinking and feeling. I'm so grateful! Amen.

DAY 330
Leader of the Pack

Do you know what it means to respect your elders (those who are older than you)? Think about the adults you know—your parents, grandparents, and church leaders. Did you realize God has placed them in your life for a reason? And He's watching you closely to make sure you treat them with the respect they deserve.

Imagine this. . . A leader at your church isn't getting a lot of respect from the kids in your class. Maybe some of your friends are talking when they should be listening or interrupting when the teacher is speaking. What can you do to help? By far the best thing you can do is treat the teacher with respect. Then encourage others to do the same.

Why treat your leaders with respect? Because it's the right thing to do!

> *Dear brothers and sisters, honor those who are your leaders in the Lord's work. They work hard among you and give you spiritual guidance.*
> **1 THESSALONIANS 5:12 NLT**

Father God, I want to understand what respect really means. I want to always show proper respect to others. Please show me, Lord. When I see other kids being disrespectful, please help me to be a good example, and show me how to be part of the solution. I want to influence other kids to follow You, Lord. I know it's the right thing to do, and I want to please You. Amen.

DAY 331
Behaving Wisely

You know the story of young David. He had proven he was responsible enough to care for his father's sheep. When wild beasts attacked, he showed wisdom in the way he protected the sheep. When he was given the task of carrying food to his soldier brothers, he probably didn't anticipate that God would use him to win an important victory, but he was prepared when it happened. While he was still young, God called upon David, who had already served as King Saul's musician, to be the next king of Israel.

Why was God able to use David this way? It's simple, really. David had determined to live wisely and maturely. He chose this path when he was a child, and you can choose it too.

> *I will behave myself wisely in a perfect way.*
> *O when wilt thou come unto me? I will walk*
> *within my house with a perfect heart.*
>
> **PSALM 101:2 KJV**

> *Father God, I am determined to walk wisely. And*
> *with Your help, Lord, I will be strong. I will follow Your*
> *lead for my life. I want others to see You through my*
> *words and actions. When they do, they will trust me. . .*
> *and they will see You use me for Your plans and pur-*
> *poses. This will draw others closer to You, Father.*
> *Use me for Your glory. I'm all Yours, Lord. Amen.*

DAY 332
White Noise

Some people can only sleep with those white-noise machines that fill their quiet bedroom with the sounds of the ocean, birds chirping, or even street clamor. Silence is just too loud. There is a lot of clatter going on around us, especially when we look for answers about faith, religion, and God. Everyone has a different opinion. And everyone thinks theirs is the right one.

Where can you go to get good advice and answers about the things of God? Your parents would be able to answer that question for you by pointing you in the direction of the people you can trust who will give you godly counsel and advice found in scripture. Make sure that, even with all the noise around you, you're listening carefully for God's voice through the chaos. He will make Himself known to you if you listen closely.

> *"For God so loved the world, that he gave his only Son, that whoever believes in him should not perish but have eternal life."*
> JOHN 3:16 ESV

Dear God, the world is a very noisy place. I'm sorry for all the times I've paid more attention to the noise than I have to You. I want to listen for Your voice above all else. Please help me to keep my focus on You, Lord. Help me know Your voice even as others shout at me and try to turn me away from You. Speak, Lord. I am listening! Amen.

DAY 333
Love Letter

MORNING •

My child,

You don't know Me well, but I have been watching you for a long time.

Do you know how much I love you? My love is so deep, so vast, that it cannot be expressed in this simple letter. It would take many letters—volumes of them! Indeed, they are written. Will you read them if I give them to you? Will you cherish My words, savor them, reflect upon them until they are written on your very heart?

I want you to trust Me. To believe in Me. I will stay by your side always and protect you as fiercely as a lion! For you are My dear one, and My most precious Gift is yours.

Will you accept My love?

I shall wait for your answer.

Eternally yours,
God

"So have I loved you."
JOHN 15:9 KJV

EVENING •

Dear God, I want to know more about You. I am amazed at how much You love me. And I love You right back, Lord! As I read Your Word, the Bible, I will get to know You so much better. I treasure Your Word, Lord. Help me to spend more time in it. I am so thankful I have You in my life, Father. You are all I need! Amen.

DAY 334
The Green-Eyed Monster

Jealousy is a hard emotion to control. No matter what sport or activity you participate in, there will always be someone better than you. That's just life. In addition, there will also always be someone better looking, smarter, richer, taller, thinner. . .the list goes on. But don't let that drive you crazy with jealousy. Just accept the fact. Forget about those who are better. . .and set your sights on becoming the best version of you! You don't ever need to worry about anyone else.

Instead of flaws, focus on your positive traits. You are unique! God made you special. You have wonderful talents and strengths. So the next time that green-eyed monster rears its ugly head, turn your head upward and thank God for making you, you!

Love is kind and patient, never jealous,
boastful, proud, or rude.
1 CORINTHIANS 13:4–5 CEV

God, feeling jealous of someone else is the worst! I don't want to feel that way about others. Remind me that it's okay when another kid is better than me at something—it's nothing to get upset about. I'm sorry for being jealous sometimes. Please help me to stop feeling jealous and instead focus on being the best version of me. . .which is what You'd like me to do, right, God? Thanks for making me, me! Amen.

DAY 335
Living Forever

MORNING •

I remember when my grandfather died. I was twelve years old. My mother told me Granddaddy had gone to see Jesus. That sounded nice, because everyone knows heaven is a great place. But I was still heartbroken.

The good news is this: I know I'll see my grandfather again in heaven. The reason I know that is because Granddaddy believed Jesus was God's Son. He believed Jesus died on the cross to take the punishment for our sins so we could spend eternity in heaven. And I believe that too. God's Word tells us that if we believe in Jesus and what He did for us on the cross, we won't ever really die. Our bodies will die, but our spirits—the part of us that makes us who we are—will live forever in heaven with Jesus and with all those who also believe in Him.

> *I write these things to you who believe in the name of the Son of God so that you may know that you have eternal life.*
>
> **1 JOHN 5:13 NIV**

EVENING •

Dear Father, I believe Jesus is Your Son and that He died in my place as punishment for my sins. Thank You for sending Him, and thank You for eternal life. Thank You also for the gift of our forever home, heaven. While I miss my loved ones who have passed away, I can be full of joy because I know I'll see them again when I get to heaven. Thank You, Father! Amen.

DAY 336
The Best Secret Keeper

It doesn't matter what made you feel upset, hurt, angry, or sad. God wants to hear what you have to say. He is the God of *all* comfort, which means He is interested in the little details as well as the humongous ones. If your friend embarrassed you at lunch or you're having parent drama, tell God all your troubles. Don't be afraid to tell Him any mean or unkind thoughts you may be having too. He can take it. He understands what you're going through.

Find a quiet, private place where you can tell Him what's going on. Hold nothing back. Share it all. He's the best secret keeper there is! Soon you'll experience a release from your burdens as you give them away to Him. He'll show you how to move forward and will comfort you as you go.

Blessed be the God and Father of our Lord Jesus Christ, the Father of mercies and God of all comfort.
2 CORINTHIANS 1:3 NKJV

Dear God, thank You for always being ready and willing to listen. I'm so glad I can talk to You, Lord. Please give me Your comfort as I share what makes me feel angry, sad, upset, or hurt. Even though I can't always trust and depend on others, I know I can ALWAYS depend on You to keep my secrets and trust You to help me find my way. I love You, Lord! Amen.

DAY 337
Liar, Liar

MORNING •

You've heard the little taunt, "Liar, liar, pants on fire." You may have even said it a time or two. Does it apply to you? Are you in the habit of telling lies? Not HUGE lies. . .but those little white lies that don't seem to make much of a difference?

The Bible is crystal clear on lying: God hates it! Even the little white lies that are meant to make others feel good. If you are really curious, look up Revelation 21:8. It describes what happens to people who make a lifelong habit of lying. Yikes! Ask God to help you be truthful in everything you say and do.

> *The Lord detests lying lips, but he*
> *delights in those who tell the truth.*
> **PROVERBS 12:22 NLT**

EVENING •

Dear heavenly Father, thank You for the Bible that is crystal clear about how to live my best life. When I'm unsure, I just need to read Your Word, and I'll find the best advice and guidance there is. I know You hate lies, Father. Please help me to avoid lying at all times. . .and remind me that even lies that don't seem that big of a deal are a very big deal to You. I want to walk in truth. Amen.

DAY 338
Obey. . .It's the Safest Way

It's not always easy to obey, is it? So many times we want to have our own way, to do our own thing. If you read today's scripture, you can see that God makes a promise to us when we obey our parents. Our lives will be filled with many good things if we just follow the proper direction.

Imagine you're crossing the street on your way to school. The crossing guard blows her whistle, letting you know that traffic is coming. If you disobeyed her warning and stepped out into the street, what would happen? You could get badly injured! The same is true with God's directions. We must obey for our own safety. If we do, He promises us a long life filled with great things! So stay safe. Obey!

Children, as Christians, obey your parents. This is the right thing to do. Respect your father and mother. This is the first Law given that had a promise. The promise is this: If you respect your father and mother, you will live a long time and your life will be full of many good things.

EPHESIANS 6:1–3 NLV

God, it's not always easy to obey! I struggle sometimes. I just want to have my own way, to do what I want to do. Please remind me that my ideas and wants aren't always the best for me. No, Lord, You are the only one who will lead me in the right direction every single day. Thank You for showing me how to obey, even when I don't feel like it. Thank You, Father, for caring for me and loving me so much! Amen.

DAY 339
Send Your Gorillas Running

MORNING •

When I was seven years old, my sister and I went to a circus. Halfway through the show, two men rolled out a male gorilla in a cage. One of the men opened the cage and the gorilla jumped over the chain-link fence and ran up the bleachers. All the kids sitting in front of me screamed and ran away. I did too.

When I got older, I discovered that the gorilla was just a man in a gorilla suit!

I learned something important from this funny event: what you think and believe will affect how you act. So if you let your mind fill up with bad thoughts, then you'll behave badly. If you let your mind fill up with fearful thoughts, you'll act afraid.

If you want to be strong and live the way God wants, focus your mind on true thoughts from the Bible like Philippians 4:13, which says, "I can do all this through him who gives me strength" (NIV).

Finally, brothers and sisters, whatever is true, whatever is noble, whatever is right, whatever is pure, whatever is lovely, whatever is admirable—if anything is excellent or praiseworthy—think about such things.

PHILIPPIANS 4:8 NIV

EVENING •

Lord, help me control my thoughts when they threaten to run out of control. Remind me that my thoughts aren't always reality. Sometimes my thoughts are untrue. Help me to rely on You and Your Word instead, Lord. Thank You for giving me strength and courage when I focus on Your truth. Always help me to fill my mind with Your comforting and reliable thoughts. Amen.

DAY 340
The Whole Puzzle

MORNING •

Our lives on earth are like a big, complicated jigsaw puzzle. We cry out to God, asking for His help to make sense of the jumbled problem pieces we have on earth that we can't sort out. God is the only one who knows what the finished picture looks like. He sees how the happiness and trouble in our lives fit together in the end.

He answers our prayers, telling us to give our burdens to Him. He helps us work them out, arranging the pieces of our puzzles in a way that will make the picture full and complete in the end. We won't always understand why He's doing what He's doing, so He asks us to follow Him in faith.

What trouble pieces do you have in your life? Ask God to take care of those problems by placing them in the right spot so they will ultimately work together for good.

> *And we know that in all things God works*
> *for the good of those who love him, who have*
> *been called according to his purpose.*
> **ROMANS 8:28 NIV**

EVENING •

God, some puzzles are super complicated and hard to put together. This is kind of like life sometimes. It can be a real mess, and I need Your help to sort it out. I am so thankful that You see the entire picture of my life as it's meant to be. I trust You to help me put the pieces together according to Your perfect plan. With Your help, the pieces will fit together, just as they're meant to. Thank You, Lord! Amen.

DAY 341
No Revenge

Did you ever have someone you thought you could trust give away a secret? You may have wanted to teach her a lesson by doing the same to her. Or how about when someone pushed you? Did you ever feel like pushing him right back?

It's not hard to want to treat others the same way they treat you. But God wants you to love them even when they don't seem loveable. But here's what's so cool. When you treat others the way God wants you to—by loving them, doing good to them, and praying for them no matter what—you will be so much happier with yourself. And you may be very surprised by the change of heart they might have by your kindness toward them.

> *"But I say to you, love your enemies, bless those who curse you, do good to those who hate you, and pray for those who spitefully use you and persecute you."*
>
> **MATTHEW 5:44 NKJV**

Father, when someone treats me badly, I want to treat them the same way. I am so tempted to get even—but I know it's not the right thing to do. I know it's not what You want me to do. Your Word tells me to love other people . . .even those people who aren't very easy to love. This is going to be hard for me, Lord. But I know You'll help me do the right thing, God. I trust You and I love You. Amen.

DAY 342
Go. And Sin No More!

MORNING •

We're humans. . .born sinners. But there's good news! God forgives us (Colossians 2:13)! He sent Jesus—the pure, sin*less* Son of God—to die as a living sacrifice for *our* sins. That means we're forgiven. . .we've been set free (Galatians 5:1)!

That freedom isn't something we should take advantage of or take for granted. Some Christians continue in sin because "they're forgiven no matter what." But God says that's wrong (Galatians 5:13, 24–25).

We've died to the world. . .we're alive in Christ (1 John 2:15–17; Philippians 1:21; 1 Corinthians 15:22; Ephesians 2:4–6). As Christians, Jesus calls us to show others the light of salvation and His perfect, everlasting love (Matthew 5:13–16).

Christ *died* for us so we can *live*.

Live for *Him*!

> **And Jesus said, "I do not condemn you, either.**
> **Go. From now on do not sin any longer."**
> **JOHN 8:11 NASB**

EVENING •

Lord, I know that I'm a sinner. I can't even imagine why You've forgiven me. . .why You've cleansed me. But Your Word says You have. And so I believe it. Help me to walk in Your Spirit and not in sin. I don't ever want to take Your promise of freedom for granted. Help me to live with a thankful heart every single day. In Jesus' precious name. Amen.

DAY 343
How Many Times?

Forgiveness can be strange. Some people who have hurt you may not even care that you won't forgive them. Others might have simply made a mistake and are truly sorry. Holding a grudge, even if you think it's deserved, creates a dark sore in your heart. All the bad feelings you have about others will only make things worse. And maybe, if you wait too long to forgive someone, you just might ruin the chance for a lifetime friendship.

Think how wonderful it will be if you choose to forgive. You'll experience the joy of living without that ugly grudge in your heart. And who knows what other amazing things might happen because you chose to say, "I forgive you"?

Make the decision to forgive, even if you don't really feel like it. God will bless your offer to let go of a grudge.

Then Peter came to Him and asked, "Lord, how many times will my brother sin against me and I forgive him and let it go? Up to seven times?" Jesus answered him, "I say to you, not up to seven times, but seventy times seven."
MATTHEW 18:21–22 AMP

Dear Lord, the world is full of imperfect human beings . . .and sometimes people are unkind to each other. I don't want to hang on to my bad feelings when I have been hurt by others. And I don't want to turn against anyone who has hurt me either, Lord. Please help me learn to forgive, and teach me how to be a good example. And thank You for forgiving me first! Amen.

DAY 344
The Cry of Your Heart

Have you ever been afraid you might not be doing this "Christian thing" right? Maybe you're worried that you aren't good enough or that you'll somehow mess it up.

The truth is, you're probably NOT going to get it right all the time. None of us do. The thing to remember is this: God's grace is bigger than your sin. And if you really have a desire in your heart to make Him proud, you can pray Psalm 139:23–24. God will always honor that prayer. He'll send the Holy Spirit to nudge you and let you know when something isn't right. He'll make sure you stay on the path of everlasting life because He wants the best for you.

Search me, O God, and know my heart; test me and know my anxious thoughts. Point out anything in me that offends you, and lead me along the path of everlasting life.

PSALM 139:23–24 NLT

Dear God, although I want to please You all the time, I know there are times when I don't. And when I mess up, I'm truly sorry. I'm glad that You love me no matter what. Please help me to be a reflection of You. Know my heart, and guide me in the way that I should go. Keep my focus on You and You alone, Father. I want to honor You every day, Lord, with both my words and my actions. Amen.

DAY 345
Finish Strong!

If you've ever run track at school or competed in any kind of race, you might have heard your coach yell, "Finish strong!" as you headed toward the finish line. The desire to "finish strong" pushes runners farther than they knew they could go and faster than they thought they could run.

We have a coach up in heaven giving us the same direction to "Finish strong!" No matter how hard life gets, God wants us to keep going. No matter how you're feeling, God wants you to know that He is on your side. He is cheering you on to victory. He has already given you everything you'll ever need to run your race. Just keep your eyes on Him and finish strong.

Let us run with perseverance the race marked out for us, fixing our eyes on Jesus, the pioneer and perfecter of faith.
HEBREWS 12:1–2 NIV

God, some days are tough. Some days I wonder if I'll be able to accomplish my goals. Some days I feel like no one cares about me. Some days are just terrible, horrible, bad days! On those days when I'm struggling, I need Your help, Father. Help me to keep my eyes on You. I want to run and finish the race You have set before me. I want to run my very best race. Help me to finish strong. Amen.

DAY 346
With Open Arms

MORNING •

God comforts you—just like a warm blanket wrapped around your shoulders on a cold day. Open His Word and discover the healing you can find in scripture. God is always there, offering His warmth and His love to your broken heart.

When you suffer a loss isn't the only time the heavenly Father will wrap you in His loving embrace. He's there to hold your hand when you don't get the spot on the team you wanted so badly. He's there when you get sick on the night you had special plans. He's there—with open arms to comfort you—*always*.

> *Even though I walk through the darkest valley,*
> *I will fear no evil, for you are with me; your*
> *rod and your staff, they comfort me.*
>
> **PSALM 23:4 NIV**

EVENING •

God, thank You for friends and family who try to comfort me when I'm hurting. They do the best they can—and they truly do help me to feel a little better. But sometimes I need more. On those days, I need the best comfort there is. . .YOURS. Thank You for Your comfort, Lord. Wrap me in Your loving arms. Let me experience Your unconditional love. Amen.

DAY 347
Wow—He Loves Me!

MORNING •

Have you ever had someone in your life who really got on your nerves? Even though you probably really disliked—possibly even hated—this person, did you know that God loves them just as much as He loves you?

It's a hard pill to swallow. But think about it this way: God made the world. He made all the rules. And then all of humankind disobeyed. We sinned. We lied and murdered and cheated. Bullied, stole, annoyed others. But guess what? God showed us He loved us by sending His Son to pay the price—even though we were sinners! (And obnoxious and annoying!)

Today, take some time to remember how much He loves you—even though you're a sinner—and share that love with someone that may even get on your nerves. You'll be glad you did.

> ***But God demonstrates His own love toward us, in that while we were still sinners, Christ died for us.***
> **ROMANS 5:8 NKJV**

EVENING •

God, there are people on earth who get on my nerves ...people I really don't like very much. But instead of ignoring them and hoping they'll go away, I can be a good example and share Your love with them. Help me share Your love today with someone who needs it. And when someone is mean to me or annoying me, please remind me that You love them just as much as You love me and that I'm supposed to love them too. Amen.

DAY 348
Hiding Place

A few years ago, I had a pet fish. Whenever I stood near the bowl and looked at him, he would hide among the ivy. We must have looked pretty scary to him, peering through the bowl!

Sometimes life can be scary. Whether we're frightened of bullies or a hard test or a new school, God says we can hide in Him. He'll comfort us and keep us safe. He'll protect us from trouble and help calm us down so we're not afraid anymore. He sings peaceful lullabies into our spirits and lets us know everything will be okay.

The next time you see trouble headed your way, run to God. He'll wrap you in His comforting arms and let you bury your face in His neck. You can know that everything will be okay as long as you use God as your hiding place.

You are my hiding place; you will protect me from trouble and surround me with songs of deliverance.
PSALM 32:7 NIV

Dear Father, when life gets scary, I want to run away and hide. But that's not really possible. I know I can't hide from my fears and problems. But You do make a way for me to feel safe and secure. I can run to You. . .and You will comfort me. I can "hide" in Your love and care. Thank You for letting me hide in You and for delivering me from all kinds of trouble. With You in my life, I don't ever have to be afraid. Amen.

DAY 349
All the Way to Your Toes

What do you do when you hear some interesting gossip? Do you lean in so you can hear it a little better? Do you chime in with more gossip to make the story more shocking?

What if those hurtful words are about your best friend? Do you stand up for your friend, or do you say nothing? It takes courage to stand up for what's right. Being courageous isn't a lot of fun, and it isn't easy.

But God will give you the strength to stand strong. To be able to walk away when you need to. Or to be able to speak up in love when you know you should. It'll make you feel good inside—not only all the way to your toes, but all the way to your heart!

Finally, be strong in the Lord and in his mighty power.
EPHESIANS 6:10 NIV

Lord, it is so hard to be courageous—especially when I'm the only one who seems to speak up and do what's right. When I hear gossip or unkind words, help me shut it down. I don't want to be a part of the problem, Lord; I want to be part of the solution. I want to make things better. And I want to be a good example. Help me to always know what is right, and then give me the courage to follow through and do the right thing. Thank You! Amen.

DAY 350
Precious Goods

MORNING •

Almost every kid on the planet has felt that their parents have been unfair at some point, so you shouldn't feel bad if you do too. If you were to ask your parents, they would probably admit that sometimes they *are* unfair. Sometimes they really don't understand, and sometimes they won't let you do what your friends get to do.

Why?

Because they love you.

God has tasked your mom and dad with a very serious responsibility: taking care of precious, irreplaceable you! So make it easy for them. Your parents aren't perfect. They *do* make mistakes, but their decisions—especially if they are Christians—are meant to help you be the best that you can be.

***Children, obey your parents in all things:
for this is well pleasing unto the Lord.***
COLOSSIANS 3:20 KJV

EVENING •

Dear God, sometimes it's hard to obey my parents. I feel like some of their rules are unfair...especially when I'm not allowed to do something my friends have permission to do. When I disagree with their rules, please help me to show respect. It's hard for me, but I know it pleases and honors You, Lord. Remind me that when I obey my mom and dad, I'm really obeying You. Amen.

DAY 351
Bad News

Do you watch the news? It seems like a new tragedy strikes somewhere every single day. People get hurt, and natural disasters destroy homes and even entire towns. Sadly, it's the bad news that gets our attention in the headlines. It's what people notice. There's always something, and it's always scary.

Yes, God does allow for things to happen; and yes, it can be scary. But the blessing is that He has called us to be a light for His truth in this dark world, and He will give us the strength we need to carry out that mission. Be thankful for His presence in your life, and be willing to follow the call He has for you no matter what's happening around you. Rest in Him, and trust in the protection of His mighty hand.

> *Be of good courage, and He shall strengthen*
> *your heart, all you who hope in the LORD.*
> **PSALM 31:24 NKJV**

Lord, bad things have happened in the world—and bad things will continue to happen. Please help me to be strong and courageous as I face a world full of hard things. Help me to be a voice that spreads the truth of Your Word to hurting people. Please give me strength and courage. Even in a world that is hurting, I can share the hope I have because of You. So many people in the world need Your hope, Lord! Amen.

DAY 352
Salty Christians

Imagine you're at a fast-food place and have just ordered a cheeseburger and french fries. You taste the fries, only to discover there's no salt on them. You go ahead and eat the fries, but they're not very tasty, are they? It's not like you need a lot of salt to fix the problem. Just a little bit would be enough.

That's how it is when you share your faith with people who don't know the Lord. Just a pinch here and there goes a long, long way. They don't need you to preach to them. They just need little sprinkles, enough to make them thirsty for the Gospel.

That's our job, after all—to make people thirsty for the Lord. He calls us to reach others for Him. What an adventure! So grab that salt shaker! God's got work for you to do!

> *"You are the salt of the earth. But if the salt loses its saltiness, how can it be made salty again? It is no longer good for anything, except to be thrown out and trampled underfoot."*
> **MATTHEW 5:13 NIV**

Heavenly Father, help me to spread little pinches of salt everywhere I go! Introduce me to people who need to know You, Lord. And then give me the courage and strength to begin sharing just a little of You with them. Hopefully once they get a small taste, they'll want more. Thank You, Lord, for being You! Amen.

DAY 353
Dig In!

If you've ever used a shovel, you know that digging up dirt is tough work, but so worth it when you're done—especially if you're doing something fun, like planting a garden. The deeper the roots, the stronger the plants will grow!

The same is true with reading God's Word. It's not enough to just quickly read a verse or two. God wants you to dig, dig, dig! Ask Him to "uncover" some new truths so that you can learn more every time you read. Sure, reading can feel like work at times, but the payoff is great! After digging through the stories in His Word, you will learn so much! You'll be like those plants, deeply rooted and ready to grow strong and beautiful. So grab your spiritual shovel, and let's start digging!

Your word is a lamp to my feet and a light to my path.
PSALM 119:105 ESV

Lord, thank You for giving me the Bible. It's more than just a book full of stories. It's a lamp to light my way in life. Help me to dig deep in Your Word so I can grow strong in You. Just a few verses here and there is not enough. I need to dig deep enough to uncover the truths You want me to know deep in my heart, Father. I want my faith to grow strong roots! Amen.

DAY 354
A Blob of Goo

MORNING •

God created us to be unique. No matter how hard you tried, you could never look exactly like another person or think exactly like another person. And you will make yourself miserable trying to do either of those things.

Have you ever poured gelatin into a mold? It flows right into the mold, and when it sets, it comes out looking exactly like the original mold. Now imagine putting peanut butter into that same mold. It would be sticky and messy and never set up right—coming out looking like a big blob of brown goo.

Comparing yourself to someone else is kind of like putting peanut butter into a gelatin mold. You'll always come out looking like a blob of goo!

> **But when they measure themselves by one
> another and compare themselves with one
> another, they are without understanding.**
> **2 CORINTHIANS 10:12 ESV**

EVENING •

God, please help me not to compare myself to others. Comparison just isn't wise. And deep down I know that. But it's hard to avoid. Remind me that comparison will make me feel unhappy, even when I really don't have anything to be unhappy about. There are so many wonderful things in my life that I should be focusing on, Lord! Help me to just be me and to be happy about that! Amen.

DAY 355
The Finish Line

Have you ever run a race? A runner must wear light clothes that add as little extra weight as possible. In fact, good clothes for runners are designed to help with speed and agility, wick away sweat, and let the air flow freely to cool the body.

Christians are running a big race. We must plan ahead like a marathoner and choose carefully what we're going to carry with us on the journey. If we run our race bogged down with sin, temptation, and fear, our race will be slow. But if we allow Jesus to carry those burdens for us, we can run free.

> *Do you not know that in a race all the*
> *runners run, but only one gets the prize?*
> *Run in such a way as to get the prize.*
> **1 CORINTHIANS 9:24 NIV**

Dear Jesus, please carry my burdens for me so I can run the race free from the weight of this world. If I try to carry the weight of my burdens all by myself, I'll never win the race. In fact, I'll end up coming in last place. I want to cross the finish line and celebrate as I claim my prize, Lord. And I can't do that unless I allow You to carry my burdens for me. Will You do that, Lord? Thank You! Amen.

DAY 356
A Free Do-Over

MORNING •

Have you ever done something you really regretted? Like telling your mom a little lie to get out of trouble? Or maybe giving an unpopular kid at school the cold shoulder? The guilt can be overwhelming. You may feel like you've turned down a dark path.

There's good news! Jesus died on the cross so that you wouldn't have to be burdened by guilt. No matter how far you've wandered, Jesus can rescue you. If you ask for forgiveness, He will erase your sins—big and small. His grace never runs out; it's like a river that never runs dry. Just as parents delight in giving their child a gift, so does Jesus delight in giving you a free do-over.

> **But God shows his love for us in that while**
> **we were still sinners, Christ died for us.**
> **ROMANS 5:8 ESV**

EVENING •

Jesus, thank You for loving me enough to die for me.
Please forgive me for anything I've done that has hurt You
and others. Thank You for giving me unlimited do-overs
whenever I ask for them. When I am tempted to do
something I shouldn't, please give me the strength and
courage to do the right thing. Thank You, Lord! Amen.

DAY 357
God Wants Me to Do Right

MORNING •

Sometimes it's hard to do the right thing—especially when friends are telling you it's okay to do what you know is wrong. They say it's not really *that* bad, and "everyone else is doing it." It's hard to stand up for what God wants you to do when you're worried that your friends will make fun of you or leave you out of their future plans and activities. But remember you will never completely be able to enjoy doing something that you know is wrong anyhow. You'll feel guilty for saying yes when you should have said no. You know what God wants you to do. Ask Him to give you the courage, and then do it.

For it is better, if it is the will of God, to suffer for doing good than for doing evil.
1 PETER 3:17 NKJV

EVENING •

Dear God, I admit that sometimes I want to go along with my friends, even when I know I shouldn't. Please help me to be strong and to do what I know I should. Please help me to stand up for what's right and encourage my friends to do the right thing too. We can find something better to do with our time—something pleasing to You. Please give me the desire in my heart to always do what's right. Thank You, Father. Amen.

DAY 358
An Invitation to Rest

MORNING •

There are times things just don't go according to plan. The burdens can add up, making it feel like there's a heavy weight on your shoulders.

But Jesus offers an invitation to all His children to come to Him. He isn't looking for the "perfect" ones—the ones who look like they have everything all together. Because really, no one does. Everyone has weariness and heavy burdens at times.

So take Him up on His offer. Go to Him and give Him the hard things you're going through. He wants to listen. But it doesn't stop there. He also wants to give you rest. He may not take away the tough times, but He will comfort you as you go through them.

Then Jesus said, "Come to me, all of you who are weary and carry heavy burdens, and I will give you rest."
MATTHEW 11:28 NLT

EVENING •

Dear Lord, thank You for caring about the times that I struggle. Whether my best friend breaks a promise or I fail a test at school or my family member is sick, You care about ALL of it. And so I will share all my cares and concerns with You, Lord. Thank You for wanting to hear from me and for promising to give me rest and comfort, even while I'm going through hard times. Amen.

DAY 359
Do You Feel Like You Don't Fit In?

MORNING •

Maybe there are times that you feel like you don't fit in. It might seem like the kids around you are standing *in* a circle together, and you are standing *outside* the circle—alone.

God has a very special plan for you. This is why there will be times when you can't—and shouldn't—do what everyone else is doing. You won't look like them, wear the same clothes, or have the same interests because God has something special for you to do that they can't do. God made you different on purpose for a purpose.

Remember: sometimes being great for God means you need to be different.

> ***Now you are the body of Christ, and
> each one of you is a part of it.***
> **1 CORINTHIANS 12:27 NIV**

EVENING •

Lord Jesus, thank You for making me special. In the same way that You made the animals different, the planets different, and the stars different, You made me different. I am Your amazing creation. Help me to remember this when I feel like I don't fit in. Remind me of my worth. Remind me of my purpose. I want to do great things for You, Lord. Amen.

DAY 360
Fighting the Lies

Just as your ears hear different voices, your heart can hear different voices too. They usually come from your mind. They're lies that you've heard—lies the devil plants in your brain.

Have courage! There's truth throughout the Bible that contradicts Satan's lies. God knows when you're struggling. And He supplied a way to help you in the hard times (1 Corinthians 10:13). His comfort is within reach. . .right at your door.

God gave you an amazing gift for the rough times: prayer. He's always here to listen. And He asks you to call out to Him (Matthew 7:7–8).

> *"Do not let your heart be troubled;*
> *believe in God, believe also in Me."*
>
> **JOHN 14:1 NASB**

Father, I don't know why I go through hard times. And I have no idea how to handle those situations. I feel confused sometimes. Help me to trust You, Lord. Thank You for Your everlasting love, Your always-within-reach comfort, and the wonderful gift of prayer. You know my heart, and You will help me every step of the way. Thank You, Lord. In Jesus' holy name, I pray. Amen.

DAY 361
Encourage Yourself!

MORNING •

Everybody deals with discouragement once in a while—even mighty men and women of God. Remember David in the Bible? He was called a man after God's own heart, yet he battled discouragement too.

Especially on one particular day. . . David was doing exactly what God had told him to do—fighting battles for God—but when he and his men returned from war, they found their city had been burned and all their wives and children had been taken. Talk about a reason to be discouraged! To make matters worse, all of David's men got mad at him and wanted to kill him! Things looked pretty bad, but David didn't give up. Instead, the Bible says David encouraged himself in the Lord. And it wasn't long before the entire situation turned around in David's favor. In fact, seventy-two hours later, they had all their possessions and families back, and David was made king!

> *. . .but David encouraged himself in the Lord his God.*
> **1 SAMUEL 30:6 KJV**

EVENING •

God, I sometimes feel like giving up. Life gets hard. School is stressful. My best friend is mad at me. Mom or Dad wants me to do so many chores! I just want to scream, "I'm done!" Help me to keep on going. . .and to deal with hard situations. Because with You, I can do it! I can be quick to encourage myself by thinking about You and Your goodness to me. Thank You for everything You do for me, Father. Amen.

DAY 362
You Are Always on His Mind

MORNING •

No matter who you are, no matter how popular, no matter how shy, no matter how smart—there are probably days when you feel invisible. You wonder if anybody notices you at all. Maybe your teachers seem to overlook you. Maybe your parents seem more concerned about their own problems than you. Or you feel like the odd one out even when you're with your friends.

But you never have to worry about being invisible to God. He thinks about you all the time. His love for you will last forever. You are His "handiwork, created in Christ Jesus to do good works" (Ephesians 2:10 NIV). No matter what happens, God will fulfill His purpose for you. He will not abandon the works of His hands. (That's you!)

> *How precious are your thoughts about me,*
> *O God. They cannot be numbered!*
> **PSALM 139:17 NLT**

EVENING •

Dear God, it makes me sad when I feel like I'm invisible. Like no one sees me and no one cares. I am so thankful that I am important to You, Lord. I'm thankful that You are always thinking of me. I'm grateful that You love me and created me for a special purpose. Help me to always walk close to You so I can be all You created me to be. Amen.

DAY 363
Hidden in My Heart

It's been a long six weeks. You've been memorizing dozens of scriptures from the Old and New Testaments. You want so badly to earn a new Bible that your Sunday school teacher has promised as a reward—if, and only if, you pass her test on Sunday.

You've studied hard. You've spent hours in your room thumbing through your Bible and repeating scriptures in your head.

Then Sunday comes, and the nerves hit! You say a quick prayer for God to calm your pounding heart.

At the end of class, the teacher announces that you passed. Next Sunday, you will receive a new Bible! And best of all, you have hidden God's Word in your heart, for today and always.

Your commands are always with me and
make me wiser than my enemies.
PSALM 119:98 NIV

Thank You, God, for Your Word. It holds nothing but truth. It's a reliable guide for everyday living. When I am confused, scripture can help me sort things out. I am so thankful for my Bible. Your Word encourages me and gives me advice that will help me to live my best life today and every day. Thank You, Lord! Amen.

DAY 364
Tutti-"Fruitti"

Did you know that people recognize you by your fruit? The fruits of the Spirit, that is: love, joy, peace, patience, kindness, and so on. If you stick close to Jesus (like vines clinging to the branch of a tree), you will bear good fruit, but if you wander far away, you will bear bad fruit.

When people look at you, they either see good fruit or bad fruit. They either see love, joy, and patience, or they see someone who's grumpy, hard to get along with, and impatient! They either see someone who has a helpful attitude or someone who always wants to get their own way.

So which is it? Good fruit? Bad fruit? Happy fruit? Or sad fruit? The decision is up to you.

> *"Make a tree good and its fruit will be good,*
> *or make a tree bad and its fruit will be bad,*
> *for a tree is recognized by its fruit."*
>
> **MATTHEW 12:33 NIV**

Heavenly Father, help me to always walk closely with You so I can bear the good fruit that Your Word talks about. I want to be loving, kind, patient, and all the things You created me to be. I want other people to be able to see Your goodness in me, Lord! I want to be recognized as Your child. I praise You today! Amen.

DAY 365
Bright Future

Come closer, child, and look into my crystal ball. See how the colors swirl about! They are the clouds that obscure your future. Now, I will part them and reveal. . .

What?

Your high school graduation? Your future spouse? It couldn't hurt to take a little glimpse into the years to come. Or could it?

Even if you could get your hands on a crystal ball, knowing the future wouldn't prepare you for it. That's why God has chosen not to show you what lies ahead. He wants you to live moment by moment, *trusting Him*! Every step that you take on the winding path of life's journey has been specially designed for you by your heavenly Father. He has everything planned for your good!

Take therefore no thought for the morrow: for the morrow shall take thought for the things of itself.
MATTHEW 6:34 KJV

Dear Father, You don't want me to worry about what's next in my life. I don't have to worry about it, because You already know what's coming—and You've got it under control. Remind me that no matter what the future holds, You've got my back. Your plans for me are good, Lord! And I'm so grateful for the gift of this life that You've given to me. I won't waste a single second of it! Amen.

Contributors

MICHELLE MEDLOCK ADAMS: Days 1, 22, 60, 81, 96, 114, 136, 151, 168, 188, 211, 273, 294, 334, 345, 361

Michelle Medlock Adams is an award-winning journalist and bestselling author. Michelle has written more than 1,000 articles for newspapers and magazines and has published dozens of books since graduating with a journalism degree from Indiana University. Michelle is married to her high school sweetheart, Jeff, and they have two daughters, Abby and Allyson.

JANET LEE BARTON: Days 9, 12, 27, 44, 61, 80, 93, 106, 120, 147, 169, 180, 190, 213, 223, 248, 263, 315, 341, 357

Janet Lee Barton was born in New Mexico and has lived in Arkansas, Florida, Louisiana, Mississippi, Oklahoma, and Texas. She and her husband now live in Oklahoma, where they feel blessed to live near one daughter and her family. Janet loves researching and writing Christian fiction.

EMILY BIGGERS: Days 5, 17, 31, 49, 68, 84, 101, 117, 130, 149, 167, 182, 195, 210, 228, 241, 259, 278, 296, 307

Emily Biggers is a Tennessee native living in Arlington, Texas. She teaches gifted and talented students in first through fifth grades. She loves to travel, write, spend time with family and friends, and decorate.

DEBORAH BATES CAVITT: Days 64, 85, 109, 128, 146, 165, 186, 219, 244, 268, 302, 321, 346, 363

Deborah Bates Cavitt lives with her husband near Dallas, Texas. She has contributed to *Hello Future*, *Angel Digest*, and *Heaven Humor for the Teacher's Soul*. She has also written lesson plans and articles for *Library Media Connection* and published a children's book, *Amber's Fairy Tale*, in 2011. Deborah enjoys reading and writing devotions.

CHERYL CECIL: Day 12

Cheryl Cecil lives in Fort Wayne, Indiana. Two married daughters and three granddaughters inspire her to write for girls of all ages. She loves finding any reason to celebrate life.

JAN CLINE: Days 3, 18, 35, 58, 73, 90, 111, 124, 137, 156, 175, 209, 225, 239, 260, 279, 303, 343

Jan Cline is an author, freelance writer, and speaker from the Northwest. She also directs a Christian writers' conference and leads a writers' group in her area. Jan has seven grandchildren and loves to travel and play golf.

DEBORA M. COTY: Day 320

Debora M. Coty is a popular humorist, speaker, and award-winning author of numerous inspirational books, including the best-selling *Too Blessed to Be Stressed* line. Deb considers herself a tennis junkie and choco-athlete (meaning she exercises just so she can eat more chocolate). A retired piano teacher and orthopedic occupational therapist, Debora currently lives, loves, and laughs in central Florida with her husband, Chuck, and three grandbuddies and one grandprincess.

REBECCA GERMANY: Days 230, 232

Rebecca Germany works full time as a fiction editor and has written and compiled several novellas and gift books. She lives in Ohio, where she enjoys country life.

RENAE BRUMBAUGH GREEN: Days 7, 23, 38, 50, 77, 134, 153, 176, 192, 207, 222, 240, 254, 270, 287, 304, 335, 348

Renae Brumbaugh Green lives in Texas with her handsome country-boy husband, her noisy children, a rowdy dog, and a bunch of chickens and ducks. She's published more than 25 books and a whole bunch of articles. Her favorite color is blue, unless you're talking about nail polish, in which case her favorite color is bubblegum pink.

JENNIFER HAHN: Days 24, 41, 55, 63, 78, 98, 113, 132, 157, 174, 179, 193, 208, 229, 246, 272, 291, 314, 358

Jennifer Hahn resides in Lancaster County, Pennsylvania, with her husband and three children. She loves homeschooling her kids and is also active in her church, working with the youth and assisting with editorial and proofreading tasks. Her desire is that, through her writing, readers will strengthen their relationship with Christ.

ANITA HIGMAN: Days 2, 52, 100, 141, 183, 224, 269, 295, 349

Best-selling and award-winning author Anita Higman has dozens of books published (several coauthored) for adults and children. She's been a Barnes & Noble "Author of the Month" for Houston and has a BA degree, combining speech communication, psychology, and art. Anita loves good movies, exotic teas, and brunch with her friends.

GALE HYATT: Days 15, 30, 46, 72, 97, 119, 138, 154, 173, 214, 220, 245, 266, 285, 289, 333, 350, 365

Gale Hyatt discovered her passion for writing in the third grade. Since then, she has written numerous songs, poems, articles, short stories, and devotionals. She continues to write while home educating her three children in beautiful Lithia, Florida.

WENDY LANIER: Days 8, 28, 42, 66, 87, 102, 121, 140, 161, 184, 200, 216, 237, 256, 271, 290, 309, 325, 344, 362

Wendy Lanier is an author, teacher, and speaker who writes for children and adults. She has written books for Lerner Books, KidHaven Press, Lucent, and Capstone Press, as well as articles in online and print publications, such as *Highlights for Children* and *Clubhouse Magazine*.

KELLY MCINTOSH: Days 29, 171, 185, 194, 199, 201, 203

Kelly McIntosh is a wife, mother of twins, and editor from Ohio. She loves books, the beach, and everything about autumn (but mostly pumpkin spice lattes).

HILLARY MCMULLEN: Days 16, 36, 75, 123, 142, 233, 319, 356

Hillary McMullen received a BA degree in English from Sam Houston State University, and she has had a short story published in the *SHSU Review*. After graduating, Hillary gained editorial experience by critiquing Christian fiction and nonfiction. Writing, music, and youth ministry are a few of her passions. Hillary currently lives in Houston, Texas, with her husband.

BRIGITTA NORTKER: Days 48, 91

Brigitta Nortker lives and works in Nashville but takes every opportunity to travel that she can. In her free time, she enjoys an excellent book, a cup of coffee, and spending time with friends and family.

NICOLE O'DELL: Days 34, 54, 62, 83, 95, 112, 129, 148, 163, 205, 217, 235, 252, 264, 277, 280, 281, 286, 305, 306, 318, 324, 332, 351, 355

Youth-culture expert Nicole O'Dell resides in Paxton, Illinois, with her husband and six children—the youngest of which are toddler triplets. She writes and speaks to preteens, teenagers, and parents about how to prepare for life's tough choices.

MARILEE PARRISH: Days 4, 11, 13, 32, 47, 53, 59, 70, 86, 99, 107, 110, 118, 126, 135, 144, 152, 158, 162, 164, 177, 191, 204, 212, 215, 226, 234, 238, 250, 255, 262, 275, 284, 298, 308, 313, 316, 328, 337, 354

MariLee Parrish lives in Colorado with her husband, Eric, and children. She's a freelance musician and writer who desires to paint a picture of God with her life, talents, and ministries.

RACHEL QUILLIN: Days 25, 39, 150, 310, 331

Rachel Quillin is the author of several gift books and coauthor of the devotional prayer book *Prayers & Promises for Mothers*. She makes her home on a dairy farm in Ohio with her husband and children.

SHANA SCHUTTE: Days 14, 43, 57, 65, 89, 115, 131, 198, 231, 249, 267, 283, 299, 317, 339, 359

Shana Schutte is an author and speaker. She is a former editor for *Focus on the Family*, has authored more than 300 articles, and hosts a nationwide radio program called *Beyond Imagination* that airs daily on more than 400 Christian stations. Shana also leads seminars across the country.

MELANIE STILES: Days 6, 37, 79, 108, 125, 143, 159, 172, 189, 206, 227, 242, 261, 297, 312, 336

Melanie Stiles has won numerous writing awards and accumulated hundreds of bylines in various publications. Her recent book, *The Heart of a Ready Scribe*, continues to be well received. She is a Christian Life Coach specializing in author services and personal one-on-one sessions.

JANICE THOMPSON: Days 40, 56, 71, 76, 92, 104, 116, 133, 160, 178, 247, 258, 276, 288, 293, 322, 329, 330, 338, 352, 353, 364

Janice Thompson hails from south Texas. She is a Christian author and mother of four grown daughters. Janice has written over forty books.

ANNIE TIPTON: Days 74, 94, 236, 251, 257, 300, 327, 340

Annie Tipton made up her first story at the ripe old age of two when she asked her mom to write it down for her. (Hey, she was just two—she didn't know how to make letters yet!) Since then, she has read and written many words as a student, newspaper reporter, author, and editor. Annie loves snow (which is a good thing because she lives in Ohio), wearing scarves, sushi, Scrabble, and spending time with friends and family.

KAYLA WOODHOUSE: Days 20, 21, 26, 45, 67, 82, 103, 122, 145, 166, 181, 196, 197, 221, 243, 265, 282, 301, 323, 342, 360

Kayla Woodhouse loves the Lord and wants to share His Word with others—especially teens. Living with a rare nerve disorder, Kayla has been featured all over national television and in hundreds of magazines and newspapers.

KIMBERLEY WOODHOUSE: Days 10, 33, 51, 69, 88, 105, 127, 139, 155, 170, 187, 202, 218, 253, 274, 292, 311, 326, 347

Kimberley Woodhouse is a multipublished author of fiction and nonfiction. A popular speaker/teacher, she's shared her theme of "Joy through Trials" with more than 150,000 people at more than 1,000 venues across the country. She lives, writes, and homeschools in beautiful Colorado with her husband of twenty-plus years and their two awesome teens.

Scripture Index